P9-DGX-394

SMALL
GARDEN
DESIGN
BIBLE

An Hachette Livre UK Company

First published in Great Britain in 2008 by
Hamlyn, a division of Octopus Publishing Group Ltd
2–4 Heron Quays, London E14 4JP
www.octopusbooks.co.uk

Distributed in the United States and Canada by
Sterling Publishing Co., Inc.
387 Park Avenue South, New York, NY 10016-8810

ISBN 978-0-600-61649-8

A CIP catalogue record for this book is available
from the British Library

Printed and bound in China

10 9 8 7 6 5 4 3 2 1

SMALL GARDEN DESIGN BIBLE

hamlyn

Tim Newbury

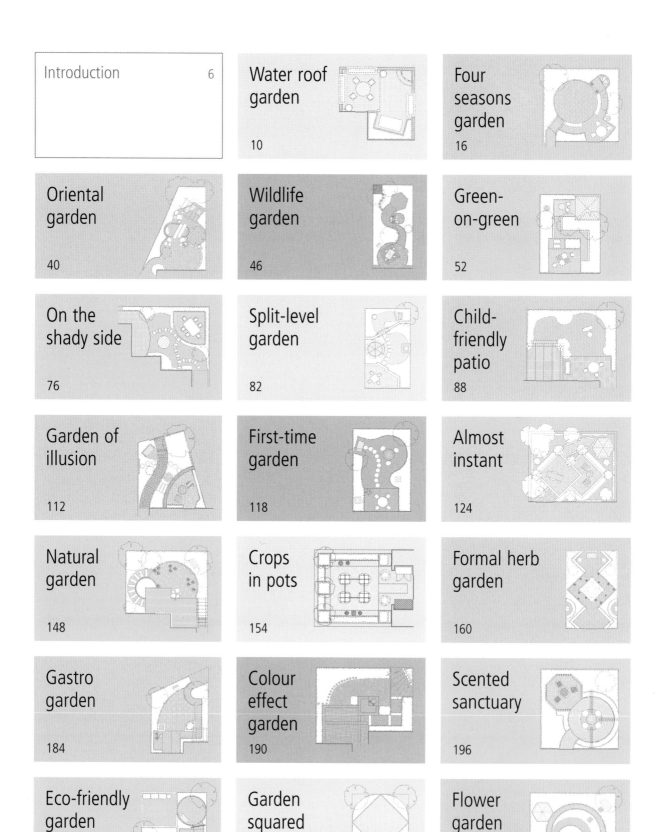

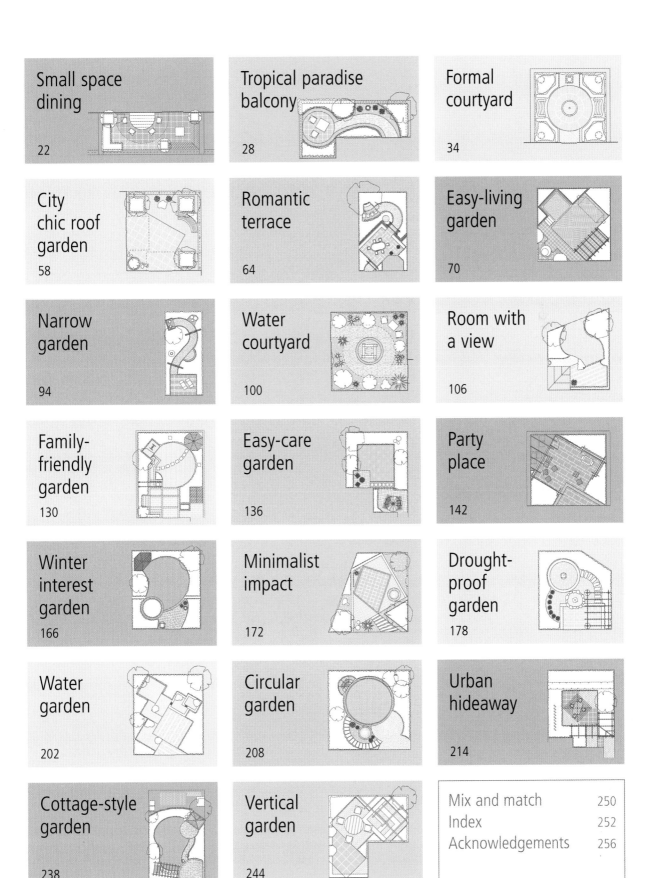

Introduction

As space for housing becomes increasingly limited, gardens have become smaller. Although defining a small or large garden is largely subjective, most gardens are at least the same width as the house, and in this book the plans have been prepared for gardens of roughly this minimum size – that is, ranging from about 4m (13ft) to 8m (26ft) wide and often not much longer.

Thinking ahead

Designing a garden that will happily accommodate the often competing demands of the entire family can be difficult. Finding space for children to play while their parents relax or entertain friends and at the same time grow some attractive plants as well as perhaps fruit and herbs and a few vegetables is never easy, but in a small garden the challenge can appear overwhelming.

Large gardens often simply evolve, with new features being added on an ad hoc basis as homeowners' interests, priorities and needs change. In a small garden, however, this approach will lead to a muddled, rather messy layout that satisfies no one. If you have moved into a new house with a small garden it is far better to think about how you will use the entire space from the beginning. Of course, the work can still be staged and carried out over several seasons, but ultimately the

overall appearance of your garden will be coherent and satisfying.

If you are fortunate enough to have a garden that is much larger than the dimensions suggested here, there is, of course, nothing to stop you taking some of the ideas from these small gardens, such as the Romantic Terrace (see pages 64–69) or Winter Interest Garden (see pages 166–71), and using them as part of an overall design.

Many roof gardens and most balconies are at the lower end of the size mentioned above – indeed, they are usually smaller – but even so they still offer plenty of scope for producing wonderful effects. Don't forget that many of the materials used – flagstones, compost, gravel and so on – are heavy, so check with a surveyor or other professional first to make sure that your balcony or roof can bear the extra weight, and as you draw up your plans consider the practicalities of transporting these heavy materials from ground level to the finished height – their weight or dimensions will have a bearing on your final design.

Budgeting and planning

Even in a small garden it is easy to get carried away and end up spending far more than you would have thought possible. Try to decide on a budget before you begin and are too involved in the minutiae of

your design. Look at alternative materials and suppliers to get the best prices, particularly when it comes to the most essential and usually most expensive elements, such as paving and feature plants. If your initial budget is limited but you know that you will have more to spend later on, try to phase the work, carrying out the basics first and then adding more details at later stages. Start with your patio or paving and the boundaries, such as fences, so that your garden is secure and accessible, and at the early stages carry out any other major excavation and hard construction for features such as ponds and terraces.

Even if you haven't decided whether you will need water or electricity at different points in the garden, make sure that you schedule the work of laying conduit, such as 50mm (2in) plastic pipes, under paths, patios and other paved areas in the early stages so that you can thread water pipes or electricity cables through them later on without having to disturb the ground.

Choosing features

Most homeowners want their garden to include a secluded space where they can sit and relax and entertain

Small gardens don't need to be boring. With imagination and hard work you can create your own green haven.

Sometimes just a few plants are needed when the hard landscaping details are thoughtfully constructed.

You'll also need to think of the more mundane aspects of your garden. Where do the rubbish bins go? How does the laundry get dried? Where can garden tools and furniture be kept in winter? Don't forget to consider these at the planning stage – there are several clever ideas in this book that will help you introduce valuable storage space into a small garden.

Organizing the work

When you begin work on your garden remember that space is limited, so think ahead about the way it will progress. How will you get rid of excess spoil? Where are you going to store materials until they are needed? What arrangements will have to be made for access and parking while the work is going on? You might find that you need to have some materials delivered in two or more small batches rather than all at the same time because you simply don't have room to store a huge pile of gravel or stack of paving stones. If this is the case check with your supplier that subsequent batches will be of identical size, quality and colour, especially when you are buying paving flags, bricks, gravel and bark mulch.

Planting

The planting plans list all the plants suggested for each garden design. However, if you can't get hold of a particular variety or cultivar, ask your

friends. Positioning the patio so that it is accessible from the kitchen or dining room will often be a priority, but you must also make sure that it is large enough to accommodate a table and chairs comfortably. The style and colour of the paving you choose will dominate the rest of the garden, so take plenty of time to make your choice and consider all the available options before you commit yourself.

There are few gardens that won't benefit from the addition of even a small water feature. Choose your fountains, waterfalls or cascades carefully and avoid irritatingly drippy or splashy types. Gently gurgling ones will be far more relaxing in a confined space. Wildlife ponds are always valuable, regardless of size, but they can take some time to mature, so if you want a pond for an instant effect you might decide to go for something more formal, such as a raised pool or wall-mounted dish.

If entertaining on the patio is going to be important, you might want to consider arranging some form of outdoor lighting. There is an increasingly wide range of garden light fittings available, ranging from spotlights, uplights and downlights that can be used to highlight individual features to lights that can be inserted in patios. For safety, you might also want to light steps and changes of level. Make sure that any lighting you do install does not spill over into your neighbours' gardens.

nursery or garden centre to suggest another similar plant that will do the same job.

Put in long-term plants first – trees, hedges, large shrubs – and add smaller plants as final touches later on. Although it might be tempting to buy large specimen plants for an instant effect, such plants are rarely worth the money. They are not only expensive, eating into your budget, but can be difficult to establish. Smaller, immature plants are generally better value and will soon reach the dimensions you want if you look after them well.

By their nature, small gardens are frequently overlooked, and privacy can be a problem. Although it can be a temptingly easy solution, don't just plant a hedge around your boundary. The gardens illustrated here suggest other sensitive and inspiring ideas for screening and blocking views to create a secluded space.

Before you make your final plant choices, check your soil to see if it is acid, neutral or alkaline with a simple pH testing kit. Acid-loving plants, such as rhododendrons and camellias, need an acid soil – that is, soil with a pH below 7 – so you should avoid these if your soil is alkaline – that is, has pH of 7 or above. Check with your local nursery or garden centre to see which type of plants are best for your soil.

Your choice of plants will also be affected by your garden's aspect and microclimate. If the size and shape of your garden roughly match one of the examples here but the direction of the sun is different, try to identify where the shady areas will be and look at some of the other designs with similar shady areas for other planting ideas that will suit your garden.

Small gardens are often more sheltered than large ones, and they can be warmer by one or two degrees, particularly in built-up areas. Take advantage of this by experimenting with one or two more exotic plants that perhaps wouldn't thrive in a colder, more exposed garden. You might be pleasantly surprised by what will thrive in your garden.

Doing the work

If you are fairly handy and practical you will probably want to carry out all or most of the work yourself.

However, there are some aspects of garden construction for which you should seek professional help, particularly anything electrical, such as pond pumps and filters and garden lighting. In addition, even if you do the work yourself, you should always seek professional advice before undertaking structural elements, such as retaining walls or tall, free-standing walls.

While the gardens illustrated in this book are all complete designs, don't be afraid to take elements that you like from different examples and combine them to make your own unique design. A garden should reflect the personality of the family that lives in it, so choose features from different gardens and combine them to make the design that suits your life and hopes.

Growing suitable plants in containers is a classic and effective way to enhance a roof garden or balcony.

Water roof garden

Water – especially moving water – can add light, sound and movement to a garden as well as attracting all kinds of wildlife and offering a habitat for beautiful plants. However, water is heavy, and if you want to incorporate some kind of water feature in a roof or balcony garden you must bear this fact in mind when you are deciding on the type of feature you would like and also where it will be located in the design. If you have any doubts, seek the advice of a qualified surveyor.

Why this works

✓ A large cascading water feature makes a focal point from anywhere in the garden.

✓ Troughs of plants mounted on the surrounding wall provide low greenery and flowers.

✓ A swing seat allows you to relax in the sun.

✓ A lightweight overhead structure with climbers gives shade when it becomes too hot or bright.

✓ Taller plants around the swing seat provide scale and soften the walls of the building behind.

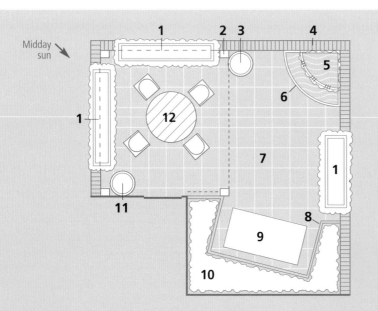

Garden elements key

1 Wall-mounted trough
2 Post for shade structure
3 Climber in pot on shade structure
4 Balustrade wall
5 Marginal planting in water feature
6 Water feature
7 Terracotta floor tiles

8 Raised perimeter
  planter
9 Swing seat
10 Planting

11 Climber in pot
  trained on to wall
  and shade structure
12 Patio furniture

Mix and match
If you like this garden but would prefer
a different feature, see pages 250–51 for
possible variations.

Garden dimensions
5m x 5m (16ft 6 in x 16ft 6in) approx.

Key features

Water feature

This cleverly designed water feature makes a dramatic focal point. Much of the weight is carried by the surrounding balustrade walls and the strongest part of the floor structure, which is in the corner. As long as you don't intend to keep fish or grow aquatic plants that need extra depth, your water feature need only be a few centimetres (inches) deep to be effective.

Wall-mounted troughs

These troughs are a convenient way of both softening the boundaries of your garden and using up otherwise dead space, leaving more usable room for your patio area. For the best results make sure you use a good-quality compost or growing medium to plant in and, if possible, install a simple automatic or manual irrigation system.

Overhead shade structure

One of the most enjoyable aspects of a garden is being able to sit in a cool, shady position on a hot, still day. Overhead structures for this purpose need to be strong enough to withstand gusts of wind without being heavy and overpowering. In this design most of the shade is provided by climbers in pots growing on wires, which are light but strong. Use deciduous climbers, so that in the winter, when you don't need shade, they'll lose their leaves and let through the low sun.

Water feature

One of the limiting factors in building a water feature in a roof garden is the amount of weight the roof can safely support. To overcome this design your feature so that some, if not all, of the weight is carried by the edge structure of the roof space. Placing it in a corner is desirable both structurally and visually. Keep the container that will hold the water shallow and make it from thin but strong materials, such as fibreglass or sheet aluminium. Don't forget to provide a safe access for any electric supply at the design stage of your garden for a submersible pump or lights.

Small carefully detailed water features can look superb in a limited space.

You will need

2 shallow containers, 1 large, 1 small, that can fit into a corner
Submersible pump and submersible lights (optional)
At least 1m (39in) of 19mm (¾in) flexible corrugated pond hose
2 x 19mm (¾in) hose clips
6mm (¼in) angle iron, sufficiently long to make a triangular support for the small container (see diagram); alternatively, use hardwood or treated softwood, 47mm x 70mm (1¾in x 2¾in)
4 x 8mm (⅓in) anchor bolts and drill bit to suit
Small pieces of perspex, plastic, aluminium or stainless steel sheet to construct 'cascades'
Waterproof mastic
Aquatic plants
19mm (¾in) plumber's tank connector
Crushed slate or small pebbles

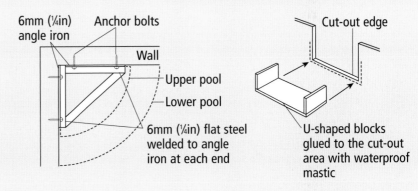

Marginal plants in aquatic containers
Wall
Anchor bolt through angle iron
Cascade
Upper pool
Water level
Hose
Lower pool
Submersible pump
Plumber's tank connector to feed return hose through; use a longish piece of hose so that the pump can be pushed to the back, out of sight

6mm (¼in) angle iron
Anchor bolts
Wall
Upper pool
Lower pool
6mm (¼in) flat steel welded to angle iron at each end

Cut-out edge
U-shaped blocks glued to the cut-out area with waterproof mastic

Step by step

1 Put the larger (lower) container tight into the corner of the walls, leaving a narrow gap of 6–8mm (¼–⅓in) on one side so that you can conceal the electric cable.

2 Cut the angle iron with a hacksaw or angle grinder into three pieces and weld or bolt them together to make a triangle slightly smaller than the small container. Drill four 8–10mm (about ⅓in) holes in the side pieces to take the anchor bolts.

3 Position the metal triangle in the corner 10–15cm (4–6in) above the larger container. Mark the position of the four holes, making sure that the triangle is level, and drill four

matching holes in the wall. Fix the metal triangle to the wall with the anchor bolts to form a bracket.

4 Cut one or more shallow, rectangular notches in the front lip of the smaller container, about 2.5cm (1in) high by 5cm (2in) wide. Take the spare pieces of metal or plastic sheet, cut and mastic them to form small, U-shaped blocks to match the size of the notches in the lip. Glue these to the outside edge of the notches.

5 Place the submersible pump and lights (if used) in the lower container. Connect one end of the 19mm (¾in) hose to the pump using the hose clip. Drill a hole in the bottom of the

small container, fit the tank connector to the hole and fix the other end of the hose to the bottom end of the tank connector with a hose clip. Take a short length of hose and fix it to the top end of the connector and position the open end so that it sits just below the water level in the upper container to make sure that the water doesn't drain down into the lower container when the pump is switched off.

6 Plant the aquatic plants in suitable pots and position in the upper container. Spread a thin layer of crushed slate or pebbles over the bottom of the lower container and make sure the pump is out of sight.

Planting

8

9

12

25

The best plants for this garden

All the plants have been selected because of their suitability for a roof garden. There is a good mix of colour, shape and texture, with a vine growing on the overhead structure for summer shade. All these plants can tolerate periods of fairly dry conditions, making them ideal for containers and troughs.

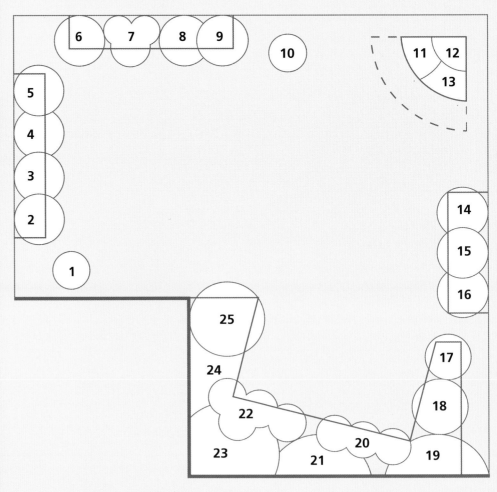

Planting key

1 *Actinidia kolomikta*
2 *Euphorbia* x *martini*
3 *Geranium* x *cantabrigiense* 'Cambridge'
4 *Berberis thunbergii* f. *atropurpurea* 'Dart's Red Lady'
5 *Tsuga canadensis* 'Cole's Prostrate'
6 *Diascia barberae* 'Blackthorn Apricot'
7 *Carex buchananii*
8 *Lavandula pedunculata* subsp. *pedunculata*
9 *Convolvulus cneorum*
10 *Vitis vinifera* 'Ciotat'
11 *Caltha palustris* var. *alba*
12 *Iris laevigata* 'Variegata'
13 *Filipendula ulmaria* 'Aurea'
14 *Sedum* 'Indian Chief'
15 *Pinus mugo* 'Mops'
16 *Hypericum olympicum*
17 *Hakonechloa macra*
18 *Anthemis tinctoria* 'E.C. Buxton'
19 *Escallonia* 'Red Elf'
20 *Festuca glauca* 'Blauglut'
21 *Philadelphus* 'Manteau d'Hermine'
22 *Helianthemum* 'The Bride'
23 *Garrya elliptica* 'James Roof'
24 *Crambe cordifolia*
25 *Fuchsia magellanica*

Plants that have silver or grey foliage, such as *Achillea*, are an ideal choice for roof gardens.

Plants for roof gardens and balconies

Because roof gardens and balconies are well above ground level they tend to be exposed to greater extremes of weather, particularly wind. You should, therefore, select plants that are suitable for these conditions. Remember, too, that most of the planting will be in containers, which tend to dry out faster and more frequently than plants in the open ground, so avoid anything that won't tolerate some dryness at the roots.

Best perennials for roof and balcony gardens

- *Miscanthus sinensis* 'Yakushima Dwarf'
- *Achillea* cvs.
- *Festuca glauca* 'Blaufuchs'
- *Artemisia* 'Powis Castle'
- *Eryngium variifolium*
- *Euphorbia polychroma*
- *Geranium renardii* 'Zetterlund'
- *Oenothera macrocarpa*
- *Anthemis tinctoria* 'E.C. Buxton'
- *Centaurea montana* 'Parham'

Best shrubs for roof and balcony gardens

- *Hebe* (low, small-leaved cvs., such as *H. topiaria*)
- *Pinus mugo* cvs.
- *Lavandula angustifolia* 'Loddon Pink'
- *Brachyglottis* (Dunedin Group) 'Sunshine'
- *Salvia officinalis* cvs.
- *Viburnum* (evergreen spp., such as *V. davidii* and *V. tinus*)
- *Rosmarinus officinalis* 'McConnell's Blue'
- *Cytisus* x *kewensis*
- *Cistus* x *lenis* 'Grayswood Pink'
- *Salix hastata* 'Wehrhahnii'

Four seasons garden

Although gardening is usually thought of as a seasonal pastime – with the peak of interest tending to be through the summer months – you need to think about how it will look throughout the year. A good design will provide a backbone of interest and structure to your garden at all times.

Why this works

✓ A bold circular design centres around the lawn, making the garden feel more spacious and creating generous planting areas.

✓ The small seat under an arbour provides an alternative sitting area to catch the sun during the middle of the day.

✓ Plant choice ensures there is some interest in the garden at any time, from flowers, stems and foliage.

✓ Climbers on the boundary wall hide and soften the brickwork and provide shade beneath the pergola.

✓ A water feature is positioned making a focal point that can also be viewed from the house.

✓ The dwarf, evergreen hedge and path accentuate the circular theme.

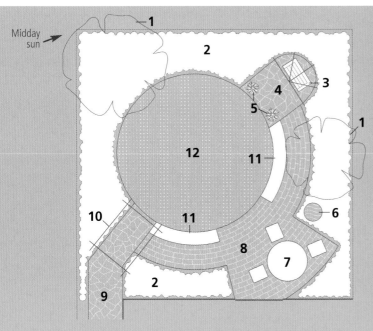

Garden elements key

1 Small tree
2 Mixed border
3 Arbour and seat
4 Crazy paving
5 Pots or urns
6 Water feature
7 Patio furniture
8 Sett paving patio
9 Crazy paving path
10 Pergola
11 Dwarf hedge
12 Lawn

Mix and match
If you like this garden but would prefer
a different feature, see pages 250–51 for
possible variations.

Garden dimensions
8m x 8m (26ft x 26ft) approx.

Key features

Year-round interest

Choose plants with coloured stems or interesting bark; those with bold, coloured or variegated foliage; those that bear fruit and berries; and evergreens to give your garden colour, structure and greenery all year round.

Sett paving

Paving is an integral part of a design, not just as a necessary piece of hard landscaping. The choice of material, colour and even the pattern of laying can have an effect on the rest of the garden. To unify a design, use the same paving materials throughout, although you might want to vary the style of laying. Alternatively, you could differentiate between areas of paving by using different materials entirely – here the neat, uniform setts form a strong contrast with the stone crazy paving.

Pergola

Pergolas are ideal for supporting a range of climbing plants. Where the climbers are vigorous or evergreen they will probably quite quickly hide posts and overheads, so in this case your pergola need be no more than a simple supporting structure. However, for slower-growing climbers or plants with a delicate, open habit, pay attention to the choice of pergola so that it can hold its place in the garden even without climbers growing on it.

Boundary walls and fences

A feature that is, almost without exception, common to all gardens is the fact that they are defined by boundaries, if for no other reason than to demarcate limits of ownership in the legal sense. Boundaries can be low key – a post and wire fence – or they can be significant solid structures – a high brick or stone wall or even the back of another building.

Regardless of the type of boundary, you will need to

Sensitively detailed boundaries don't need to be completely clad in plants to be effective.

decide how you want to incorporate it into your garden design. This is particularly so in a small garden, where the boundaries are much more obvious and therefore require extra thought. Of course, if you are in a position to replace a boundary structure with one of your own choice or to put in a brand-new one if you are having a new house and garden built from scratch, then it's less of a problem. If, however, you inherit a garden with boundaries that cannot be changed structurally, you should consider how to incorporate them into your design.

- Use good-quality bricks with attractive colour and texture or natural stone in warm colours and a mellow finish.
- Instead of only using plain brick or stonework use contrasting brick or stone for copings or in-built patterns, add piers or perhaps even create false 'arches' in which you can place a feature plant or a small statue.
- Light the walls from the ground with soft lighting for extra night-time effect.
- Limit the use of climbers and wall shrubs so that they complement the walls or fence rather than hide it.
- Use different coloured stains on fencing and maybe combine lower solid panels with open or trellis panels on top, or perhaps alternate two different styles (or colours) of fencing panel.
- Make your own board or palisade fence using three or four different widths of vertical boards in a random pattern.
- Liven up an existing plain wall with small panels of ornamental trellis, or hang pots and ornaments from it.

Establish a striking theme by staining or colour washing fences and walls to complement your plant colours.

How to disguise an ugly boundary

If your wall is unsightly but sound, colour wash it. Choose a pale, pastel colour to bring light into the garden or a darker shade to tone it down into the background. You can do the same with fencing, but use appropriate woodstain.

In gardens where space is limited, use climbers to hide the boundary. You will have to erect a system of parallel wires or a trellis to support them, and if you are using trellis, fix it to battens so that air can circulate around the plant. Stain the trellis beforehand in dark or muted colours so that it doesn't stand out, and if possible attach it with hinges along the lower edge and hooks at the top so that you can fold it down from the wall for easy access for painting or general maintenance.

If there's enough room, plant a border in front of the boundary with tall shrubs at the back and smaller plants to the front, but remember that walls often create a rain shadow and you might have to water these plants more often than other plants in the garden. Use additional climbers to complete the screening.

Planting

The best plants for this garden

For year-round interest your garden should have a basic structure of one or two small trees and several larger shrubs, particularly evergreens. This garden has these plants, and they are linked together with a wide range of smaller shrubs, perennials, climbers and grasses. Each plant has been selected for a particular quality – or qualities – which ensures that at any time there will always be highlights in the garden, whether they are flowers, foliage, berries or shape.

Planting key

1 *Juniperus horizontalis* 'Blue Chip'
2 *Rudbeckia fulgida* var. *deamii*
3 *Chaenomeles speciosa* 'Geisha Girl'
4 *Erysimum* 'Bowles Mauve'
5 *Ophiopogon jaburan* 'Vittatus'
6 *Clematis* 'Gipsy Queen'
7 *Iris foetidissima*
8 *Lonicera periclymenum* 'Serotina'
9 *Helleborus niger*
10 *Rosa* 'Pink Perpétué'
11 *Hebe albicans* 'Red Edge'
12 *Elaeagnus pungens* 'Frederici'
13 *Astilbe* 'Sprite'
14 *Phlox paniculata* 'Mount Fuji'
15 *Clematis* 'Constance'

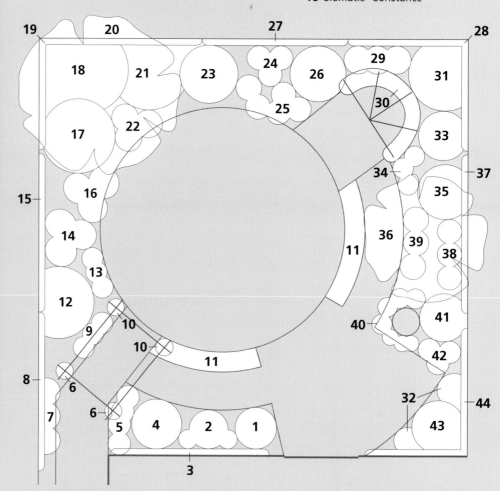

16 *Crocosmia* x *crocosmiiflora* 'Solfatare'
17 *Hydrangea aspera* 'Mauvette'
18 *Osmanthus* x *burkwoodii*
19 *Hedera colchica* 'Sulphur Heart'
20 *Betula utilis* var. *jacquemontii* 'Jermyns'
21 *Ligustrum* 'Vicaryi'
22 *Astrantia major* 'Claret'
23 *Phormium cookianum* subsp. *hookeri* 'Tricolor'
24 *Thalictrum flavum* subsp. *glaucum*
25 *Sedum spectabile* 'Iceberg'
26 *Cornus alba* 'Sibirica'
27 *Schizophragma hydrangeoides* 'Roseum'
28 *Clematis cirrhosa* 'Wisley Cream'
29 *Ageratina altissima* 'Chocolate'
30 *Rosa* 'Meg'
31 *Pyracantha* 'Mohave'
32 *Schizostylis coccinea* 'Fenland Daybreak'
33 *Miscanthus sinensis* 'Malepartus'
34 *Eryngium* x *tripartitum*
35 *Carpenteria californica*
36 *Arbutus unedo* f. *rubra*
37 *Jasminum nudiflorum* 'Aureum'
38 *Actaea simplex* Atropurpurea Group 'Brunette'
39 *Anemone hupehensis* var. *japonica* 'Bressingham Glow'
40 *Erica carnea* 'Pink Spangles'
41 *Caryopteris* x *clandonensis* 'Kew Blue'
42 *Helenium* 'Moerheim Beauty'
43 *Ilex* x *attenuata* 'Sunny Foster' (female)
44 *Campsis* x *tagliabuana* 'Madame Galen'

Hollies, such as this *Ilex aquifolium* 'Pyramidalis', make excellent evergreen hedges in both formal and informal situations.

Hedges for small gardens

In small gardens space is invariably at a premium, and large or fast-growing plants are not desirable. Fortunately, there are many plants that you can use to create hedges that are much better suited to smaller gardens.

Best plants for dwarf hedges
- *Berberis thunbergii* f. *atropurpurea* 'Bagatelle'
- *Lavandula angustifolia* 'Blue Cushion'
- *Buxus sempervirens* 'Suffruticosa'
- *Hebe* 'Margret'

Best plants for low–medium hedges
- *Euonymus fortunei* cvs.
- *Potentilla fruticosa* 'Primrose Beauty'
- *Viburnum davidii*
- *Spiraea betulifolia* var. *aemeliana*

Best plants for medium–tall hedges
- *Osmanthus heterophyllus* cvs.
- *Taxus cuspidata* 'Straight Hedge'
- *Viburnum tinus* 'Eve Price'
- *Pittosporum tobira*
- *Prunus lusitanica*

Small space dining

Designing a small garden is often far more challenging than a larger one simply because there is less space available to include all the features you would like to see. Any design features or devices that take up less space are therefore invaluable, and you should incorporate them whenever you can. For balconies or tiny roof gardens this simple but effective folding dining table, combined with stacking or folding chairs that can be stored away, and a bench seat that doubles up as a plant stand are ideal in limited space.

Why this works

✓ Room for up to four people to sit and eat at the dining table, which can be folded away and the chairs stored, leaving room for more casual patio furniture, such as a sunbed or loungers.

✓ A simple bench seat doubles as an extra sitting area, and when it is not in use as a seat it can be used as a stand for a selection of containers.

✓ A raised planter with a cupboard underneath is large enough to accommodate four stacking or folding chairs, and the underneath of the planter at the opposite end of the balcony could be used as another cupboard for storing smaller items, spare pots, tools or cushions.

✓ A small number of carefully selected, easily managed plants gives a range of colour and shape throughout the year.

✓ Paving, walls and garden features are in light or bright colours to lift the whole space, even in winter.

Midday sun

Garden elements key

1 Common wall
2 Chair store cupboard with planter on top

3 Broken line indicates outer edge of minimum space required for dining area
4 Folding dining table

5 Stacking or folding
  chairs

6 Fixed planter

7 Bench seat/plant
  stand with storage
  for cushions

8 Table

9 Balustrade/railings

10 Temporary position
   for containers when
   bench seat is in use

Mix and match
If you like this garden but would prefer
a different feature, see pages 250–51 for
possible variations.

Garden dimensions
5m x 2m (16ft 6in x 6ft 6in) approx.

Folding dining table

Dining tables that can be folded flat against a wall when they are not in use are great space-savers. If you like you can leave a narrow 'shelf', about 30cm (12in) wide, at the back when the table is folded and not in use, on which you can place small plants in containers or a selection of ornaments for a little extra colour and interest.

Store cupboard or planter

A store cupboard that doubles up as a planter is an ingenious way to make the most of a very small space. To make it more of a design feature, extend the cupboard upwards and create a shallow planter. Make sure the inside of the planter section is waterproof and put drainage holes at the bottom outside edges of the planter section so that any excess water doesn't drain directly into the cupboard.

Bench seat

In a small space, try and make everything serve more than one purpose. This simple bench seat can be softened with cushions for sitting. In winter store the cushions and use the seat as a plant stand to give a display of late-season flowers, stem colour and foliage shapes. To make the most of the space use the area under the bench to store spare pots, bags of potting compost and watering implements.

Folding dining table

This folding dining table accommodates four people, but you can alter the size and shape to suit your own purposes, as long as there is a blank wall that is long enough. Try to find wooden folding chairs that can be stained to match the table; alternatively, buy small plastic stacking chairs and adjust the table colour to match or complement them.

Folding chairs and collapsible tables are the perfect solution for tiny seating areas.

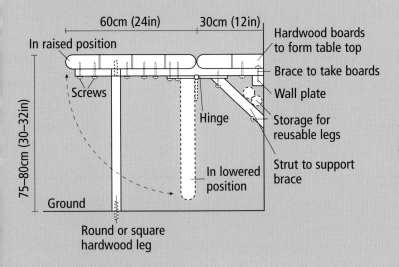

End section

60cm (24in) 30cm (12in)

In raised position

75–80cm (30–32in)

Screws

Hinge

In lowered position

Ground

Round or square hardwood leg

Hardwood boards to form table top

Brace to take boards

Wall plate

Storage for reusable legs

Strut to support brace

Plan

Screws and plugs to hold wall plate

Hinge

Leg

1.45m (4ft 9in)

Brace

Wall plate

Board

Optional table shape if extra room available

You will need

5cm x 15cm (2in x 6in) uniform hardwood or softwood boards 8–10m (26–33ft) long (depending on the table size) for the table top

5cm x 7.5cm (2in x 3in) long sawn softwood, 6–7m (20–23ft) long, for the bracing, struts and wall plate

5–7.5cm (2–3in) square or round-section hardwood or treated softwood for the legs, about 1.5m (5ft) long

4 large gate-type hinges

7 x 7.5cm (3in) screws plus wall plugs to match

18 x 32mm (1¼in) screws

32 x 6.5cm (2½in) screws

13mm (½in) diameter steel rod or hardwood dowel

Weatherproof adhesive

Paint, woodstain or wood oil

Step by step

1 Cut the 5cm x 15cm (2in x 6in) boards to the desired length. Smooth the edges and top using a wood plane and decreasing grades of glass paper.

2 Cut the wall braces, struts and wall plate using the 5cm x 7.5cm (2in x

3in) softwood, mitring the ends of the angled strut.

3 Drill and fix the wall plate horizontally to the wall with the 7.5cm (3in) screws and plugs. Drill and screw the braces and struts to the wall plate with the 6.5cm (2½in) screws and to the wall with the 7.5cm (3in) screws to form triangular supports. Screw two of the table top boards on top of these to form the 'shelf' section of the table.

4 Use the remaining 5cm x 7.5cm (2in x 3in) softwood to make braces for the 'hinged' section of the table, making sure they line up exactly with the triangular braces. Fix the remaining table top boards to these with the 6.5cm (2½in) screws.

5 On the braces, fix the hinges to both the 'fixed' and 'hinged' sections of table top with the 32mm (1¼in) screws.

6 Cut the 5–7.5cm (2–3in) sections to form two equal 'legs'. Drill each end 5cm (2in) deep to take the rod or dowel. Cut 7.5cm (3in) lengths of the rod or dowel and glue into both ends of each leg, leaving 2.5cm (1in) protruding. Drill 2.5cm (1in) deep holes in the floor tile and the underside of the table top directly above.

7 Lift the 'hinged' section slightly above horizontal, drop the dowelled ends of the legs into the floor holes and lower the table so that the dowels at the top of the legs locate in the appropriate holes in the underside of the table. When the table is not in use, store the legs under the 'shelf' in the space created by the triangular bracing.

8 Finish off with one or more coats of your selected stain, paint or wood oil, applied according to the manufacturer's instructions.

Planting

The best plants for this garden

Emphasis is on providing as much colour, texture and shape as possible from a limited number of plants. Evergreens are prominent to provide softness and structure in winter. Even in this small space there is sufficient room to grow a selection of annuals or herbs in pots to display on the 'shelf' section of the table.

Planting key

1 *Juniperus procumbens* 'Nana'
2 *Abelia* x *grandiflora*
3 *Phormium* 'Jester'
4 *Genista pilosa* 'Vancouver Gold'
5 x *Halimiocistus sahucii*
6 *Sasa veitchii*
7 *Cornus sanguinea* 'Midwinter Fire' and *Crocus* 'Lilac Beauty' (in pot)
8 *Erica* x *darleyensis* 'Kramer's Rote' (in pot)
9 *Skimmia japonica* 'Rubella' (in pot)
10 *Galanthus nivalis* and *Erica carnea* 'Myretoun Ruby' (in pot)
11 *Ilex crenata* 'Golden Gem' (female; in pot)

Alternative foliage planting

1 *Pinus mugo* 'Ophir'
2 *Prunus laurocerasus* 'Otto Luyken'
3 *Berberis thunbergii* f. *atropurpurea* 'Dart's Red Lady'
4 *Juniperus squamata* 'Blue Star'
5 *Yucca flaccida* 'Golden Sword'
6 *Pittosporum tobira* 'Nanum'
7 *Hosta* 'Honeybells'
8 *Dryopteris erythrosora*
9 *Calamagrostis arundinacea*
10 *Bergenia* 'Abendglut'
11 *Hedera helix* 'Ivalace'

Alternative blue and white planting

1 *Juniperus horizontalis* 'Blue Chip'
2 *Caryopteris* x *clandonensis* 'Heavenly Blue'
3 x *Halimiocistus wintonensis*
4 *Hebe* 'Caledonia'
5 *Ceratostigma willmottianum*
6 *Ceanothus thyrsiflorus* var. *repens*
7 *Scabiosa caucasica* 'Miss Willmott'
8 *Festuca glauca* 'Blauglut'
9 *Iris sibirica* 'Perry's Blue'
10 *Carex morrowii* 'Variegata'
11 *Agapanthus* 'Bressingham White'

alternative position for pots when not located on bench

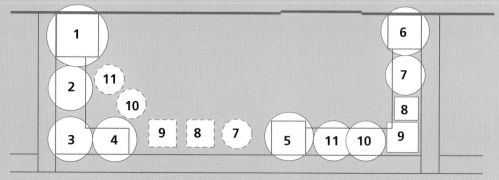

Alternative colour schemes

Small areas of planting that you are most likely to find on balconies and roofs are the perfect size for developing a theme in your garden. There are various ways in which you could achieve this: with a scheme that has flowers and leaves of either a single colour, such as gold, or a combination of two, such as blue and white. A foliage theme can be particularly effective in small spaces: use different colours, textures, sizes and shapes of leaf and plant, or limit your choice to just one or two colours such as purple and/or silver. A third option that could work well in a tiny garden, although not so much in a larger one, is to limit your plants to one type, such as grasses, ferns or dwarf conifers.

In a small area choosing the colour of your plants is even more important than in a large garden. Pale blues and mauves, for example, have the effect of appearing to be further away than they actually are, while reds and oranges always seem to be nearer, crowding in on the viewer. It is always better, too, to select plants that have flowers and foliage that are in a fairly close colour range, because a multitude of colours and shades will appear spotty and bitty and create a rather restless effect.

Pastel blues, pinks and yellow always go well together, creating a peaceful, hazy atmosphere, although even these will benefit from the occasional splash of a brighter or contrasting shade. In a small area avoid deliberate colour clashes. Purple and orange or pink and orange might work well in a long border, where you have space to make this sort of statement, but they are too confrontational and disturbing to be seen at close quarters every day. However, it's perfectly acceptable to brighten up a predominantly blue planting scheme with yellow, while a largely foliage area can benefit from a splash of bright red.

Linking your plant colours to the furniture, containers and ornaments makes for a very harmonious solution.

Remember, too, that even species that you select for their foliage are available in a wide range of colours. *Hosta* 'Sum and Substance' has lime green leaves, while *H.* 'Halcyon' has glaucous (blue) leaves. Conifers are not all the same green, either. If your colour scheme is based around yellows and the sharper greens on the spectrum look out for the upright *Cupressus macrocarpa* 'Goldcrest', but if the emphasis in your scheme is on shades of blue you will want a blue-green conifer like *Juniperus scopulorum* 'Skyrocket'.

Tropical paradise balcony

A balcony garden doesn't need to be a bland, uninteresting place. With a little imagination and effort it can be turned into a mini-tropical paradise. This design uses simple curves, interesting materials and container-grown tropical plants cleverly disguised to look as if they are growing in a bed to create an exotic oasis.

Why this works

✓ A striking ground plan of curves and circles breaks up the otherwise long, narrow area into interesting spaces.

✓ Small trees add height, structure and a feeling of seclusion and at the same time frame a desirable view.

✓ An attractive screen for shelter and privacy can be removed occasionally to let in more sun or to allow you to admire the view.

✓ Flexible log edging disguises the containers, gives the impression of a larger planted area and introduces a change of level.

✓ Planting suitable for warm climates gives a tropical, exotic feel to the garden space.

✓ Trellis on the building's walls offers support for rampant, prolifically flowering climbers to add to the effect.

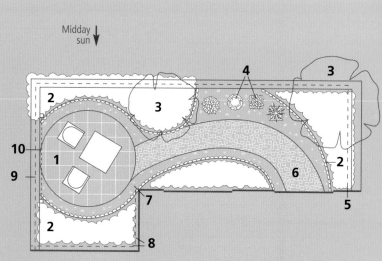

Midday sun ↓

Garden elements key

1 Tiled circle
2 Raised bed with flexible log edging
3 Small tree
4 Containers with low planting to keep view open
5 Trellis on common wall with climber

6 'Mosaic' path

7 Stone chippings

8 Trellis on apartment
wall with climber

9 Railings

10 Movable screen

Mix and match
If you like this garden but would prefer
a different feature, see pages 250–51 for
possible variations.

Garden dimensions
6m x 3.3m (20ft x 10ft 9in) approx.

Key features

Movable screen

To get the best position for a screen or screens like this, observe the weather patterns and views from the balcony. You can then site a screen so that it most effectively provides shelter from the wind or the midday sun. Alternatively, use one or more screens to block out an unsightly view or to give you more privacy.

Raised bed

Flexible log edging is a good way to create the effect of a raised bed: it allows you to grow your plants in containers while making it appear that they are actually growing in a bed. To complete the effect, fill the gaps between the containers and on top to cover the rims with ornamental-grade bark. Make sure you know exactly where the centre of each container is located so that you don't miss any plants when you are watering, or, even better, put in an irrigation system.

Tropical plants

Tropical planting is effective because of the exotic combination of bold, dramatic foliage and bright, flamboyant flowers. Densely planting the beds adds to the overall character of this style of garden. Remember to secure taller or upright plants to take account of gusty winds. The containers with trees and large shrubs in them might need to be fixed in some way so they cannot blow over.

Removable screen

This is a simple yet effective and quick way to make a screen where your roof or balcony space is surrounded by a balustrade wall at least 30cm (12in) high. Use the screen to provide shade or shelter, give privacy to a small section of the balcony or as a simple divider.

Lightweight screens or trellis can be used to divide or shelter a small space without being overpowering.

Balcony section

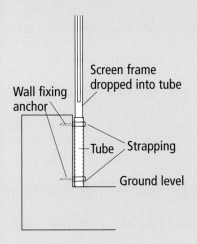

Screen frame dropped into tube

Wall fixing anchor

Wall fixing anchor

Tube

Strapping

Ground level

Square or circular tube to suit diameter of support post

Wall fixing anchor

Log edging

Square or circular tube

Galvanized flexible steel strapping

You will need

1 trellis panel, size to suit but about 1.5m x 1.8m (5ft x 6ft)

2 uniform round or square 6cm–7.5cm (2¼–3in) wooden posts, each 30cm (12in) longer than the side of the trellis panel

2 metal or heavy-duty rigid plastic tubes, each 30–40cm (12–16in) long, with inside diameter to match the diameter of the posts

About 1m (39in) flexible galvanized steel pre-drilled strapping, available from good builders' merchants

8 x 6mm (¼in) anchor bolts, at least 5cm (2in) long, or 8 x 5cm (2in) screws and wall plugs

6 x 6.5cm (2½in) screws

Woven mesh, rolled bamboo screen or similar for extra shade or protection (optional)

Step by step

1 Fix a post to each side of the trellis panel using 6.5cm (2½in) screws. To avoid splitting the trellis, pre-drill the holes slightly smaller than the screw shank diameter. Make sure you leave 30cm (12in), or the height of the balustrade wall if greater, of post

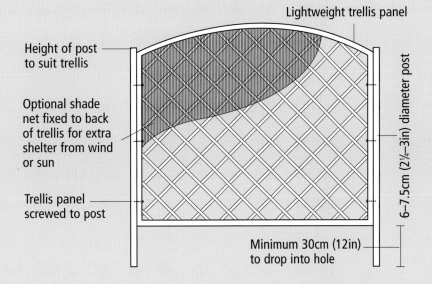

Height of post to suit trellis

Optional shade net fixed to back of trellis for extra shelter from wind or sun

Trellis panel screwed to post

Lightweight trellis panel

6–7.5cm (2¼–3in) diameter post

Minimum 30cm (12in) to drop into hole

projecting below the bottom of the trellis panel.

2 Cut the tubes to the height of the wall, at least 30cm (12in), drill and fix them to the wall with clamps formed from the flexible strapping. Use the anchor bolts or 5cm (2in) screws and wall plugs. Put one clamp at each end of the tubes and set them at the same distance as the posts on the trellis, making sure they are plumb.

3 Drop the lower ends of the post and trellis screen into the tubes to

finish. For a really tight fit make some thinly tapered wedges from narrow pieces of wood or pieces of sheet lead and tap them into the narrow gap between the post and the inside wall of the tube. You can also fix additional coverings, such as woven mesh or bamboo, to the trellis for more shade or to create a windbreak.

4 Make sure that the tubes are fixed to the wall so that they are behind – and therefore concealed by – the flexible log edging.

Planting

The best plants for this garden

All the plants in this garden are tropical or nearly so in their requirements, needing a minimum temperature of about 10°C (50°F) to perform best. There is a mixture of bold flowers and foliage, giving colour and texture throughout the year. To add to the effect, perfumed plants, including jasmine (*Jasminum*) and lemon-scented geranium (*Pelargonium crispum*), are incorporated into the design.

To achieve a comparable effect in a temperate climate you will need to select your plants with care, choosing species that are hardy or can be easily protected from cold weather. You will find that the best show is from late spring until late autumn, but if you want to extend the season of interest, you could plant up some pots with dwarf late-winter or early-spring bulbs, such as aconites (*Eranthis*), snowdrops (*Galanthus*), crocuses and chionodoxas.

Planting key

1 *Nerium oleander*
2 *Canna indica* 'Purpurea'
3 *Eriobotrya japonica*
4 *Brugmansia suaveolens* (in pot)
5 *Pelargonium crispum* (in pot)
6 *Cyrtanthus elatus* (in pot)
7 *Aloe vera* (in pot)
8 *Plumbago auriculata*
9 *Callistemon viminalis* 'Captain Cook'
10 *Aspidistra elatior*
11 *Begonia masoniana*
12 *Jasminum polyanthum*
13 *Strelitzia reginae*
14 *Cycas revoluta*
15 *Agapanthus africanus*
16 *Bougainvillea* 'Closeburn'
17 *Musa basjoo*
18 *Caladium bicolor*
19 *Abutilon* 'Boule de Neige'
20 *Aeonium arboreum* 'Atropurpureum'
21 *Heliotropium arborescens* cv.

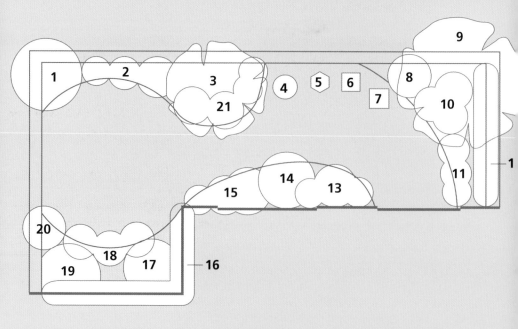

Alternative planting for a temperate climate

1 *Viburnum tinus* 'Variegatum'
2 *Acanthus spinosus*
3 *Amelanchier* x *grandiflora* 'Ballerina'
4 *Delphinium grandiflorum* 'Blue Butterfly' (in pot)
5 *Schizostylis coccinea* 'Pink Princess' (in pot)
6 *Penstemon* 'Blackbird' (in pot)
7 *Zantedeschia aethiopica* 'Crowborough' (in pot)
8 *Ceratostigma plumbaginoides*
9 *Arbutus unedo* (standard)
10 *Hosta sieboldiana* var. *elegans*
11 *Ajuga reptans* 'Catlin's Giant'
12 *Jasminum* x *stephanense*
13 *Crocosmia* x *crocosmiiflora* 'Star of the East'
14 *Polystichum aculeatum*
15 *Agapanthus* Headbourne hybrids
16 *Rosa* 'Galway Bay'
17 *Sasa palmata* f. *nebulosa*
18 *Arum italicum* subsp. *italicum* 'Marmoratum'
19 *Abutilon megapotamicum*
20 *Euphorbia characias* subsp. *wulfenii* 'Humpty Dumpty'
21 *Campanula carpatica*

There are lots of unusual houseplants around to create an exotic, jungle effect.

Tropical and sub-tropical planting

The easiest way to give a balcony or patio an exotic, tropical atmosphere is to move some of your houseplants outdoors in summer. Ferns, such as *Didymochlaena truncatula* and Boston ferns (*Nephrolepis exaltata* 'Bostoniensis'), and palms, such as *Cocos nucifera*, that spend winter indoors can safely be left outside from the last frost of spring until the first frost of autumn. They will benefit from late-spring and summer showers and from the extra space.

Some slightly tender perennials can be successfully grown in containers. Cannas, which flower from mid- to late summer into autumn, are ideal for this treatment. They produce large, lush, often colourful leaves and vivid red, yellow and orange flowers. The rhizomes must be lifted and stored in cool, but frost-free conditions before the first autumn frosts and replanted into fresh compost the following spring.

If you have space for more permanent planting grow a passion flower (*Passiflora caerulea*). These evergreen climbers produce spectacular blooms in late spring and summer, and although they are not 100 per cent hardy, they will survive in all but the coldest of winters, and even if apparently killed off, may surprise you by reshooting in spring.

Best tropical and sub-tropical plants

* *Musa basjoo* 'Burmese Blue'
* *Brugmansia* 'Canary Bird'
* *Canna* 'Black Knight'
* *Bougainvillea* 'San Diego Red'
* *Tulbaghia violacea*
* *Ensete ventricosum*
* *Hymenocallis* x *festalis*
* *Chusquea culeou*
* *Microlepia strigosa*
* *Leptospermum scoparium*

Formal courtyard

It's easy to overfill a tiny garden such as this small courtyard with lots of different plants, features and garden ornaments. More often than not the result will look busy and cluttered. Designing small spaces along formal lines, using symmetry, simple geometric lines or shapes and a restricted plant palette will always result in a quiet, refined and noteworthy garden.

Why this works

✓ The design is strong yet simple.
✓ There is bold use of symmetry, both left to right and end to end.
✓ The selection of plants emphasizes the symmetrical ground plan and garden style, especially the trimmed yew (*Taxus*) and lavender (*Lavandula*) hedge.
✓ Flowers are chosen for their complementary, yet restrained, colours.
✓ The focal points – statue, pool, benches – are framed by carefully trained climbing roses.
✓ Maintenance is minimal – trim at each end of the growing season and tie in and deadhead the climbing roses in summer.

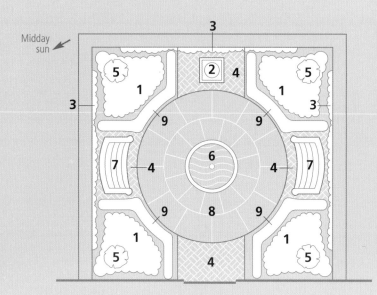

Midday sun

Garden elements key

1 Low planting
2 Statue
3 Climbing roses
4 Herringbone old brick paving
5 Evergreen
6 Low pool and fountain
7 Curved bench seat
8 Circular 'stone-effect' paving
9 Low hedge or edging

Mix and match
If you like this garden but would prefer
a different feature, see pages 250–51 for
possible variations.

Garden dimensions
4m x 4m (13ft x 13ft) approx.

Key features

Pool and fountain

Any garden can be improved with a water feature, and formal gardens are no exception. Choose a feature that is in keeping with the rest of the design: regular shapes, such as circles, squares and rectangles, are ideal. In general, the smaller the garden the simpler your pool and fountain should be. Don't forget to make provision for an underground electric supply to the site of the pool before you build the patio or terrace.

Statue

Statues are an elegant way to make focal points in many gardens. Like pools and fountains, make the size of your statue fit the space, and positioning is all-important, given that symmetry is a key design feature. Bear in mind the type of background that it will be seen against – a pale, marble statue will be lost if it is set in front of a creamy limestone wall.

Trimmed yew

Yew (*Taxus baccata* spp.) is a perfect plant for a formal garden. It can be trimmed to a range of sizes and shapes, and, as long as it is planted in well-prepared ground and is kept adequately fed and watered after planting, it will endure for many years. It is also one of few conifers that can be trimmed severely in the winter and will then sprout later in the spring from old, bare stems, which can be useful if you ever need to regenerate a neglected specimen.

Choosing and placing sculpture

Pieces of sculpture, either set individually or in thoughtfully arranged groups, add an extra quality to any garden. Like all other garden elements, they should be treated as part of the initial design process and not just added as an afterthought and put in any convenient gap or space. How they are positioned is critical, and the background against which they are seen

Choose sculpture carefully to harmonize with the garden, such as this romantic setting.

Use simple yet formal obelisks to break up and contrast with delicate soft planting.

Use simple, contrasting backgrounds to maximize the effect of a sculpture – in front of an ivy-clad wall or a tightly trimmed yew (*Taxus*) hedge, for example. Alternatively, for a softer, less obvious statement, you could place it among low planting, or with foliage from an adjacent shrub or climber just overlapping it and slightly obscuring it.

Consider including in your design arrangements for lighting your sculpture at night to make it a dramatic focal point and add another quality to your garden. Side-lighting from ground level will create contrasting light and shadow and will be more effective than a spotlight.

To make the most of your sculpture place it on a pedestal of stone or brick so that it is lifted above the surrounding ground. If your water feature is large enough stand the statue in the centre of a pool with submerged lighting for dramatic night-time viewing.

should allow pieces of sculpture to be fully appreciated.

Decide where pieces of sculpture are to be placed early on in the planning process, even if you haven't acquired them yet. Use them as focal points to be seen from different parts of the garden and place one or two in less obvious places, not to be discovered until you walk around the garden.

Make sure that the size of your chosen sculpture is in keeping with your garden. Occasionally, a massive sculpture can look dramatic if it forms the main centrepiece of a design, but generally keep them in proportion to the other features.

Sculptures should be blended into your garden design as part of the structure.

Planting

The best plants for this garden

In this small courtyard garden the plants have been chosen to reflect and enhance the formal style: the neatly trimmed yew, the low, uniform lavender hedge, the even groundcover of geraniums and the beautifully regular tulip stems and flowers. The flower colours are muted and restrained – soft

pinks and purples stand against the silvery foliage of the lavender and the dark green yew. All the plants in this garden are reliable, helping to minimize maintenance and upkeep. Apart from trimming the lavender each year and trimming the yew when it needs it, the only demanding work is to prune and train the climbing roses in late winter to create elegant arches behind the two matching benches.

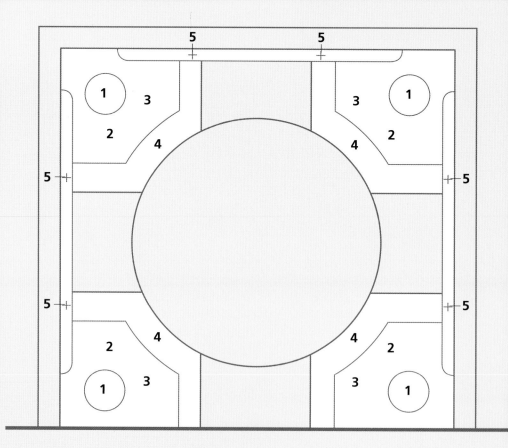

Planting key

1 *Taxus baccata* (formally trimmed)
2 *Geranium* x *cantabrigense* 'Biokovo'
3 *Tulipa* 'Douglas Bader'
4 *Lavandula* x *intermedia* 'Twickel Purple'
5 *Rosa* 'New Dawn' (climber)

In a formal garden, there are few perennials to beat irises for dramatic impact.

Plants for formal gardens

Carefully trimmed and uniformly shaped plants are an essential part of a formal garden. They also need to be reliable growers. There is nothing worse than planting a perfect hedge and then to have a single plant die unexpectedly five or six years later, making it difficult to fill the gap.

Best low hedges
- *Buxus sempervirens* 'Suffruticosa'
- *Lavandula angustifolia* 'Hidcote'
- *Euonymus japonicus* 'Microphyllus'
- *Nepeta* x *faassenii*
- *Berberis buxifolia* 'Pygmaea'
- *Erica* x *darleyensis* 'Silberschmelze'

Best evergreens for trimming
- *Viburnum tinus* 'French White'
- *Taxus baccata*
- *Buxus sempervirens*
- *Ilex aquifolium* cvs.
- *Osmanthus* x *burkwoodii*
- *Thuja plicata* 'Atrovirens'

Best perennials
- *Agapanthus* cvs.
- *Iris* (tall bearded)
- *Allium* spp. and cvs.
- *Euphorbia amygdaloides* cvs.
- *Geranium renardii*
- *Heuchera* cvs.

Best climbers and wall shrubs
- *Wisteria floribunda*
- *Rosa* (climbing)
- *Garrya elliptica* 'James Roof'
- *Hedera helix* (green-leaved cvs.)
- *Euonymus fortunei*
- *Pyracantha*

Oriental garden

Simplicity is especially relevant to gardens devoted to an oriental style. Even in a tiny space a flowing design that avoids hard, straight edges and corners, coupled with natural materials – rock, bamboo, wood and water – can result in a wonderfully secluded and peaceful oasis. Make sure that every part of the garden, whether it's a feature or a plant, serves a purpose.

Why this works

✓ An elegant, yet uncomplicated layout makes good use of limited space.
✓ Plants are chosen for harmonious colour and shape combinations.
✓ Structure is provided by small trees and bamboo, with low perennials and grasses pulling the planting together.
✓ Features – pool, pergola, lanterns – serve a specific purpose within the design and are placed thoughtfully.
✓ Contrary to initial appearances, the garden is practical and low maintenance, with sufficient space for outdoor sitting and entertaining.

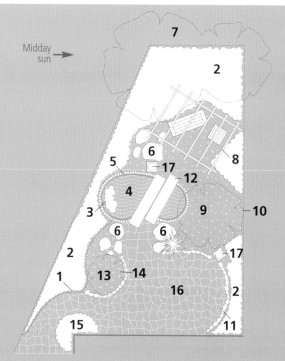

Garden elements key

1 Low bamboo or reed edging
2 Background planting
3 Marginal aquatic planting
4 Small pool

5 Log edging
6 Rocks
7 Slow-growing trees
8 Rustic bamboo pergola
9 Crushed stone

10 Small tree

11 Stone edging

12 Plank 'bridge'

13 Dwarf pine

14 Bark chippings

15 Evergreen shrub

16 Slate 'crazy' paving patio

17 Japanese lantern

Mix and match

If you like this garden but would prefer a different feature, see pages 250–51 for possible variations.

Garden dimensions

6.5m x 8m (21ft 6in x 26ft) approx.

Key features

Bamboo pergola

Pergolas built from large-diameter bamboo canes are light in weight and easy to build. Despite their appearance, they are quite strong, and they are also flexible in a way that heavier wooden pergolas are not. Use natural cord or twine to bind the canes to each other. This type of fixing will absorb movement without tending to pull apart.

Pool

Position pools so that they can be seen from key areas – in this example the pool is not only seen from both the patio and pergola sitting area but actually provides a link between them. Although fish – particularly koi and other forms of carp – are regarded as an essential part of a Japanese garden, bear in mind that pond maintenance will increase if you decide to include more than just one or two small koi.

Rocks

The placing of individual rocks or groups of rocks is as important as positioning a plant or patio. In any garden such features should appear as an integral part of the design. Bed the lower end into the soil or loose materials, such as gravel and bark, so that they give an appearance of emerging upwards. It is generally more effective to use rocks or boulders of the same type of stone, although occasionally you can mix different colours in small groups.

Bamboo pergola

Pergolas, like arches, are a great way to grow and display climbers. If your chosen climbers are vigorous and leafy they are likely to completely cover your pergola in a relatively short time, so there's no point in making your pergola elaborate (and probably expensive) as it will soon be hidden from view. However, you might want to limit the climbing plants to one or two modest growers, or even none at all, so that the structure and design of the pergola itself become the focal points.

Though an obvious choice, bamboo structures add an extra degree of refinement and authenticity.

You will need

4 large-diameter, 7.5–10cm (3–4in), bamboo poles about 2.7–3m (9–10ft) long or 4 rustic softwood poles of similar size to form the uprights

2 medium-diameter, 5–7.5cm (2–3in), bamboo poles about 2.4m (8ft) long to form the front and back rails

6 (or more) medium-diameter, 4–5cm (1½–2in), bamboo poles or thick canes to form the top cross-rails or rafters

1 small-diameter, 15mm (¾in), bamboo pole about 80cm (32in) long to form pegs

Heavy-duty natural twine, or thick copper wire or, if you can obtain it, thin, flexible bamboo strips (as used in basket making)

Concreting sand and aggregate (or combined ballast)

Cement

Selection of paddle stones or other interesting, smooth pebbles

Proprietary waterproofing agent (for external use)

Lengths of reed or split bamboo fencing (optional)

Step by step

1 Mark out a square for the four uprights and dig a neat circular hole at each position about 30cm (12in) across and 45cm (18in) deep.

2 Liberally coat the lower 50cm (20in) of each 10cm (4in) diameter upright with the waterproofer. If possible, make sure a node is at the bottom because this is easier to paint and is also more durable. If you are using softwood posts, make sure they are well soaked or use ones that have been pressure treated. At the top end

Front view

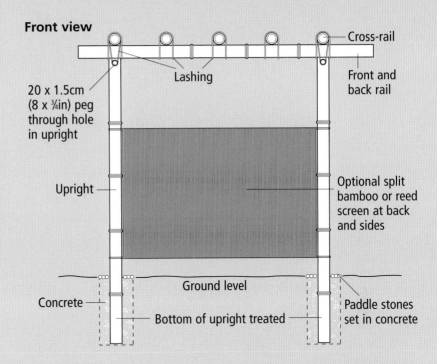

20 x 1.5cm (8 x ¾in) peg through hole in upright

Upright

Cross-rail

Lashing

Front and back rail

Optional split bamboo or reed screen at back and sides

Ground level

Concrete

Bottom of upright treated

Paddle stones set in concrete

cut a shallow V, slightly less than the diameter of the post, to form a notch in which the front and back rails can sit. Just below the V, drill a 15mm (about ¾in) diameter hole through the upright, sideways to the V.

3 Mix wet concrete using 6 parts ballast (or 4 parts aggregate, 2 parts sand) to 1 part cement and pour it into the holes, centering each post and making sure they are upright, the tops are level – not less than 2.1m (7ft) above the ground – and the V-shaped notches of the front and back pairs of posts are in line to take the rails.

4 While the concrete is wet, press the paddle stones or other pebbles or slate pieces into the surface to make crazy paving circles at ground level.

5 Select a piece of cane about 15mm (about ¾in) in diameter and cut a section 10cm (4in) longer than the diameter of the post – about 20cm (8in) total length. Cut the section

from between the nodes so that it's a uniform diameter. Repeat so that you have four pieces altogether.

6 Push the 20cm (8in) cane lengths into the 15mm (about ¾in) holes at the top of each post, leaving about 5cm (2in) protruding from each side.

7 Place the front and back rails in their respective pairs of Vs, leaving an equal overhang at each end. Take your twine, bamboo strips or wire and lash each end of the rail tightly to the top of the uprights, using the projecting 15mm (about ¾in) bamboo pieces as anchors.

8 Mark out the front and back rails in equal spaces and fix the cross-rails on top by lashing them tightly in a criss-cross fashion.

9 If you like, stretch the panels of reed or split bamboo between the uprights and tie in place to create shade or privacy.

Planting

The best plants for this garden

In small gardens the number of plants you can use is often quite limited, so you need to choose varieties that are ideal for your style of garden. Here, although the plants are essentially ornamental, they are nevertheless in perfect harmony with the controlled, yet informal layout and blend in with the colour and texture of the materials and features around. Bright or strong colours are avoided, and the overall structure of the planting provides the main interest at all times.

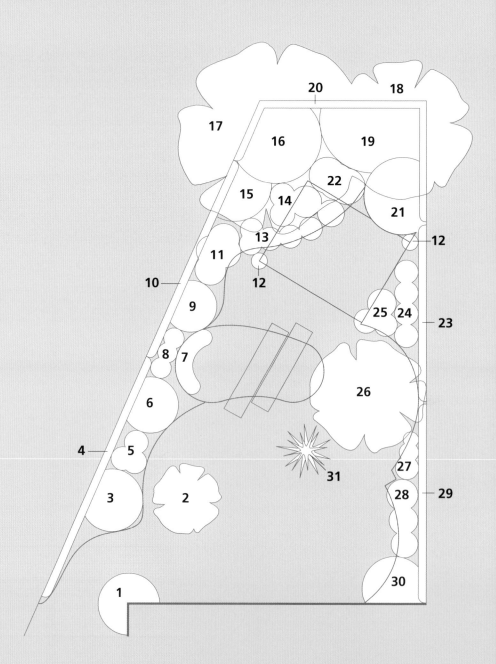

Planting key

1 *Itea ilicifolia*
2 *Pinus sylvestris* 'Beuvronensis'
3 *Fargesia nitida* 'Nymphenburg'
4 *Clematis tangutica*
5 *Astilboides tabularis*
6 *Rhododendron* 'Bruce Brechtbill'
7 *Iris laevigata*
8 *Astilbe* 'Deutschland'
9 *Cornus alba* 'Kesselringii'
10 *Lonicera sempervirens*
11 *Kirengeshoma palmata*
12 *Jasminum* x *stephanense*
13 *Ajuga reptans* 'Catlin's Giant'
14 *Helleborus argutifolius*
15 *Rhododendron* 'Gibraltar' (azalea)
16 *Hydrangea serrata* 'Grayswood'
17 *Prunus* 'Ukon'
18 *Acer capillipes*
19 *Rhododendron ponticum* 'Variegatum'
20 *Clematis* 'Apple Blossom'
21 *Viburnum* x *juddii*
22 *Darmera peltata*
23 *Solanum laxum*
24 *Iris sibirica*
25 *Hosta* 'Big Daddy'
26 *Acer palmatum* 'Bloodgood'
27 *Maianthemum racemosum* (syn. *Smilacina racemosa*)
28 *Carex elata* 'Aurea'
29 *Clematis* 'Gravetye Beauty'
30 *Ilex aquifolium* 'Myrtifolia' (male)
31 *Juniperus chinensis* 'Kaizuka'

You should use bamboos where there is a need for vertical emphasis and height.

Bamboos

Bamboos make an elegant addition to any garden, but many species are at first glance not suitable for small gardens, either because of their height or because of their rampant, spreading habit of growth. However, there are three ways in which you can grow bamboos in a small garden.

First, choose a suitable bamboo that will not outgrow its allotted space. The best to choose are forms of *Fargesia murielae* and *F. nitida*, which make neat, dense clumps, with tall, slender canes and small, delicate leaves.

Second, many bamboos, including forms that grow too large or too fast to be put in the ground, can be grown in large containers. This is a particularly good way of displaying those bamboos grown for their attractively coloured stems and large or variegated leaves, such as *Phyllostachys nigra*, *Sasa palmata* f. *nebulosa* and *Pleioblastus viridistriatus*.

Third, you can plant your bamboo in the ground but in such a way that its root spread is physically restricted. Do this by leaving a suitably sized hole, either within a paved area or at the edge of the paving, in a space backed by walls to create a triangular bed in the corner of your garden. For all but the dwarfest forms, make sure that the construction of your paving is solid, with a deep base to deter strong culms (rhizomes) from penetrating sideways. As an added precaution, you could line the edge of your planting hole with 60 x 60cm (24 x 24in) paving flags on edge to enclose the bamboo's root system.

Wildlife garden

You don't need a large garden in the country to encourage and help wildlife. Even the smallest of gardens can make a valuable contribution at some level at a time when natural habitats are under pressure, and gardens are known to provide 'corridors' for wildlife to move from one habitat to another.

Why this works

✓ A natural pond with marginal and aquatic planting and a shallow 'beach' area gives easy access for a variety of birds, small mammals and amphibians.

✓ Dense planting, particularly evergreens, creates a safe, desirable environment especially for nesting birds.

✓ Heavy prunings and leaf litter are stockpiled as a potential hibernation zone and to encourage worms and beetles.

✓ The general planting includes cultivars that will provide food in the form of leaves, nectar, pollen, seeds and berries and nesting material.

✓ Plenty of climbers give additional wildlife habitat on the boundaries.

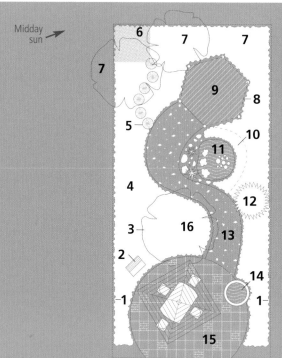

Midday sun →

Garden elements key

1 Evergreen wall shrub
2 Bird table
3 Fruiting tree with bird food holders
4 Mixed border
5 Log 'stepping stones'
6 Leaf litter or log pile
7 Trees and dense shrub planting
8 Bamboo screen
9 Raised deck
10 Bog garden

11 Pond
12 Bamboo
13 Shale path
14 Bird bath
15 Patio
16 Groundcover and bulbs

Mix and match
If you like this garden but would prefer
a different feature, see pages 250–51 for
possible variations.

Garden dimensions
5m x 10.5m (16ft 6in x 34ft 6in) approx.

Key features

Log stepping stones

Use natural log rounds 5–10cm (2–4in) thick to make access paths through planted areas. Sink them into the ground, leaving about 2.5cm (1in) above soil level, and mulch around them with bark. Use untreated wood, which will slowly rot beneath, making ideal conditions for earthworms and other insects. For safety, cover the tops of the 'stones' with pieces of galvanized chicken wire fixed down with fencing staples to make them non-slip.

Bird bath

Birds appreciate water in the garden so they can drink and bathe. Almost any shallow container will suffice. It doesn't need to be more than about 5cm (2in) deep at its deepest. Alternatively, you can use a purpose-made bird bath. For a really natural effect, you can sink it into the ground to appear like a tiny pond.

Pond

Ponds provide valuable habitats for creatures whose lifecycle involves water, such as frogs, toads and newts, and insects, including dragonflies and hoverflies. As long as there is a shallow area where wildlife can get easy access, artificial ponds made from liners or preformed plastic are a good basic. However, to be really effective you will need to have a layer of low-nutrient soil (such as heavy subsoil) in which aquatic plants can root and underwater insects can make a home.

Bird bath or splash pool

A sunken bird bath can make a natural feature in the garden, especially if you can locate it near the patio or by a window where the activity it generates can be appreciated at close quarters. This version can be built as part of a patio if you want, and you can even adapt it as a splash pool for small children. At the end of the splashing session, just pull out the 'plug' and the water drains away, and it's safe until the next time you need it.

Wide, shallow containers are best for bird baths and watering stations.

You will need

About 1.35m x 1.35m (4ft 6in x 4ft 6in) heavy-duty black polythene or pond liner

19mm (¾in) plastic waste pipe

19mm (¾in) tank connector

2 x 20mm (¾in) 90° bends

19mm (¾in) extension connector

Ballast (or concreting sand and shingle)

Cement

Smooth, flattish pebbles

Step by step

To build this into your patio, omit a section of paving 1.2m x 1.2m (4ft x 4ft), the equivalent to four 60cm x 60cm (24in x 24in) flags. For a mini-pool omit one flag.

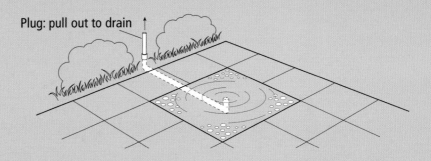

Plug: pull out to drain

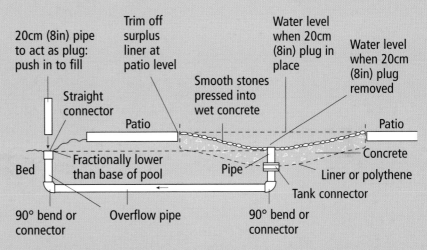

20cm (8in) pipe to act as plug: push in to fill

Trim off surplus liner at patio level

Water level when 20cm (8in) plug in place

Water level when 20cm (8in) plug removed

Straight connector

Smooth stones pressed into wet concrete

Patio

Patio

Bed

Fractionally lower than base of pool

Pipe

Concrete

Liner or polythene

Tank connector

90° bend or connector

Overflow pipe

90° bend or connector

1 Dig a narrow trench from the centre of the pool to the downhill edge of your patio to take the overflow pipe.

2 Connect a 90° bend at the lower half of the tank connector to one end of the plastic pipe. Place this in the dug trench, with the bend or connector at the centre of the pool, about 15cm (6in) below the finished patio level. Backfill the trench with damp, lean concrete (1 part cement to 10 parts ballast), making sure there is a slight slope down the pipe away from the pool centre.

3 Complete the laying of your patio, omitting the four slabs to form the splash pool.

4 Excavate the pool area if necessary to form a gentle scallop, 7.5cm (3in) deep at the edge and 15cm (6in) deep at the middle.

5 Cut a small circular hole in the centre of the polythene or liner about 19mm (¾in) across. Place the liner in the scallop excavation so that the top end of the tank connector comes through the hole. Screw down the top section of the tank connector to trap the liner and make the join watertight.

6 Cut a 20cm (8in) length of pipe and push it into the top of the tank connector. This will form the plughole.

7 Mix concrete (1 part cement to 6 parts ballast) and pour it on to the liner, about 7.5cm (3in) thick, making sure that the edge of the liner projects up just beyond the level of the flags. Make the mix just stiff enough so that you can make it follow the contours of the 'scallop'.

8 Press the pebbles into the wet concrete and leave it to set.

9 When set and hard, trim off the excess liner and saw off the pipe flush with the pebbles.

10 Cut the buried pipe just beyond the edge of the patio and fix the other 90° bend. Push another length of pipe into the upright part of the bend. Cut this off so that when you push the extension connector on to the end, the top of it will be slightly lower, by 1–2cm (½–¾in), than the centre of the pool base.

11 To use the pool, take a 20cm (8in) length of pipe and push it into the top of the extension connector. Fill up the pool to the top of the pebbles. To empty the pool, pull out the pipe and the water will drain away by gravity into the bed at the side of the patio. Leave the pipe out until you want to refill the pool.

Planting

The best plants for this garden

The planting has been carefully chosen to break up the narrowness of this garden. While the overall appearance is a prime consideration, the individual plants have been selected because of the way in which they add to the wildlife-attracting quality of the garden. Planting is generally dense with a good proportion of evergreens, which most wildlife will appreciate because of the cover and protection they provide, but there are also more open areas of lower planting for variety.

Planting key

1 *Pyracantha* 'Orange Glow'
2 *Lavandula angustifolia* 'Hidcote Pink'
3 *Geranium himalayense* 'Gravetye'
4 *Choisya ternata* 'Sundance'
5 *Alchemilla alpina*
6 *Ajuga reptans* 'Palisander'
7 *Pachysandra terminalis* 'Variegata'
8 *Sorbus hupehensis*
9 *Hypericum prolificum*
10 *Chaenomeles* x *superba* 'Rowallane'

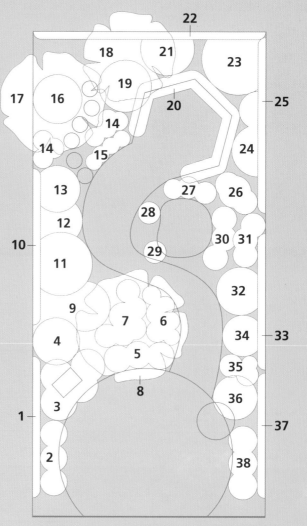

11 *Leycesteria formosa*
12 *Sarcococca hookeriana* var.
   digyna
13 *Aronia melanocarpa*
14 *Digitalis purpurea* Excelsior Group
15 *Briza media*
16 *Rhododendron* 'Cunningham's
   White'
17 *Euonymus planipes*
18 *Prunus x subhirtella* 'Autumnalis
   Rosea'
19 *Ilex aquifolium* 'Golden van Tol'
   (female)
20 *Rosa* 'Alchymist'
21 *Berberis darwinii*
22 *Hedera helix* 'Buttercup'
23 *Buddleja davidii* 'Royal Red'
24 *Mahonia x wagneri* 'Undulata'
25 *Akebia quinata*
26 *Hosta* 'Frances Williams'
27 *Primula japonica* 'Postford White'
28 *Deschampsia cespitosa*
   'Bronzeschleier'
29 *Caltha palustris*
30 *Iris laevigata*
31 *Aster novae-angliae* 'Andenken
   an Alma Pötschke'
32 *Fargesia murieliae* 'Simba'
33 *Rosa* 'Handel'
34 *Cistus ladanifer*
35 *Eryngium planum*
36 *Erica erigena* 'Irish Salmon'
37 *Cotoneaster sternianus*
38 *Centranthus ruber* var. *coccineus*

Butterfly border

It's quite easy to attract butterflies and other beneficial insects into your garden by planting a selection of plants that will supply colour, nectar and pollen. Make sure your selection includes at least one early-flowering species to provide sustenance on a sunny, mild late-winter or early-spring day when the first insects are appearing.

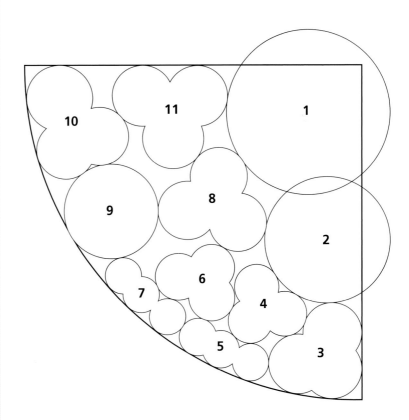

1 *Buddleja* 'Pink Delight'
2 *Hebe* 'Midsummer Beauty'
3 *Erica x darleyensis* 'Ada S. Collings'
4 *Aster x frikartii* 'Mönch'
5 *Thymus serpyllum* 'Pink Chintz'
6 *Centranthus ruber* 'Albus'
7 *Centaurea bella*
8 *Coreopsis verticillata* 'Moonbeam'
9 *Lavandula angustifolia* 'Folgate'
10 *Sedum* 'Herbstfreude'
11 *Clematis recta* 'Purpurea'

Green-on-green

This modest garden relies on a combination of natural materials and carefully chosen foliage planting for its interest. Flowers are present of course but they are secondary to the leaves and stems of the plants in terms of both colour and size. The layout is based on bold, straight lines and right angles, which provide a strong contrast to the softness of the leaves.

Why this works

✓ A crisp, organized ground plan includes a path linking two patio areas, which are separated by small trees and low planting.

✓ The summerhouse provides excellent covered space for bad weather and is tucked away in one corner, partly screened by trees and other plants.

✓ The paved areas are constructed from natural stone and timber edging, which are in harmony with the foliage planting and the natural wood of the summerhouse.

✓ Plants have been selected not only for their different qualities of foliage – size, colour and shape – but also for their easy-going nature, requiring little in the way of special conditions or pampering.

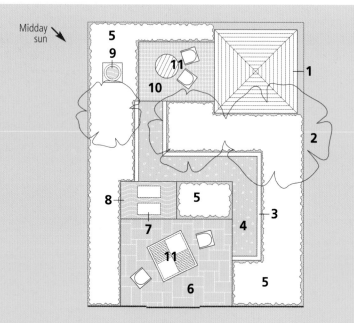

Garden elements key

1 Summerhouse
2 Tree
3 Timber edging
4 Gravel path
5 Planting
6 Cotswold stone patio
7 Stepping stones over pool
8 Pool
9 Bird bath
10 Sett paving
11 Patio furniture

Mix and match
If you like this garden but would prefer a different feature, see pages 250–51 for possible variations.

Garden dimensions
5.25m x 6.75m (17ft x 22ft) approx.

Key features

Geometric pool

You can add an extra dimension to a simple geometric pool by leading a 'path' across it via stepping stones. The easiest way to build these is to construct your pool with a firm, level bottom and then build small piers made from concrete blocks or bricks where the 'stepping stones' are to go. Finish off with paving flags, making sure the lower edge of the flags is at the final water level.

Foliage plants

You can create wonderful plant combinations without the need for flowers. Use different coloured or variegated foliage for extra effect and introduce silver or grey leaves, which work well in linking other colours. Don't look only at different leaf shapes for contrast, but also at the overall habit of the whole plant, so that you can place tall, narrow species next to wide-spreading ones.

Cotswold stone patio

Stone paving associates well with all kinds of plants as well as with other natural hard landscaping materials. How you use the stone will depend on the style of garden you are trying to achieve: regular, sawn flags look good in geometric or formal layouts, while hand-hewn pieces in random sizes are excellent for old-fashioned or informal designs, especially where the joints are left unpointed and are filled instead with fine gravel or even soil to encourage mosses and small plants to self-seed and grow.

Making the best use of foliage plants

As you look through gardening books and magazines or spend time going around local plant nurseries you will soon become aware of the wide range of plants that have interesting and attractive leaves. However, selecting plants for their individual merit is only part of the process of creating a beautiful foliage garden: how you place them in juxtaposition to each other and against different backgrounds can have a marked influence on the final effect.

Plants with insignificant flowers but interesting foliage can be very garden-worthy.

Combinations of plants with contrasting sizes and shapes of leaves make attractive edging for patios and decking.

Dramatically shaped leaves will look best against a fairly plain background – dark foliage against light walls, say, and coloured or pale foliage against a darker background. With coloured or variegated foliage, this will look more pronounced where it can catch some sunlight, particularly early or late in the day when the sun is lower and there will be more shadows and contrasts.

If you are grouping plants of similar colours, perhaps two or three shades of green, you'll need species with a greater contrast of leaf shape and size or a different overall habit of growth so that they don't all merge into a single mass.

Strong colour contrasts, such as the dark purple of *Corylus maxima* 'Purpurea' against the light yellow of *Physocarpus opulifolius* 'Dart's Gold', can be dramatic, but don't fill your garden with too many of these combinations because in a small space they can be overpowering and distracting to the eye.

Plants with silver foliage are excellent in any garden for linking different colours, and their leaves will act as a natural backdrop for darker shades and greens.

Be aware that although your plants are selected primarily for their foliage qualities, many will still produce flowers, and so you need to consider the impact these may have – for example, the brilliant orange of *Geum* 'Borisii' may look garish against the pinky stripes of *Phormium* 'Jester'.

Combine plants to take advantage of their different habits of growth. The upright, narrow leaves of iris contrast beautifully with the wide-spreading, palmate fronds of rodgersia, and the delicate, silver-veined, arching Japanese painted fern (*Athyrium niponicum* var. *pictum*) complements the large, simple, glossy leaves of *Bergenia* 'Abendglut'.

Try to keep a 'visual' balance – for example, a single small *Ajuga reptans* 'Atropurpurea' will look completely out of scale alongside a mature specimen of *Phormium* 'Yellow Wave'. You will probably want a drift of five or even more to maximize the effect.

Finally, try to include a basic framework of evergreens so that even in the depths of winter there will be something attractive to look at.

Break up areas of low planting using upright varieties such as these iris and acorus.

Planting

The best plants for this garden

Primarily chosen for their foliage and overall shape, the plants in this green-on-green garden create a wealth of contrasts in colour, shape and texture. The low edging plants soften the borders and contrast with the straight, angular ground pattern of the paths, pool and other paved areas.

The trees are used to divide the garden into two parts, and cultivars that are appropriate for the limited space available have been selected.

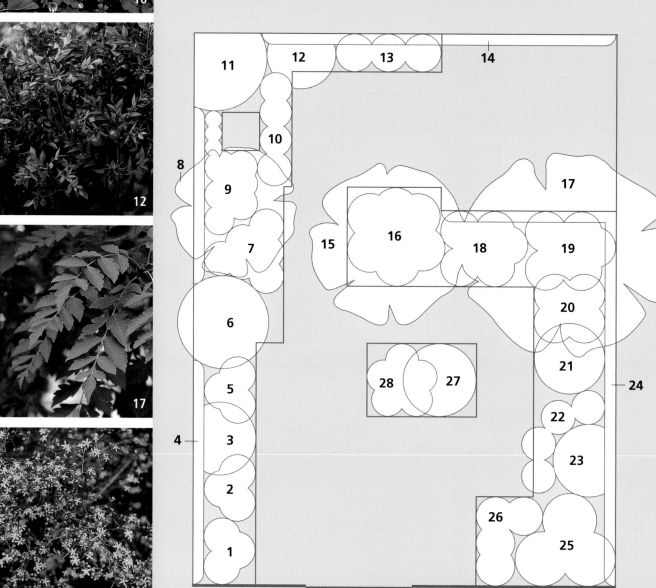

Planting key

1 *Miscanthus sinensis* 'Gracillimus'
2 *Trifolium repens* 'Purpurascens'
3 *Rheum* 'Ace of Hearts'
4 *Jasminum officinale* 'Argenteovariegatum'
5 *Carex testacea*
6 *Cornus alba* 'Sibirica Variegata'
7 x *Heucherella* 'Viking Ship'
8 *Acer griseum*
9 *Athyrium niponicum* var. *pictum*
10 *Geranium renardii*
11 *Hydrangea quercifolia* 'Snowflake'
12 *Ruscus aculeatus*
13 *Hosta* 'Ground Master'
14 *Lonicera henryi*
15 *Aralia spinosa*
16 *Tellima grandiflora* Rubra Group
17 *Koelreuteria paniculata*
18 *Iris foetidissima*
19 *Darmera peltata*
20 *Helleborus* x *sternii*
21 *Ilex aquifolium* 'Ferox' (male)
22 *Astrantia major* 'Sunningdale Variegated'
23 *Corokia cotoneaster*
24 *Vitis amurensis*
25 *Nandina domestica* 'Richmond'
26 *Koeleria glauca*
27 *Pinus mugo* subsp. *mugo*
28 *Iris pallida* 'Argentea Variegata'

Alternative planting

1 *Miscanthus sinensis* 'Zebrinus'
2 *Lysimachia nummularia* 'Aurea'
3 *Artemisia absinthium* 'Lambrook Silver'
4 *Jasminum officinale* 'Aureum'
5 *Carex oshimensis* 'Evergold'
6 *Cornus sericea* 'White Gold'
7 *Lamium galeobdolon* 'Hermann's Pride'
8 *Laburnum* x *watereri* 'Vossii'
9 *Dryopteris erythrosora*
10 *Tiarella cordifolia*
11 *Philadelphus coronarius* 'Aureus'
12 *Daphne odora* 'Aureomarginata'
13 *Hosta* 'Gold Standard'
14 *Clematis* 'Moonlight'
15 *Acer palmatum* 'Aureum'
16 *Melissa officinalis* 'Aurea'
17 *Gleditsia triacanthos* 'Sunburst'
18 *Iris pseudacorus*
19 *Euphorbia palustris*
20 *Zantedeschia aethiopica* 'Crowborough'
21 *Ilex aquifolium* 'Ferox Aurea' (male)
22 *Stachys byzantina* 'Primrose Heron'
23 *Brachyglottis* (Dunedin Group) 'Sunshine'
24 *Vitis vinifera* 'Incana'
25 *Coronilla valentina* subsp. *glauca* 'Variegata' (1 only)
26 *Carex elata* 'Aurea'
27 *Pinus mugo* 'Ophir'
28 *Iris pseudacorus* 'Variegata'

Galtonia viridiflora is a lovely late summer-flowering bulb to use as a highlight within foliage planting.

Foliage for shade

In some small gardens you might find a corner that gets little or no sun due to a wall or fence or perhaps due to the overhang of a small tree or large shrub. Use a selection of suitable foliage plants to liven up such a difficult spot.

Best green plants

- *Paris polyphylla*
- *Pachysandra terminalis*
- *Hosta* 'Honeybells'
- *Hacquetia epipactis*
- *Asplenium scolopendrium*
- *Helleborus multifidus* subsp. *hercegovinus*
- *Hedera helix* 'Maple Leaf'
- *Ilex crenata* 'Mariesii'
- *Galtonia viridiflora*
- *Heuchera* 'Green Ivory'

City chic
roof garden

In the centres of towns and cities space for creating gardens at ground level is frequently limited. However, opportunities for creating roof gardens above ground level do exist. Contemporary designs can take advantage of modern materials and techniques and can be developed to reflect the urban environment. In these situations, a simple, bold planting scheme is often more effective than a fussy, over-complicated one.

Why this works

✓ The simple yet bold design is in keeping with the surroundings.

✓ Modern materials emphasize the architectural style of the design.

✓ Elegant clear screens allow views out of the garden and provide shelter from prevailing winds and turbulence.

✓ Large shrubs trained into 'tree' shapes are an ideal size for giving structure and height within a small space.

✓ Accessories, such as the sculpture, bench and boulders, are simple and restrained, in keeping with the rest of the garden.

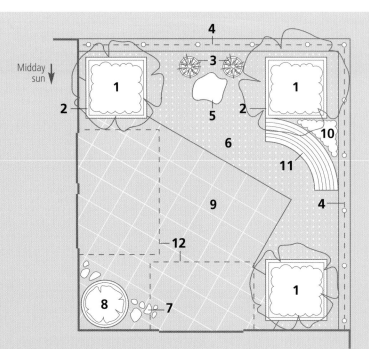

Garden elements key

1 Small tree and underplanting

2 Planter

3 Formal evergreens in pots

4 Glass or perspex screen with stainless steel frame

5 Sculpture

6 AstroTurf

7 Boulders

8 Concrete planter and
    large evergreen
9 Paving
10 Planting
11 Bench seat
12 Retractable awning

Mix and match
If you like this garden but would prefer
a different feature, see pages 250–51 for
possible variations.

Garden dimensions
4.3m x 4.7m (14ft x 15ft 6in) approx.

Key features

Planters

Paving flags are ideal for making plant containers large enough to hold specimen shrubs or small trees. There are many sizes, colours and textures available so you can design planters to fit your own space and theme. By their nature, these planters are heavy, so before you embark on making one check that your roof is strong enough to bear the weight.

Trees

The effect of trees is obtained by carefully pruning large-growing shrubs. You can plant small sizes of your selected species and prune them as they develop over several seasons, or, if your budget allows, buy large specimen shrubs and shape them for instant effect. Another advantage of this method of growing plants is that it leaves space immediately beneath for additional low-growing plants, especially creepers and trailers to hang over and soften the edges of the planters.

Screen

Glass and stainless steel are combined to make this simple screen. In some roof and balcony gardens you may need one or two panels to produce the shelter you need, but other positions might need to be completely enclosed. Safety glass is the best material to use, because apart from being safe it's easy to clean and won't deteriorate over time, although it may be relatively costly.

Paving flag planters

With a little skill, planning and a spare pair of hands, these planters are relatively quick and easy to build. The huge range of flag paving available means that you can personalize them to exactly meet your own needs.

Note: because of the weight assemble your planter directly in its final position.

The crisp, neat shape of this square planter is an excellent foil for the arching silver foliage of *Leymus arenarius*.

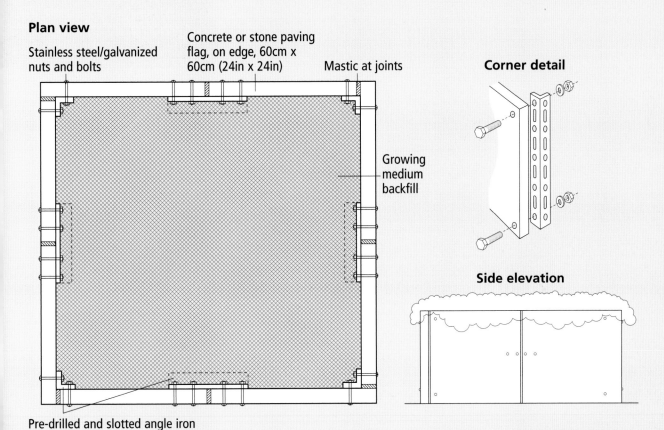

Plan view

Stainless steel/galvanized nuts and bolts

Concrete or stone paving flag, on edge, 60cm x 60cm (24in x 24in)

Mastic at joints

Growing medium backfill

Pre-drilled and slotted angle iron

Corner detail

Side elevation

You will need

For each planter

8 x 60cm x 60cm (24in x 24in) paving flags

4 x 60cm (24in) lengths of plain angle iron

4 x 30cm (12in) lengths of the same angle iron

32 x 8mm (⅓in) (M8) x 7.5cm (3in) stainless steel or galvanized nuts, bolts and washers

External-quality mastic and applicator

Step by step

1 Take the 60cm (24in) lengths of plain angle iron and drill an 8mm (⅓in) hole at each end of one of the flanges, 2.5cm (1in) from the end. Repeat on the other flange, but 5cm (2in) from the end so that the corner bolts don't foul each other. Take the 30cm (12in) lengths of angle iron and repeat, on one flange only, making two holes 2.5cm (1in) from each end and two holes 12.5cm (5in) from each end (four holes in total per length).

2 Take two flags and stand them on edge, corner to corner, to form a right angle. Place a 60cm (24in) piece of the angle iron tightly into the corner and mark through all the 8mm (⅓in) holes on to the flags with a pencil or marker pen. Drill 8mm (⅓in) holes at

the marked positions through the flags with a masonry drill.

3 Pull the flags apart and run a bead of mastic along the end of one flag. Push the flags back tightly together, reposition the angle iron and secure with the nuts, bolts and washers.

4 Take a third flag, place it on edge and butt it up to the outer vertical edge of one of the corner flags, making sure the holes for the 'corner' are in the right position. Take a 30cm (12in) length of angle iron and place it horizontally across the butted edges of the flags, mark and repeat as for the corner.

5 Continue around the planter until the square is complete.

Planting

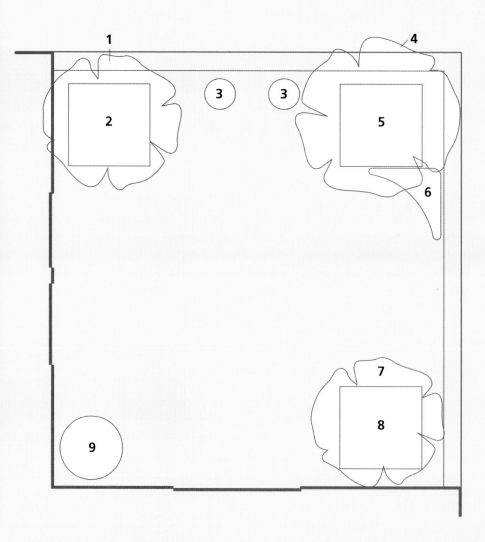

The best plants for this garden

In this small garden only a few species are used to avoid a fussy, cluttered look. Flower colour is limited and low key, and instead the emphasis is on the form and structure of leaves and stems. The tree-like shrubs are perfectly in scale with the space and will thrive in a roof garden like this. The selected plants are easy to maintain, and none of them requires any special treatment.

Planting key

1 *Euonymus europaeus* 'Red Cascade' (half-standard)
2 x *Fatshedera lizei variegata*
3 *Taxus baccata* (topiary)
4 *Aralia elata* (multi-stemmed specimen)
5 *Hedera helix* 'Buttercup'
6 *Iris sibirica* 'Papillon'
7 *Photinia serratifolia* (standard)
8 *Geranium wlassovianum*
9 *Viburnum* x *rhytidophylloides*

Trees from shrubs

One of the disadvantages of a small garden – especially roof gardens – is that it's not always easy or advisable to plant trees because of their size and vigour.

A possible solution is to 'convert' a large shrub into a tree-like form, which will give you the benefits of a small tree that is much more manageable and suitable for a limited space. There are basically two ways you can produce this type of 'tree', both of which rely on judicious pruning to achieve the end result.

The first approach is to find a suitable shrub – that is, one that already has or that can be encouraged to produce a strong main stem or leader. Pruning off the sideshoots from the lower part of this stem will produce a 'trunk', while the upper part of the plant can be trimmed to produce a crown, the result being a standard 'tree'. The amount of pruning depends on the species of shrub or conifer you have selected.

The second method is to take a large specimen shrub, preferably one with several strong main stems. Again, remove the lower branches to leave these main stems clean. This will produce a multi-stemmed 'tree'.

In both cases, as the 'tree' develops and new shoots begin to appear on the clean stem or trunk or at ground level, it is a simple matter to remove them before they grow too large.

Small-leaved shrubs can be trained into 'mini-trees' for planting in limited spaces.

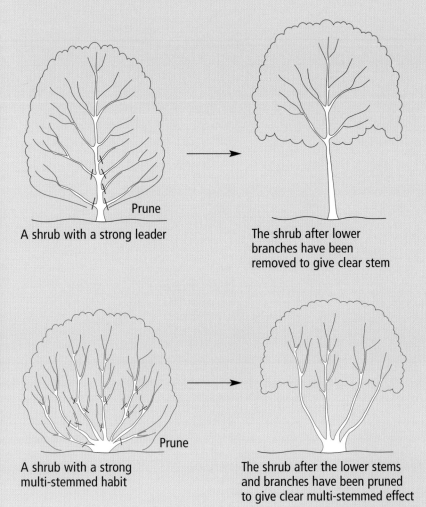

Prune

A shrub with a strong leader

The shrub after lower branches have been removed to give clear stem

Prune

A shrub with a strong multi-stemmed habit

The shrub after the lower stems and branches have been pruned to give clear multi-stemmed effect

Best shrubs to grow as standard trees

- *Photinia* x *fraseri* 'Red Robin'
- *Arbutus unedo*
- *Enkianthus campanulatus*
- *Ilex aquifolium* cvs.
- *Taxus baccata*
- *Laurus nobilis* 'Aurea'
- *Pittosporum tenuifolium* cvs.
- *Cytisus battandieri*
- *Cornus mas*
- *Ceanothus thyrsiflorus*

Best shrubs to grow as multi-stemmed trees

- *Viburnum rhytidophyllum*
- *Aralia elata*
- *Amelanchier* x *grandiflora* 'Ballerina'
- *Elaeagnus pungens* 'Variegata'
- *Sorbus koehneana*
- *Abutilon* 'Cannington Carol'
- *Euonymus alatus*
- *Olearia macrodonta*
- *Viburnum lantana*
- *Juniperus chinensis* 'Blaauw'

Romantic terrace

Small gardens are ideally suited to producing a romantic feel because of their size and intimacy. Victorian features, such as gothic-looking, wrought-iron arches and stone balustrading, combine with soft, traditional planting that is chosen for flower and scent to accentuate this feeling. Although space is limited, there is lots of interest without creating a sense of fussiness or clutter.

Why this works

✓ An informal, yet well laid-out ground plan achieves a good balance between planting and hard areas.
✓ Features traditionally associated with the romantic style of gardening are carefully positioned and used.
✓ The loose yet well-organized planting of traditional and old-fashioned cultivars is selected for shape, colour and scent.
✓ The use of reclaimed, weathered materials, such as the brick and York stone paving, add to the impression of age and maturity.

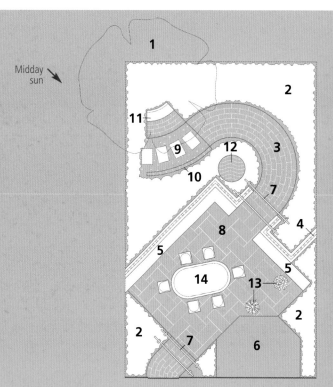

Midday sun

Garden elements key

1 Shade tree
2 Mixed border
3 Brick paving
4 Balustrade
5 Dwarf hedge
6 Sun room
7 Rose arch
8 Terrace of random rectangular York stone paving
9 York stone flags in gravel

10 Brick edge
11 Shady sitting area
12 Pool and fountain
13 Urns
14 Terrace furniture

Mix and match
If you like this garden but would prefer a different feature, see pages 250–51 for possible variations.

Garden dimensions
6m x 9.5m (20ft x 31ft) approx.

Key features

Rose arch

Wrought iron arches, arbours and gazebos in a gothic style are classic features to be found in a romantic garden. If you're going to include more than one of these, keep them in the same style and colour to provide unity. Don't plant them with climbers that are too leafy or vigorous and that will quickly cover and hide the tracery of the wrought iron. Use lighter or slower growing plants, such as roses, jasmine and clematis.

Balustrade

Classic stone balustrades are an integral part of the romantic style. They can add character to even a small terrace or paved area, and they are ideal for positioning on top of a low wall to create a change of level. For a classic finish, plant a low hedge of lavender (*Lavandula*) or catmint (*Nepeta*) between the edge of your paved terrace and the balustrade wall.

Bench seat

It can be very enjoyable to wander down your garden and to then sit and relax for a while on a bench. Think about the best place to position your bench – in the shade of a tree, in a sunny corner or maybe an alcove created in a yew or box hedge. There are dozens of styles available, so you should be able to find one that is in keeping with the style of your garden design – romantic, formal, contemporary and so on.

Microclimate

When you are selecting plants for your garden one of the main factors influencing your choice will be whether the plant is suitable for the climatic conditions found in the area where you live. For example, if you experience cold, severe winters and hot, dry summers the plants you choose must be hardy and probably drought tolerant. Alternatively, in areas of mild winters and damper

Hot, dry corners enclosed by walls and fences can be planted with succulent-type planting.

summers, your plants can be more tender and more moisture reliant.

In any garden, however, regardless of its size, you will find (or indeed can create) localized spots where – in possibly a small space – the climatic conditions can be quite different from those found in the more general area around you. These 'microclimates' can and should be used to your advantage when planning your garden, and learning to recognize them and how to modify your garden to develop specific types of microclimate are invaluable techniques.

Walls and fences that catch the midday sun are excellent places to grow plants that may not be fully hardy in an open position, for example, particularly climbers and wall shrubs, such as abutilon and passion flower (*Passiflora*). On the other hand, where these barriers obstruct the sun, you will find cool shade on the opposite side, which is ideal for plants such as astilbes, hostas and ferns that don't appreciate hot positions.

Use walls, fences and hedges to create windbreaks and provide areas of shelter, which are not only good for many delicate plants but also for sitting in. Remember that the taller and wider (end to end) a windbreak is, the greater the area downwind that will be sheltered.

You may find that the shady side of a wall or fence is dry because of the 'rain shadow' effect. If you want to create a shady area without depriving the plants of water, you will need to make vertical barriers of a more 'open' nature, using trellis or open-weave fencing or framed structures covered in horticultural shade net or laths. Alternatively, build a small pergola or overhead beams, above the area you wish to shade, on which you can lay shade net, thin battens, open bamboo screening or even a climbing plant that appreciates direct sunlight.

Plants themselves can create their own microclimates. A large evergreen, such as rhododendron or laurel (*Prunus laurocerasus*), can be planted to cast shade on to a particular area where you could grow, say, rodgersias or ligularias, while on the opposite side you will find a sunny, sheltered spot better suited to fuchsias or lavender (*Lavandula*). The area found beneath deciduous shrubs or small trees has particular value as a microclimate, being open and moist in winter and shady and dry in summer, the ideal growing conditions for many spring bulbs.

A sheltered zone is proportional to the height and width of windbreaks

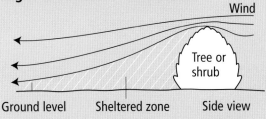

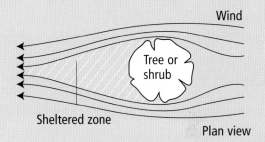

Solid barriers can create dry zones

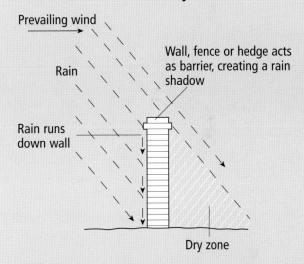

Planting can create cool, shady zones

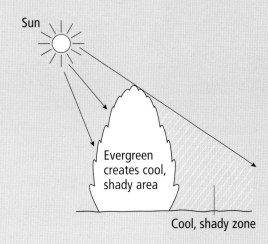

Planting

20

24

26

38

The best plants for this garden

The combinations of soft, complementary colours and mix of different plant habits and shapes are ideal for this romantic garden. A selection of larger shrubs together with climbers on the boundaries and arches provides structure and a background to the smaller, infill plants. Although this is primarily a summer garden, there is always some planting to provide interest at virtually any time of the year.

Planting key

1 *Lilium regale*
2 *Erysimum* 'Bowles Mauve'
3 *Rosa* 'Adam'
4 *Clematis montana*
5 *Euphorbia amygdaloides* 'Purpurea'
6 *Rosa* 'Bonica'
7 *Crocosmia* x *crocosmiiflora* 'Solfatare'
8 *Lavandula angustifolia* 'Munstead' (hedge)

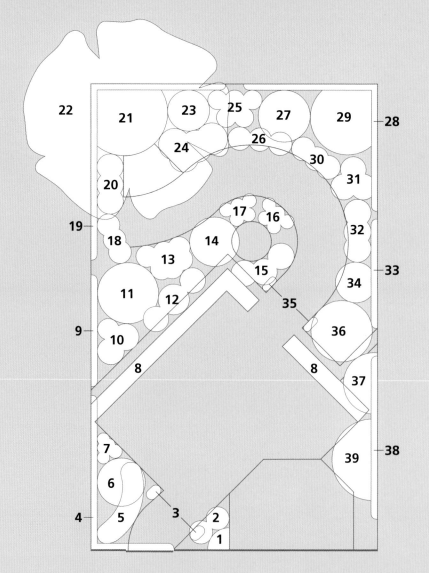

9 *Rosa* 'Galway Bay'
10 *Delphinium* Belladonna Group 'Peace'
11 *Cornus controversa* 'Variegata'
12 *Achillea* 'Anthea'
13 *Allium giganteum*
14 *Potentilla fruticosa* 'Mount Everest'
15 *Platycodon grandiflorus* 'Mariesii'
16 *Dianthus* 'Doris'
17 *Sisyrinchium striatum*
18 *Aconitum carmichaelii* Arendsii Group 'Arendsii'
19 *Lonicera implexa*
20 *Digitalis ferruginea*
21 *Hydrangea aspera* Villosa Group
22 *Prunus padus* 'Watereri'
23 *Daphne laureola*
24 *Anemone nemorosa*
25 *Ligularia przewalskii*
26 *Alchemilla mollis*
27 *Rhododendron* 'Tortoiseshell Wonder'
28 *Clematis* 'Miss Bateman'
29 *Philadelphus coronarius* 'Aureus'
30 *Dicentra* 'Adrian Bloom'
31 *Campanula persicifolia* 'Wortham Belle'
32 *Geranium psilostemon*
33 *Rosa* 'Kathleen Harrop'
34 *Ceratostigma willmottianum*
35 *Rosa* 'Céline Forestier'
36 *Cotinus* 'Grace'
37 *Hydrangea paniculata* 'Grandiflora'
38 *Clematis* 'Doctor Ruppel'
39 *Lavatera* x *clementii* 'Barnsley'

A romantic corner

Even the tiniest garden can be given a romantic makeover with a few carefully selected plants and features. Here, a thoughtfully designed corner illustrates what can be achieved in such a space.

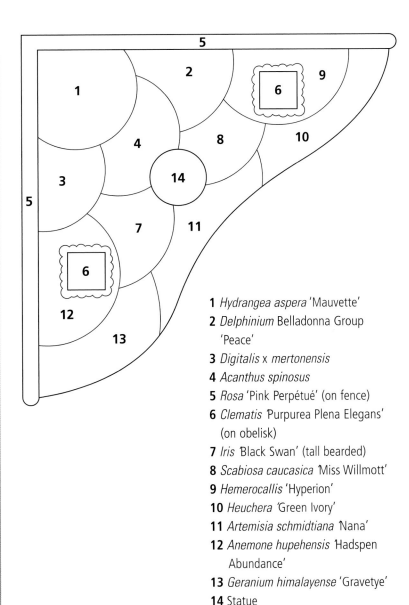

1 *Hydrangea aspera* 'Mauvette'
2 *Delphinium* Belladonna Group 'Peace'
3 *Digitalis* x *mertonensis*
4 *Acanthus spinosus*
5 *Rosa* 'Pink Perpétué' (on fence)
6 *Clematis* 'Purpurea Plena Elegans' (on obelisk)
7 *Iris* 'Black Swan' (tall bearded)
8 *Scabiosa caucasica* 'Miss Willmott'
9 *Hemerocallis* 'Hyperion'
10 *Heuchera* 'Green Ivory'
11 *Artemisia schmidtiana* 'Nana'
12 *Anemone hupehensis* 'Hadspen Abundance'
13 *Geranium himalayense* 'Gravetye'
14 Statue

Easy-living garden

Leisure time is becoming a more important and valuable part of people's lives, especially when the pressures of work are great and family commitments crowd in. Even the smallest garden, therefore, needs to be geared up to letting you make the best use of this time. In this example, a generous deck and tiled area provides plenty of space for outdoor relaxation with the added enticement of a hot tub and a barbecue area for those spa parties.

Why this works

✓ A hot tub is tucked away in a sunny, sheltered corner, softened by evergreen planting.
✓ A generous paved area, combining timber decking and terracotta tiles, gives room to spread out and relax.
✓ Generous corner plantings make the small garden seem more spacious.
✓ There is enough room on the deck for a free-standing hammock or, with concealed supports, in the planting.
✓ Conveniently placed barbecue area.
✓ When it is too hot to sit in the spa or on the deck the pergola offers a shady space.

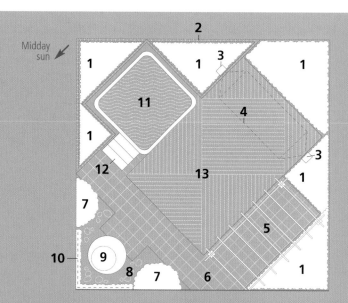

Garden elements key

1 Planting
2 Timber raised bed
3 Optional support for hammock
4 Space for hammock
5 Shade area beneath pergola
6 Tiled paving

7 Evergreen wall shrub

8 Loose stone and
cobbles

9 Barbecue area

10 Climber on trellis

11 Hot tub or spa

12 Steps up

13 Deck

Mix and match
If you like this garden but would prefer
a different feature, see pages 250–51 for
possible variations.

Garden dimensions
8m x 8m (26ft x 26ft) approx.

Key features

Hot tub

An increasingly popular feature, hot tubs can be accommodated in almost any size garden. When you are allowing for one in your design remember that you will need an electric supply (the supplier of the tub will tell you what type and where to) and that it will need to be drained occasionally. Make sure the layout of your paving allows for access to the relevant parts of the hot tub should a fault occur.

Paving and decking

In a small garden link all your paved and decked areas so that when combined they make an extra-large space for when you're entertaining or partying. If you wish, divide them up between parties with pots, planters and ornaments, which can be moved to one side when required. For maximum flexibility, keep all your paving at the same level, and introduce changes of level with raised beds around the perimeter and in the corners.

Hammock

These days, you no longer need to find two strong trees on which to hang a hammock as there are several free-standing models available. However, where space is limited, you could set a couple of substantial posts in deep concrete foundations amongst the planting on either side of a paved area so it can be quickly and easily taken down if needed.

Irrigation

Having spent a lot of time and money on building and planting your garden, you need to make sure that your investment is safeguarded by carrying out ongoing maintenance and management. Not least of this work is providing your plants with sufficient water, not just in the short term immediately after planting, when they are most vulnerable, but also in the longer term so that they continue to perform at their best.

In a small garden with a few plants you might be happy to water by hand as necessary. However, there is a fine line

Drip and porous pipe systems are best when irrigating among tall, bushy plants.

between finding that carrying a watering can around the garden is a pleasurable, relaxing task on a warm evening and it becoming a necessary, time-consuming chore. A properly planned and installed irrigation system can not only save you lots of time but can be more effective than watering by hand.

There are three basic systems to choose from: overhead sprayers or sprinklers, either fixed or 'pop-up'; porous pipes, which can be buried or laid on the soil's surface; and drip systems, which deliver water directly to individual plants. Depending on the design of your garden, you might find you will need a combination of two or even all three of these irrigation systems, which are powered by mains water pressure.

All three systems can be connected to an automatic timer, which can vary from simple devices that deliver water for a chosen length of time, typically from 0 to 60 minutes, but that have to be turned on by hand, to sophisticated electronic timers capable of running complex programmes with combinations of time, date, zoning and even sensors that cancel irrigation when it's raining. Between these extremes are a number of relatively inexpensive timers, which are ideal for when you are away on holiday.

Overhead sprayers or sprinklers

Overhead sprayers or sprinklers have adjustable or interchangeable spray heads, which can control the size, range and droplet size of the spray they produce. They are ideal for areas of open, low planting and lawns, and they allow you to see where water is falling so that you can place them accurately to give complete coverage. They are less effective among large plants, which can block the spray pattern, leading to a rain-shadow effect, and you need to avoid using them in windy situations, where again the spray pattern can be disrupted.

Porous pipe

Porous pipe is essentially a form of hosepipe that allows water to leak out along its length. One type, made from recycled car tyres, is full of thousands of minute holes,

which weep under low water pressure, and this is best used in short lengths off a ring main running around the garden because water pressure can drop, resulting in variable watering. A second type has a single hole about every 30cm (12in), which lets out a measured amount of water by way of a simple internal valve, which provides even distribution. These two systems can be laid on the surface among the plants in a serpentine fashion and covered with bark to disguise. You can also bury the pipe, which is more efficient in terms of getting water into the root zone, but you must be careful when digging not to puncture it.

Drip system

The third system of drip feeding is excellent where you need to water only a number of plants – perhaps one or two that require extra moisture and especially plants in containers. It requires a ring main of low-density polythene pipe, usually 16mm or 20mm (about ¾in) diameter, laid around the garden, with one end fixed to a tap and the other sealed tightly. All that is then required is to plug in a length of flexible, narrow-bore PVC tube at the appropriate position using a purpose-made fitting, which also controls the flow, and pegging the open or delivery end into the ground (or pot) in the root zone of your chosen plant.

Adjustable 'spider' drippers allow you to determine exactly how much water is dispensed.

Planting

3

11

15

27

The best plants for this garden

To maximize space planting is limited to the corners and angles created by the rotation of the patio, sitting areas and hot tub. Gentle flower colours, predominantly pink, blue and yellow, are used in combination with bold, lush foliage with a preponderance of evergreens to provide colour and interest all year round.

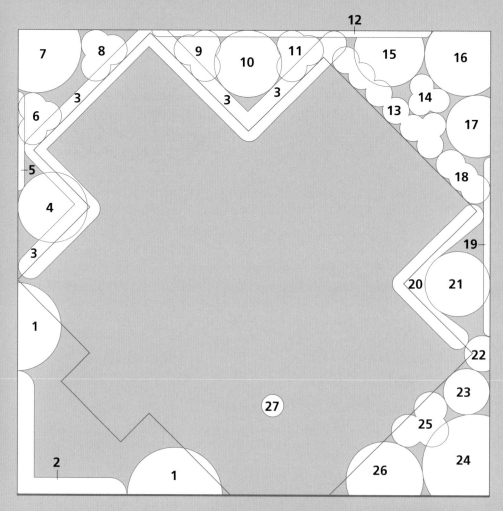

Planting key

1 *Pyracantha* 'Orange Glow'
2 *Schisandra rubriflora*
3 *Cotoneaster congestus*
4 *Pinus mugo* 'Winter Gold'
5 *Clematis* 'Markham's Pink'
6 *Molinia caerulea* subsp. *caerulea* 'Strahlenquelle'
7 *Photinia* x *fraseri* 'Robusta'
8 *Ageratina altissima* 'Chocolate'
9 *Campanula persicifolia* 'Bennett's Blue'
10 *Viburnum plicatum* f. *tomentosum* 'Pink Beauty'
11 *Ligularia dentata* 'Othello'
12 *Lonicera* x *tellmanniana*
13 *Pulmonaria longifolia*
14 *Crambe cordifolia*
15 *Hydrangea aspera* Villosa Group
16 *Rhododendron* 'Cunningham's White'
17 *Fargesia murielae* 'Simba'
18 *Hosta* 'Hadspen Blue'
19 *Hydrangea serratifolia*
20 *Heuchera* 'Pewter Moon'
21 *Pinus strobus* Nana Group
22 *Vitis vinifera* 'Purpurea'
23 *Hydrangea serrata* 'Blue Deckle'
24 *Mahonia* x *media* 'Lionel Fortescue'
25 *Zantedeschia* 'Kiwi Blush'
26 *Fuchsia* x *bacillaris*
27 *Hedera colchica*

Dwarf conifers look and grow best when they are given some space amongst low planting.

Conifers in the small garden

Conifers are not easy plants to mix with other garden favourites, such as shrubs and perennials, partly because they can look out of place with their often regular conical habit and partly because some types, like cypress (*Chamaecyparis*), react badly to close competition from plants that shade their foliage, which subsequently turns brown. This type of conifer often suits a formal design, where its shape and regular, neat habit is sympathetic to the overall scheme, and because it responds quite well to being trimmed. In informal layouts, however, these typically conical trees are more difficult to place.

There are, however, a number of conifers that are generally adaptable to a range of soils. Juniper (*Juniperus*), pines (*Pinus*) and yew (*Taxus*) can be successfully mixed with other plants, particularly shrubs and groundcover perennials, and all three have the added benefit of being quite tolerant of dryish conditions.

For the average small garden you will need to look out for dwarf or slow-growing forms or for prostrate cultivars, which will make good groundcover. Even in a limited space common yew (*Taxus baccata*) will make a decent hedge, but the cultivars *T. baccata* 'Robusta' and *T. cuspidata* 'Straight Hedge' are superior.

Do not use shears to prune junipers, because this results in a rather neat and tidy effect. Use secateurs to cut through individual stems for a more feathery effect. Although pines can't be pruned in this way, you can control them by either removing the centre leader of the end whorls in winter or by gently snapping the tip of the 'candles' from the young shoots as they emerge in spring. Yew can be trimmed with shears for a hedge, but is best treated like juniper to keep it a bit on the raggy side.

Although all three will tolerate poorish, dry conditions, they will do far better in good, well-drained soil, so make sure you prepare the planting positions as you would for any other tree, shrub or perennial.

On the shady side

Trees and buildings in and around a small garden can have a great bearing on the amount of light that falls into it. With limited space available, you need to take some time to observe the patterns of sunlight and shade so that you can select the optimum place for your patio and other garden features. At the same time, you should also give some thought to the types of plants you will need to suit the conditions.

Why this works

✓ A generous patio is thoughtfully located to receive the maximum available sun, especially in the summer months.

✓ Warm, pale-coloured paving materials give a light, airy feel to the space.

✓ Walls are painted in warm, soft colours to reflect available light back into the garden.

✓ Small-leaved climbers, which can be easily pruned, provide flower colour and will not become invasive, allowing the wall colour to show through.

✓ Carefully chosen plants will thrive in the varying conditions of light and shade and create highlights of foliage and flower.

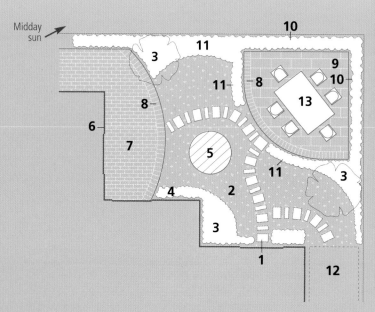

Garden elements key

1 Stepping stone path
2 Light-coloured gravel mulch
3 Highlight planting
4 Low planting at base of wall

5 Stainless steel reflection 'pool'
6 Light-coloured wall
7 Brick paving
8 Brick edging

9 Patio with flag paving to match colour of gravel

10 Wall shrubs or climbers against fence

11 Edge planting

12 Storage area

13 Patio furniture

Mix and match
If you like this garden but would prefer a different feature, see pages 250–51 for possible variations.

Garden dimensions
8m x 5.5m (26ft x 18ft) approx.

Key features

Patio

The positioning of patios and other sitting areas in a small garden is critical. As a rule, if space allows, try to make the patio larger than you think you'll actually need so that you will have room to adjust the position of garden furniture as the sun moves around. Choose paving materials that are warm and light and avoid cold or dark colours, such as greys and blues.

Reflection 'pool'

Reflection pools work by reflecting light from the sky above or sometimes from a warm-coloured wall on the other side of a garden. They don't have to contain water, however. A 'pool' made from carefully polished stainless steel sheet will do the same job and is not only maintenance free (apart from an occasional wipe clean and polish) but is also perfectly safe if you have small children.

Shade-loving plants

Plants for shady or sunless areas should be carefully chosen with two purposes in mind. First, you want plants that will grow away happily in the conditions provided, rather than just struggling to survive. Second, select plants that will actually highlight the otherwise gloomy spots in your garden. Choose cultivars with coloured, variegated or bold foliage or those with dramatic flower interest.

Selecting the best sitting area

One of the pleasures of having a garden is being able to sit out in it, and most often you will probably want to be in the sun, at least for some of the time. Choosing the best place for your sitting area is, therefore, important, especially in a small garden where your choice of locations will be limited.

The most obvious way to find the optimum spot is by observation over a period of time. In an ideal world, this would take you a year, so that you can note where the sunniest spots occur when the sun is high and low in the horizon and where surrounding features cast shadows at different times of day. Your choice will also depend, of course, on how and when you want to use the

With a little thought and imagination, your sitting area can be a delightful feature.

garden. If you're interested in sitting out only in summer, observing conditions over some or all of the summer months will be sufficient. However, if you want to use the sitting area for as much of the year as possible, you will need to observe the patterns of the sun over a much longer period.

Surprisingly, you may find situations where a shady – and therefore less desirable – spot in the height of summer can actually be warm and sunny in the middle of winter. The area beneath an evergreen tree will be in shade in summer because of the height of the sun falling down on the canopy, but in winter the rays of the sun that is now lower will be able to penetrate under the canopy and make a cosy spot in which to sit.

You will probably find that there is one particular spot that receives sun all through the year, and this should form the centre or focus of your patio or sitting area. If this spot is sufficiently large to accommodate your patio furniture, your patio can match that area in size. However, if it's smaller than the space you require, you will need to extend the patio outwards from the sunny 'core' so that you can move around to follow the sun. Try to build a patio that is larger than you think you will need if space and budget permit, and use plants in containers on the patio that can be moved around to suit your needs.

Finding the sunniest spot

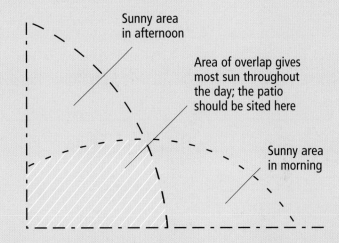

Sunny area in afternoon

Area of overlap gives most sun throughout the day; the patio should be sited here

Sunny area in morning

Proportional sun to shade

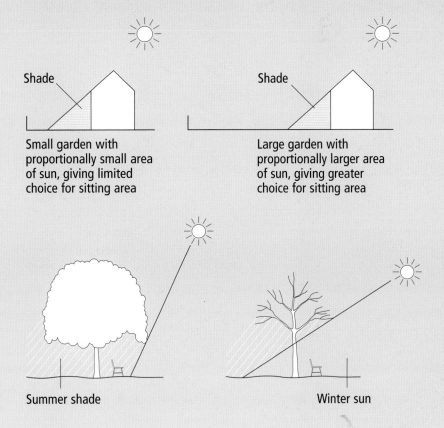

Shade

Small garden with proportionally small area of sun, giving limited choice for sitting area

Shade

Large garden with proportionally larger area of sun, giving greater choice for sitting area

Summer shade

Winter sun

Planting

3

12

16

22

The best plants for this garden

A loose, soft style of planting is used in this small, shady garden, and it complements the curved, informal shapes and edges of the paved areas nicely. All the plants have been chosen to suit the conditions where they're planted – from full sun through to varying degrees of shade. The cultivars used have been selected both to provide colour and interest throughout most of the year and also to create highlights that will lift and brighten the darker corners of the garden. The types of plants, particularly the climbers, allow the strength of the colour-washed walls to show through to add to the lightening and brightening effect.

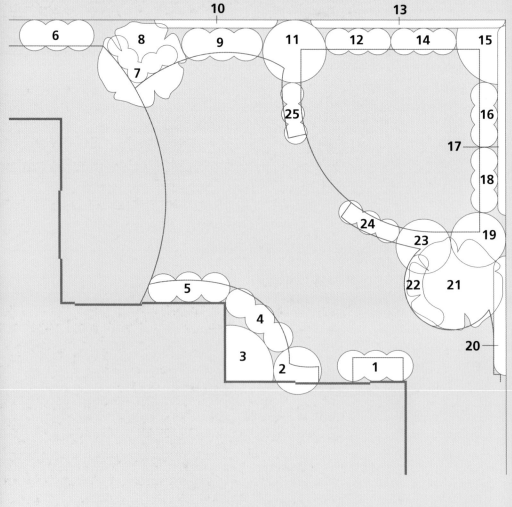

Planting key

1 *Polystichum setiferum* Divisilobum Group 'Herrenhausen'
2 *Berberis thunbergii* 'Aurea'
3 *Crinodendron hookerianum*
4 *Helleborus niger*
5 *Anemone hupehensis* var. *japonica* 'Pamina'
6 *Pleioblastus variegata*
7 *Primula japonica* 'Miller's Crimson'
8 *Acer shirasawanum* 'Aureum'
9 *Rodgersia pinnata* 'Elegans'
10 *Lonicera periclymenum* 'Graham Thomas'
11 *Rhododendron* 'President Roosevelt'
12 *Imperata cylindrica* 'Rubra'
13 *Clematis* 'Hagley Hybrid'
14 *Aconitum* x *cammarum* 'Bicolor'
15 *Ilex aquifolium* 'Flavescens' (female)
16 *Filipendula ulmaria*
17 *Clematis* 'Prince Charles'
18 *Saxifraga* 'Rubrifolia'
19 *Rhododendron* 'Klondyke' (azalea)
20 *Euonymus fortunei* 'Sheridan Gold'
21 *Hydrangea macrophylla* 'Quadricolor'
22 *Cyclamen hederifolium*
23 *Fuchsia* 'Annabel'
24 *Hosta* 'Blue Moon'
25 *Deschampsia flexuosa* 'Tatra Gold'

Anemone and arum are excellent companions for a shady corner of the garden.

Shade planting

As with other parts of any garden, the ground conditions in shady areas can vary. For example, you could have a site on a heavy soil where the sun is blocked off by a high wall or fence and the resulting shaded patch is quite damp for most of the year. On the other hand, the shade might be directly beneath a tree, whose roots make the soil dry, requiring a different selection of plants to be successful.

Best plants for dry shade

- *Lamium maculatum*
- *Liriope muscari*
- *Alchemilla mollis*
- *Geranium macrorrhizum*
- *Melissa officinalis* 'Aurea'
- *Pachysandra terminalis*
- *Rubus* 'Betty Ashburner'
- *Aucuba japonica* 'Crotonifolia'
- *Ribes sanguineum* 'Brocklebankii'
- *Digitalis purpurea* Excelsior Group

Best plants for moist, but not waterlogged, shade

- *Cornus canadensis*
- *Gaultheria procumbens*
- *Arum italicum* 'Pictum'
- *Brunnera macrophylla* 'Hadspen Cream'
- *Anemone nemorosa*
- *Hosta* 'Halcyon'
- *Luzula sylvatica* 'Marginata'
- *Blechnum spicant*
- *Sarcococca ruscifolia*
- *Viburnum davidii*

Split-level garden

Terracing is a classic way of dealing with a sloping garden, no matter how severe the fall is. Dividing a garden at the points where steps and retaining walls are most needed can also create different spaces that help to disguise the restricted proportions of the garden.

Why this works

✓ Two simple changes of level, cleverly set at an angle, divide this narrow garden into three distinct spaces or zones.

✓ A gazebo is positioned partly hidden from the rest of the garden for privacy and where it will catch the afternoon sun.

✓ The simple glazed sphere water feature is a focal point both from the patio and also the gazebo.

✓ Concealed lighting adds an extra dimension to the garden at night.

✓ Planting taller shrubs in key positions by the dwarf walls not only helps to emphasize the level changes but also adds to the space division.

✓ A statue at the far end of the garden is framed by planting and also by the arch over the steps.

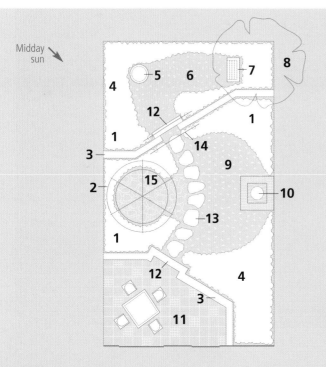

Midday sun

Garden elements key

1 Tall shrubs
2 Gazebo and climbers
3 Heavy timber dwarf wall
4 Mixed border

5 Statue or sculpture and lighting
6 Gravel
7 Bench seat
8 Tree

9 Bark

10 Water feature and lighting

11 Patio

12 Step up

13 Random stepping stones

14 Arch above step plus climber

15 Stone paving

Mix and match

If you like this garden but would prefer a different feature, see pages 250–51 for possible variations.

Garden dimensions

5m x 9m (16ft 6in x 29ft 6in) approx.

Key features

Steps

Wherever you have a change of level in your garden you will need steps. You can treat them in one of two ways: make them small, simple and discreet, perhaps with soft planting at the edges, so that they blend into the background, or develop them as a prominent feature, accentuating them with balustrades, handrails or ornaments and containers.

Gazebo

Gazebos make excellent features in any size of garden. Make sure that the one you choose is in scale with the rest of the garden and remember when you locate it that it should not only look good in that position but you need to be able to reach it comfortably. By their nature, they are fairly open structures, so don't overplant them with masses of heavy or vigorous climbers, like vines and ivy. Instead, restrict your choice to one or two light-foliaged varieties.

Patio

Paved areas are an essential part of almost any garden, and it's worth giving some thought to them when you plan your garden. Make sure their location suits your needs – you might prefer to sit in the sun, or you might want a shady location when the weather is hot. Make sure that it's large enough for your purpose, and if possible lay out your garden furniture where the patio is to be built to give you an idea of how much space you'll need.

Creating changes of level

On a naturally sloping garden the traditional way to create usable level areas is to use a process called cut and fill. This simply means moving soil from a higher part of the garden to a lower part to create one or more level terraces. Where there is no natural slope – that is, the garden is completely flat – it is still possible to build shallow terraces that will add a lot of

Even modest changes of level can add interest to your garden.

character to your garden. For this to look natural, you must avoid creating big changes of level – two changes each of say 15cm (6in), equal to a good step height, are probably enough. By keeping the levels modest you will also minimize the amount of material (soil, subsoil) you will have to excavate and move.

One of the key points to remember if you do this is that although the levels in your garden will change, where your garden meets your neighbours' at the boundaries, the ground level on their side must remain the same. To do this, therefore, you will need to retain the soil at the boundaries using gravelboards of concrete or treated heavy timber or purpose-built dwarf retaining walls in brick, concrete or stone. Where you're going to excavate below the existing ground level, to create say a sunken patio or lawn, make sure the water can drain away

otherwise the lowered area will act as a sump and become waterlogged.

If you're excavating for a patio or similar area that won't be used for planting, you can strip off the topsoil to the required depth and use it in the part of the garden to be raised. However, if the sunken area is to be a lawn or will have some form of planting on it, you will need to make sure that once the ground level is lowered there is still sufficient topsoil to support lawn or plants.

To minimize the amount of soil that you'll need to dispose of or import, try to make sure that the sunken area to be dug out is about the same size as the raised area to be built up, assuming that the depth or height of both is equal. If one of these is considerably larger than the other, you will end up with a surplus of soil or not enough.

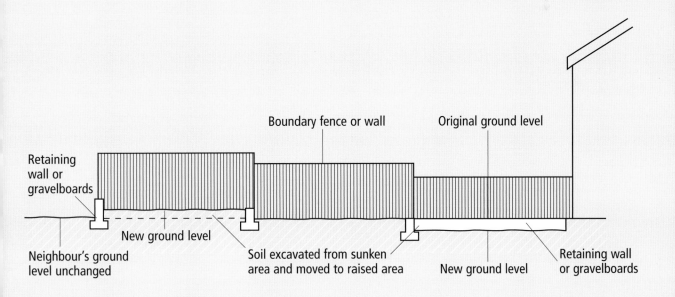

Retaining wall or gravelboards

Boundary fence or wall

Original ground level

New ground level

Neighbour's ground level unchanged

Soil excavated from sunken area and moved to raised area

New ground level

Retaining wall or gravelboards

Planting

20

26

28

35

The best plants for this garden

A carefully selected blend of trees, shrubs, perennials and climbers provides year-round interest without creating excessive work.

Flower colours are delicate shades of predominantly pink, yellow and blue, with lots of varying form and foliage shape to contrast. The heavy timber walls are softened by low planting, including anthemis, deadnettle (*Lamium*) and sedge (*Carex*).

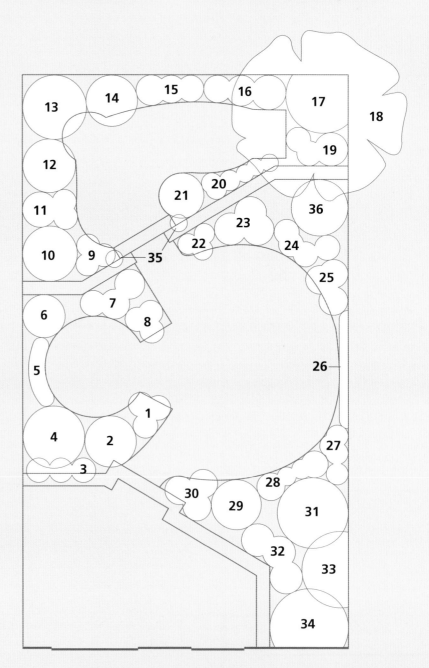

A group of smaller matching pots and plants can sometimes be more eye-catching than a single larger one.

Planting key

1 *Erigeron* 'Dignity'
2 *Syringa meyeri* 'Palibin'
3 *Lamium maculatum* 'White Nancy'
4 *Pyracantha* 'Mohave'
5 *Lonicera henryi*
6 *Kerria japonica* 'Picta'
7 *Calamagrostis* x *acutiflora*
8 *Hemerocallis* 'Eenie Weenie'
9 *Astilbe* 'Sprite'
10 *Viburnum sargentii* 'Onondaga'
11 *Geranium* x *monacense*
12 *Berberis thunbergii* f. *atropurpurea* 'Red Chief'
13 *Pieris japonica* 'Purity'
14 *Skimmia japonica* 'Fragrans'
15 *Rodgersia pinnata* 'Superba'
16 *Digitalis* x *mertonensis*
17 *Prunus laurocerasus* 'Otto Luyken'
18 *Acer rufinerve*
19 *Tricyrtis formosana* Stolonifera Group
20 *Primula florindae*
21 *Cordyline australis* 'Torbay Dazzler'
22 *Imperata cylindrica* 'Rubra'
23 *Rudbeckia fulgida* var. *deamii*
24 *Heuchera* 'Plum Pudding'
25 *Sidalcea* 'Elsie Heugh'
26 *Itea ilicifolia*
27 *Tanacetum coccineum* 'Eileen May Robinson'
28 *Sisyrinchium striatum*
29 *Cornus sanguinea* 'Midwinter Fire'
30 *Carex* 'Silver Sceptre'
31 *Acer palmatum* 'Bloodgood'
32 *Anthemis tinctoria* 'E.C. Buxton'
33 *Carpenteria californica*
34 *Mahonia* x *media* 'Charity'
35 *Rosa* 'Sombreuil'
36 *Viburnum plicatum* 'Pink Beauty'

Containers

In small gardens – especially balconies and roof gardens – plants grown in containers can form an important element of the design. It's therefore necessary to ensure that these plants are grown in the best possible conditions so that they look their best at all times by trying to match the conditions the plants would find in the ground.

Nutrients

Nutrients can be provided in two ways. Either use a proprietary growing medium that has some fertilizer already incorporated in it, or add fertilizer later on as the plant grows once the initial fertilizer has been used up.

Moisture

Moisture is essential for plant growth and health. You can provide it by manually watering your containers regularly with a watering can or by installing an irrigation system. As a rule, you should never let containers become bone dry because this stresses the plants and leads to a deterioration in the quality of foliage and flower.

Drainage

Adequate drainage is essential for healthy plant growth. Ideal drainage is provided by putting a free-draining compost into a container with one or more drainage holes so that excess water can escape freely. Raise containers off the ground on special feet or blocks so that excess water can run off.

Potting on

Containers hold a limited amount of growing medium, and sooner or later the plant's roots will extend throughout and have nowhere else to go. In order to provide more room for the roots you will either have to move it into a larger container or remove up to one-third of the solid rootball and replant it in the same size container with fresh compost to replace the third removed.

Child-friendly patio

Making gardens safe for children is one of the factors you will need to consider if you are designing a family garden. If there are young children, the most obvious safety issue is to avoid – or make childproof – any water feature. In this example of a patio garden there is plenty of space for both children and adults to enjoy leisure activities in a safe environment.

Why this works

✓ A covered deck area is suitable for outside play when it's raining.
✓ Plants are carefully selected to avoid potential hazards, such as thorns, toxic sap and poisonous berries, but still provide plenty of interest.
✓ A larger bark-covered play area is ideal for rougher activities but avoids the problems caused by wet, muddy lawns. The bark extends right into the planted areas to act as a mulch.
✓ A simple patio is ideal for outside dining, sunbathing and entertaining.
✓ A sandpit set into the deck area with a cover forms part of the deck.

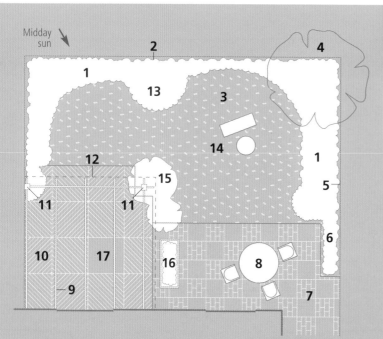

Garden elements key

1 Mixed planting
2 Climbers on fence
3 Bark groundcover (extends under plants as mulch)
4 Small to medium tree
5 Boundary fence
6 Wall shrub or climber
7 Patio
8 Patio furniture
9 Overhead structure with polycarbonate sheet covering

10 Deck
11 Post with climber
12 Edge of covered area
13 Bamboo
14 Play area
15 Shrubs
16 Mobile planter on castors
17 Sandpit with removable cover

Mix and match
If you like this garden but would prefer a different feature, see pages 250–51 for possible variations.

Garden dimensions
7m x 5.7m (23ft x 18ft 6in) approx.

Key features

Sandpit

Sandpits are traditional, popular features for small children to play in and can provide hours of fun. Having one under a covered area extends its period of usefulness in bad weather. You will also have to provide a lid so that when it is not being used it can be covered over. Peg down a piece of mulching fabric (geotextile) at the bottom of the sandpit to prevent the sand from mixing with the soil beneath and keep it clean.

Bark play area

Bark is a pleasant, safe material to use for play areas as well as a mulch for beds and borders. There are various grades available, so always check a sample before buying to make sure it's suitable for your purposes. Before you lay bark rake the area level and roll or firm it to avoid future settlement. Make sure that the area is sufficiently below the level of surrounding surfaces, such as a patio and paths, to allow for the required thickness of bark. Remember, too, to cover the ground first with a proprietary geotextile fabric and to peg or pin it down tightly before spreading the bark on top.

Mobile planter

Making larger containers mobile is a good way of using limited space in a garden. When you need extra room for a barbecue or children's party, you can simply wheel them out of the way until it's finished.

Mobile plant stand

In a small garden you can maximize the space available for planting by using containers that can be placed on your patio or other paved areas. Occasionally, though, you might want to throw a party or have a barbecue, and you will probably want as much room as possible for chairs, tables and other essentials. This means that you will need to move your containers out of the way until after the party. This isn't a problem with small containers, but large ones are not only heavy but are expensive to replace if dropped. If you put your biggest containers on mobile plant stands before you fill and plant them, temporarily relocating them becomes a simple matter.

This stylish plant stand, mounted on castors, is easy to move when you need extra space for entertaining.

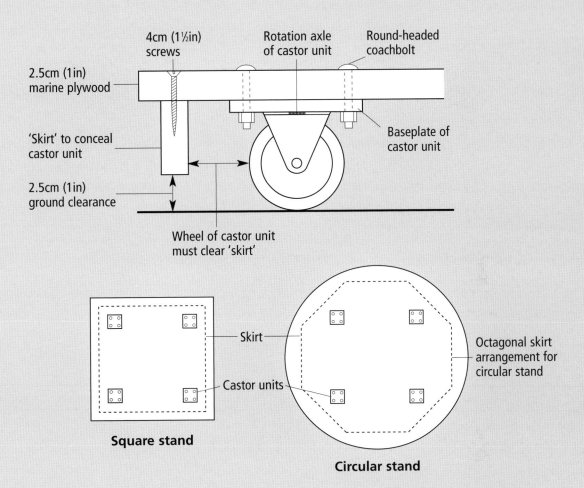

4cm (1½in) screws

Rotation axle of castor unit

Round-headed coachbolt

2.5cm (1in) marine plywood

'Skirt' to conceal castor unit

2.5cm (1in) ground clearance

Baseplate of castor unit

Wheel of castor unit must clear 'skirt'

Skirt

Castor units

Octagonal skirt arrangement for circular stand

Square stand

Circular stand

You will need

2.5cm (1in) thick marine plywood

4 rubber-wheeled castors, not less than 6.5cm (2½in) in diameter

16 x 40mm x 6mm (1½in x ¼in) nickel-chrome round-headed coachbolts and nuts

8–16 x 4cm (1½in) wood screws

Woodstain

Container

Step by step

1 Cut a square or circle of plywood to suit the shape and base dimensions of your container.

2 On the underside of the base mark a square (for a square base) or octagon (for a circular base) set in about 2.5cm (1in) from the edge.

3 Cut lengths of plywood to match the sides of the square or octagon. Make the depth of the lengths about 2.5cm (1in) less than the depth of the castor units to allow some ground clearance.

4 Fix the lengths of plywood to the underside of the base with the 4cm (1½in) screws to form a skirt.

5 Drill four holes at each corner (for the octagon, at the midway point of

four opposite sides) to take the coachbolts, lining the holes to match those of the castor unit baseplate. Make sure that each castor unit is placed to allow a small clearance between the wheel and the inside face of the skirt.

6 Fix each castor unit in place with four coachbolts and nuts.

7 Stain the completed stand with two coats of stain. Apply an extra coat of stain on any sawn edges.

8 Put your chosen container on the stand before you fill it with compost and plant it up.

Planting

The best plants for this garden

Because this garden is going to be used by small children, the planting has been selected to avoid species possessing potentially hazardous features, such as thorns or toxic sap. In addition, the selected plants are quite easy to grow and are generally robust and are likely to recover from accidental damage and suffer no long-term effects. Although the planting is simple, there is plenty of interest and variation, with climbers, such as clematis and jasmine, softening the fence, and larger, woody plants, including a small cherry tree (*Prunus serrula*) and *Photinia glabra* 'Rubens', to create some height and scale in the limited space.

1

13

14

20

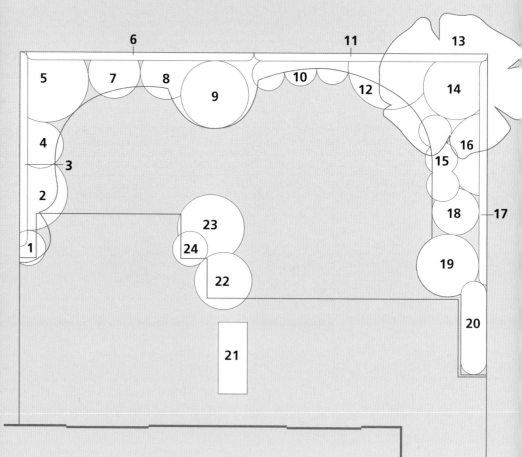

Gardens that are made safe and friendly for children don't have to be boring.

Planting key

1 *Clematis* 'Ville de Lyon'
2 *Abelia* x *grandiflora* 'Francis Mason'
3 *Lonicera henryi*
4 *Deutzia* x *kalmiiflora*
5 *Photinia glabra* 'Rubens'
6 *Clematis cirrhosa* var. *purpurascens* 'Freckles'
7 *Fuchsia magellanica* var. *gracilis* 'Aurea'
8 *Pieris* 'Forest Flame'
9 *Fargesia nitida*
10 *Bergenia* 'Wintermärchen'
11 *Parthenocissus henryana*
12 *Hydrangea serrata* 'Grayswood'
13 *Prunus serrula*
14 *Choisya ternata*
15 *Lavandula angustifolia* 'Hidcote'
16 *Potentilla fruticosa* 'Daydawn'
17 *Jasminum officinale*
18 *Miscanthus* 'Purpurescens'
19 *Weigela* 'Florida Variegata'
20 *Passiflora caerulea*
21 *Buxus sempervirens*
22 *Hebe vernicosa*
23 *Spiraea japonica* 'Gold Mound'
24 *Thunbergia alata*

Choosing safe plants

It's always a good idea to bear in mind that some otherwise attractive and desirable plants may have less desirable characteristics. This doesn't mean that you shouldn't include them in your planting scheme, but you should certainly weigh up any potential hazard to see if it could affect your plans, particularly if you have small children or pets.

Sap

A number of plants – including euphorbias, zantedeschias and agapanthus – exude milky or sticky sap. In some cases this sap is an irritant, producing discomfort to the eyes and skin, and in others it is toxic if ingested.

Fruit and berries

Small children may try to eat fruits and berries. In some cases, such as *Sorbus* and *Malus*, unless they ingest large quantities, there is little potential for harm, but there are several plants whose berries, fruits or seeds are extremely poisonous – aconites, yew (*Taxus*), laburnum, foxgloves (*Digitalis*) – and should not be included where there is any risk that they will be picked up by children.

Irritating foliage

Some plants can be deemed as undesirable because repeated contact with the leaves or stems can produce a rash on the skin. Many conifers can cause this. Other plants have leaves and stems that are covered in tiny hairs that can irritate the eyes particularly.

Spines and thorns

Thorns and spines are usually confined to the stems of plants but occasionally leaves can possess sharp points – mahonia – or even have their own thorns – some types of *Rubus*, for example. If you have pets look our particularly for some yuccas, such as *Yucca gloriosa*, which can have incredibly sharp narrow spines at the tips of the leaves and at ground level can inflict serious damage to a dog's or cat's eyes.

Narrow garden

Mix and match
If you like this garden but would prefer a different feature, see pages 250–51 for possible variations.

Garden dimensions
5m x 11m (16ft 6in x 36ft) approx.

There is no clear-cut definition of what constitutes a 'narrow' garden, but in general it could apply to any garden that is much longer than it is wide, with the width probably being no more than that of the house itself. It is, therefore, a shape that is frequently encountered in built-up areas of towns and cities where space is at a premium. While such a garden can be challenging to design, it can also be enormously rewarding once you have found the right solution to disguising its restrictive proportions.

Why this works

✓ A bold layout includes a generously sized patio and strong, curving path that draws the eye.
✓ Well-planted borders and boundaries disguise the overall shape of the plot.
✓ A succession of focal points leads the eye as you move from the patio to the arbour at the far end of the garden.
✓ Arches frame and change the direction of views within the garden.
✓ Tall shrubs subtly divide the garden into several zones without introducing solid, more obvious barriers that might be claustrophobic.

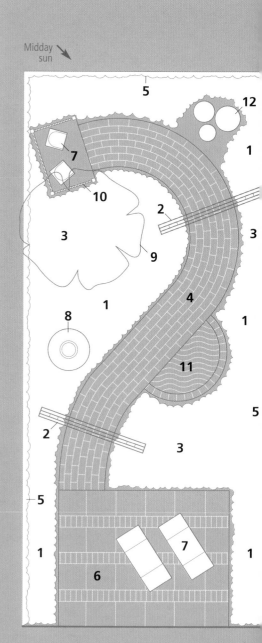

Garden elements key

1 Planting	**7** Patio furniture
2 Arch	**8** Cretan urn
3 Planting – tall shrubs	**9** Tree
4 Path	**10** Arbour
5 Climbers	**11** Pool
6 Patio	**12** Wooden 'mushrooms'

Key features

Path

Just because paths are very functional, this shouldn't preclude them from being an interesting feature. Try and avoid straight lines from A to B. Instead, make them gently curving or with subtle changes of angle from left to right and back again. Use two or even three different materials in your path design for contrast in colour, shape and texture.

Patio

Use your paved areas to 'widen' the garden visually. Here, a bold pattern of side-to-side stripes of alternating bricks and flags emphasizes the width. You can turn a rectangular or square patio through an angle to achieve a similar effect. Alternatively, make your paved areas in random informal shapes, perhaps in crazy paving, setts or brick-weave so that your eye is not drawn in any particular direction.

Arbour

In a small garden don't make your arbour too complicated or grand in scale. Simple, bold designs will be much more effective. In a narrow garden tuck the arbour away where it can't be seen until you're virtually on it. In a sunny spot you might want to keep your arbour open, with minimal planting, or you might prefer to create a shady 'grotto' effect by planting it heavily with bold-leaved vigorous climbers.

Designing a narrow garden

Narrow gardens – particularly small ones – are a challenge, and it can seem that the close proximity of two long walls or fences on either side creates a rather restrictive 'corridor' effect. However, there are several design devices that you can use to overcome this phenomenon and at the same time create a wonderfully satisfying result.

Arches, pergolas, steps and other changes of level can all be used to break up a long, narrow plot.

Boundaries

It is the boundaries that tell your eyes that your garden is long and narrow, so disguise them so they are not obvious. Use climbers to cover them, particularly species that can be left to scramble with a certain amount of untidiness. If you plant species that are naturally neat or that you regularly trim to keep tidy, you will just end up with green walls and fences rather than brown or terracotta ones. Include one or two taller shrubs as well to give some depth to your planting, thereby making it seem less flat. They will also break up the horizontal line of your boundaries, which may still be apparent even planted with climbers.

Division

Divide the garden into two or three spaces by using tall planting on its own or perhaps in a combination with an arch or some trellis fencing. Avoid really solid barriers, such as walls or conifer hedges, which will tend to make the small space feel more cramped. Make sure there is some sort of visual link between the different spaces in the garden – a narrow path or strip of lawn, for example – to suggest that there is more garden beyond.

Patio

Use alternating bands of contrasting materials to accentuate the width of your patio and make it seem wider than it actually is. Avoid strong directional patterns that run up and

A meandering, curving layout of beds and borders creates an elegant design, perfect for disguising a narrow garden.

down the garden. Another device is to rotate your patio so that it sits at an angle, encouraging your eye to look along the patio edges rather than at the boundaries. Use a circular theme for your patio and lawn (if there's room for one), which is completely non-directional and is excellent for disguising an awkwardly shaped garden.

Paths

Avoid the temptation to run a path straight from one end of the garden to the other. Instead, paths should move around the garden, perhaps at angles – like the patio – in a zigzag pattern or in long, sweeping curves. Use them to link your two or three spaces, perhaps emphasizing the link with a simple arch or with a pair of tall evergreens one on either side.

Focal points

Including a succession of focal points is worthwhile in any garden, not just small and narrow ones. Don't place them at random, however. Consider the location of each one carefully – whether it is a statue, special plant or a water feature – so that you come across it gradually, maybe as you turn a corner, or so that it is carefully framed through an arch.

Planting

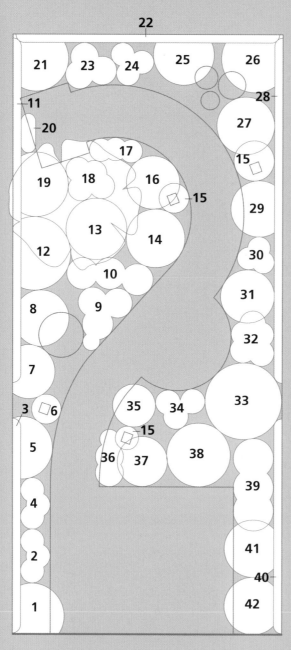

1

27

30

42

The best plants for this garden

The plants in this garden are used in a classic way: climbers mask and soften the boundaries, tall shrubs divide the garden and break up any horizontal lines, and a small tree provides additional height and structure. Perennials are used to infill between the shrubs and to soften the edges of the path and patio, creating a full, lush effect.

Planting key

1 *Cistus x purpureus*
2 *Aster novae-angliae* 'Purple Dome'
3 *Rosa* 'Leverkusen'
4 *Ballota pseudodictamnus*
5 *Potentilla fruticosa* 'Elizabeth'
6 *Rosa* 'Meg'
7 *Ilex aquifolium* 'Silver Queen' (male)
8 *Hydrangea paniculata* 'Kyushu'
9 *Clematis* x *diversifolia* 'Hendersonii'
10 *Astilbe* 'Elizabeth Bloom'
11 *Clematis montana* var. *rubens* 'Tetrarose'
12 *Cornus florida* f. *rubra*
13 *Viburnum sargentii* 'Onondaga'
14 *Phormium tenax* 'Variegatum'

15 *Rosa* 'Madame Alice Garnier' (rambler)
16 *Hebe* 'Purple Queen'
17 *Geum* 'Lionel Cox'
18 *Geranium phaeum* var. *phaeum* 'Samobor'
19 *Ligustrum* 'Vicaryi'
20 *Polygonatum multiflorum*
21 *Viburnum tinus* 'Purpureum'
22 *Lonicera japonica* 'Halliana'
23 *Aruncus dioicus*
24 *Lythrum virgatum* 'The Rocket'
25 *Weigela subsessilis* 'Victoria'
26 *Arundo donax*
27 *Hypericum* 'Hidcote'
28 *Clematis flammula*
29 *Hibiscus syriacus* 'Oiseau Bleu'
30 *Campanula takesimana*
31 *Lotus hirsutus*
32 *Crocosmia* 'Spitfire'
33 *Corylus maxima* 'Purpurea'
34 *Miscanthus sinensis* 'Undine'
35 *Rosa* 'Frühlingsmorgen'
36 *Dicentra* 'Pearl Drops'
37 *Berberis* x *ottawensis* 'Silver Miles'
38 *Spiraea thunbergii*
39 *Echinacea purpurea* 'Rubinstern'
40 *Solanum laxum* 'Album Variegatum'
41 *Caryopteris* x *clandonensis* 'Worcester Gold'
42 *Azara microphylla*

Tall, upright perennials, such as sidalcea, are perfect for suggesting division in a very small garden.

Best plants for dividing a garden

Using plants as natural dividers in a small garden is a good way to create space and 'lose' boundaries. It is not usually essential to block a view from one 'space' to the next – a suggestion of division is often quite adequate.

Best shrubs and small trees for dividing a garden

- *Aronia melanocarpa*
- *Berberis temolaica*
- *Camellia* x *williamsii* 'Donation'
- *Viburnum sargentii* 'Onondaga'
- *Cornus kousa* var. *chinensis*
- *Cotoneaster simonsii*
- *Enkianthus campanulatus*
- *Ilex aquifolium* 'Golden van Tol' (female)
- *Pittosporum tenuifolium* 'Purpureum'
- *Rubus thibetanus*
- *Trachycarpus fortunei*

Best perennials and grasses for dividing a garden

- *Fargesia nitida* cvs. (bamboo)
- *Alcea rosea*
- *Miscanthus sinensis* 'Silberfeder'
- *Delphinium* cvs.
- *Fargesia murielae* cvs. (bamboo)
- *Eupatorium purpureum*
- *Arundo donax* var. *versicolor*
- *Macleaya microcarpa* 'Kelway's Coral Plume'
- *Miscanthus sinensis* 'Malepartus'
- *Crambe cordifolia*
- *Sidalcea* 'Rose Queen'
- *Verbena bonariensis*

Water courtyard

One of the most noticeable characteristics of a tiny courtyard garden is the way in which small sounds can be reflected back and around the garden. You can take advantage of this by including in your design a small water feature to provide the sound of gently running water.

Why this works

✓ The paddle stone path around the water feature allows you to move through the courtyard and see it from different angles.

✓ There's a tiny sitting area with chairs and a table in one corner so that you can sit and listen to the sound of gently running water while you drink your morning coffee.

✓ The spot planting adds background texture, scale and colour but doesn't detract from the central water feature.

✓ Stone chippings not only act as a weed-suppressing mulch to the plants, but make a colour and textural contrast to the smooth paddle stone path.

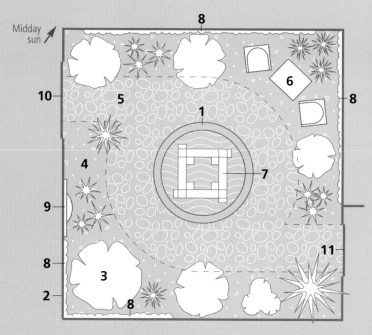

Garden elements key

1 Pool
2 Enclosing walls of courtyard
3 Spot planting through mulch
4 Stone chipping mulch
5 Paddle stone path
6 Small sitting area
7 Spiral water feature
8 Climber
9 Wall-mounted sculpture or relief

10 False doorway
11 Entrance from house

Mix and match
If you like this garden but would prefer
a different feature, see pages 250–51 for
possible variations.

Garden dimensions
4.25m x 4.4m (14ft x 14ft 6in) approx.

Key features

Spiral water feature

When you build a water feature, think carefully about where to place it for maximum effect. In this garden it is the main focal point of the courtyard. Enclosing walls and fences that are not covered in plants will reflect and magnify sound, so build your water feature with low, shallow cascades and glides that will give you gentle, soothing sounds.

Paddle stone path

Flat paddle stones are pleasant to look at and make a relatively smooth path for occasional use. For a more frequently used and comfortable paddle stone path, lay them face up in a 'crazy' or 'mosaic' style on a bed of mortar and gently press them in to about half their depth. Mix up the different sizes well to avoid large areas of plain mortar.

Spot planting

In a small space giving plants plenty of room to grow means that you can fully appreciate their individual characteristics at close quarters. This is also good for the plants themselves, allowing lots of air and light to circulate around them. You can spot-plant in different ways: setting a tree in a lawn, where it can be underplanted with spring bulbs; leaving a space in a patio for low-growing alpines or herbs; or planting in a bed or border, which you can mulch with different kinds of shingle or bark to prevent weeds encroaching and to retain moisture.

Spiral water feature

Moving water in a garden is a great way to add light and sound, particularly in a courtyard or small enclosed area. You can tailor this spiral water feature to fit your own space by varying the height of the uprights and the length of the cascades. In a tiny garden you might only need four cascades to complete one loop of the spiral, but in a larger garden you might need two, three or even four loops to achieve the desired impact. You will need to stand the spiral in a square or circular pool to act as a source of water for the cascades. You can build your own pool with concrete, brick and liner or else from a preformed container of the right dimensions, which can sit either above or in the ground according to your preferences.

This stunning series of cascades makes a perfect water feature for a small garden.

You will need

Plastic or fibreglass container, at least 30cm (12in) deep, to make the pool; it should be at least 15cm (6in) wider all round than the width of your spiral

4 round or square pressure-treated posts, diameter not critical but 5–7.5cm (2–3in) average; length to suit the chosen height of the feature

Lengths of half-round plastic, metal or bamboo for the 'cascades'; diameter to match the posts or slightly larger

8 x 2.5cm (1in) galvanized screws

Submersible pump, 13mm (½in) hose and clips to secure hose

30cm (12in) x 13mm (½in) copper pipe with one end bent to form 10cm (4in) diameter half circle

Woodstain

Plumber's U brackets to match hose diameter

19mm (¾in) marine plywood

Gutter mastic

Concreting sand and cement

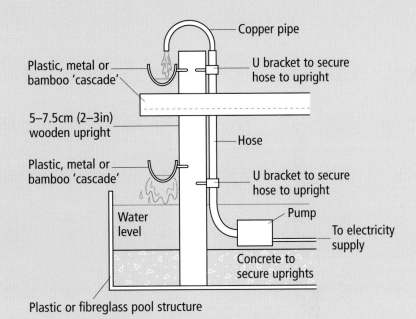

Copper pipe

U bracket to secure hose to upright

Plastic, metal or bamboo 'cascade'

5–7.5cm (2–3in) wooden upright

Hose

Plastic, metal or bamboo 'cascade'

U bracket to secure hose to upright

Water level

Pump

To electricity supply

Concrete to secure uprights

Plastic or fibreglass pool structure

Step by step

1 Level and firm the ground and set your preformed container on it to create the pool. For a sunken pool, excavate an appropriately sized hole to accommodate the container.

2 Cut the posts to suit the finished height of the spiral (allowing for the depth of water), stain them in your chosen colour, allow to dry and set them in a 7.5–10cm (3–4in) bed of concrete in the bottom of the 'pool', making sure they form a square and are vertical. Use a concrete mix of 6 parts sand to 1 part cement, and keep the mix stiff so that it is easier to stand the posts upright.

3 Cut the half-round sections of pipe or channel so that they are about 10cm (4in) longer than the outside edges of the square formed by the wooden posts.

4 Block off one end of each cascade, either with a proprietary stop-end or with a half circle cut from the marine ply and fixed in place with gutter mastic. (If you are using perspex cascades, use a piece of perspex and clear mastic or sealant.)

5 Fix the first cascade by drilling and screwing it to the tops of two adjacent posts. Keep the holes near the top edge of the cascade and use a spirit level to check that the cascade slopes gently from left to right – 1cm (½in) fall in 30cm (12in) maximum. Make sure the cascade projects about 5cm (2in) beyond the posts at each end.

6 Move to the next side of the spiral (to the right) and repeat step 5,

setting the left-hand (uphill) end of the new cascade about 7.5cm (3in) below the right-hand (downhill) end of the cascade you've previously fixed.

7 Continue fixing cascades until the last one is about 7.5cm (3in) above the proposed water level in the pool.

8 Connect the hose to the pump, place the pump in the pool and fix the hose vertically with the U brackets to the inside face of the post supporting the highest point (the start) of the spiral.

9 Push the straight end of the copper pipe into the top end of the hose and turn it so that the spout thus formed overhangs the cascade at the start of the spiral (see diagram). Secure the pipe to the hose with a hose clip.

10 Fill the pond and switch on the pump. Use the flow adjuster on the pump to achieve the optimum flow down the cascades.

Planting

The best plants for this garden

Spot planting is an essential element of this courtyard garden, and although only a limited number of plants is used, there is a wide range of shape, colour and texture. Each species is positioned either individually or in small groups to display its special characteristics to best advantage. All the plants are generally undemanding — the main requirement being an acidic soil — that is, a pH less than 7.0 and preferably nearer 5 — to suit the ericaceous azaleas and camellias. Maintenance is simple. Cut back or remove the dead growth of the perennials — hostas, irises, sedge (*Carex*), reed grass (*Calamagrostis*), crab grass (*Panicum*) and maidenhair ferns (*Adiantum*) — in autumn. Lightly prune the spring-flowering shrubs — azalea, flowering cherry (*Prunus*), camellia, mahonia and *Berberis* — as soon as they have finished flowering. Trim the juniper in late winter and midsummer, and remove the old flowering stems of the hydrangea in late spring.

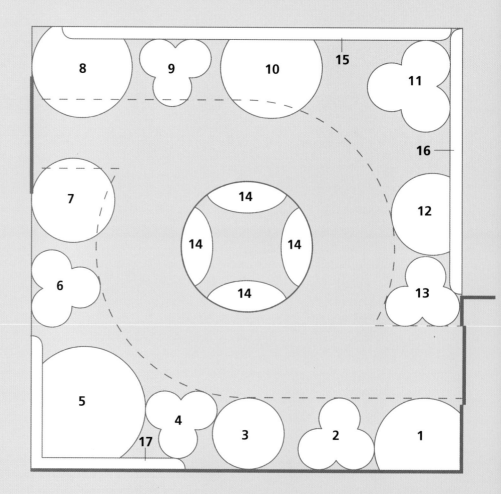

Planting key

1 *Rhododendron* 'Persil' (azalea)
2 *Hosta* 'Blue Moon'
3 *Prunus incisa* 'Kojo-no-mai'
4 *Bergenia purpurascens*
5 *Hydrangea quercifolia* 'Snowflake'
6 *Calamagrostis* x *acutiflora* 'Karl Foerster'
7 *Juniperus horizontalis* 'Prince of Wales'
8 *Camellia japonica* 'C.M. Wilson'
9 *Adiantum pedatum*
10 *Mahonia aquifolium* 'Smaragd'
11 *Panicum virgatum* 'Rubrum'
12 *Berberis thunbergii* f. *atropurpurea* 'Red Chief'
13 *Carex buchananii*
14 *Iris ensata*
15 *Clematis* 'White Moth'
16 *Rosa* 'Kathleen Harrop'
17 *Clematis* x *durandii*

A flower and foliage corner

The significance of flowers in a garden, especially those of perennials and shrubs, can sometimes be overemphasized, particularly when you think that a flowering shrub is in flower for maybe just three or four weeks in the year. You need to consider this aspect of flowering plants when you are designing small gardens because the number of individual plants you can physically include will be limited. Each plant you choose should offer good value from both flowers and foliage.

When you have selected a plant for the extra dimension that its leaves will bring to your garden – either because of its colour, shape or texture – make sure you place it where it can be best appreciated. Avoid obvious traps, such as placing similarly coloured or textured plants next to each other, and try to put one or two large-leaved species in the foreground, where the beauty of the individual leaves can be appreciated.

1 *Magnolia grandiflora*
2 *Salix purpurea* 'Nancy Saunders'
3 *Physocarpus opulifolius* 'Diabolo'
4 *Verbascum* (Cotswold Group) 'Gainsborough'
5 *Actaea simplex* Atropurpurea Group 'Brunette'
6 *Eryngium planum*
7 *Hebe topiaria*
8 *Hosta* 'August Moon'
9 *Festuca glauca* 'Elijah Blue'
10 *Heuchera* 'Rachel'
11 *Iris* 'Austrian Sky' (standard dwarf bearded)
12 *Sedum* 'Vera Jameson'
13 *Lamium maculatum* 'Pink Pewter'

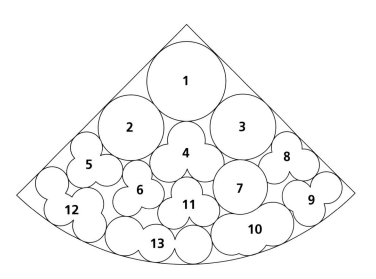

Room with a view

If the outlook from your garden is particularly attractive – perhaps looking out over a meadow to a distant wood or hills – and it would be a shame to obscure this view, it is quite possible to design your garden to make a feature of this view and even include other elements in nearby gardens, such as a specimen tree.

Why this works

✓ The far boundary is left unplanted in the centre to reveal a distant view and give the impression that the garden continues into the distance.

✓ Trees are carefully positioned in the bottom corners of the garden to frame and highlight the view.

✓ The planting of shrubs, climbers and perennials masks the side boundaries of the garden, making it feel more spacious.

✓ The pattern of the patio is angled parallel to the far boundary to make the best use of the view beyond.

✓ A removable screen can be erected along the edge of the patio to act as a windbreak when the prevailing wind is funnelled down the garden.

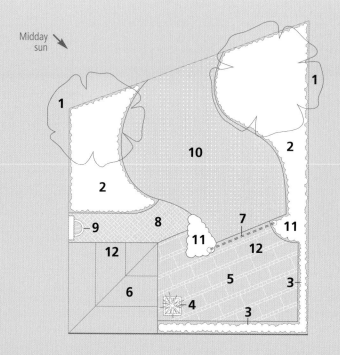

Garden elements key

1 Tree to frame view
2 Mixed border
3 Climber
4 Container planting
5 Patio

6 Conservatory
7 Removable screen
8 Brick paving
9 Wall-mounted water
   feature

10 Lawn

11 Specimen evergreen
shrub

12 View from patio/
conservatory

Mix and match
If you like this garden but would prefer
a different feature, see pages 250–51 for
possible variations.

Garden dimensions
6m x 8m (20ft x 26ft) approx.

Key features

Planter

Place planters to break up large expanses of paving when permanent beds are not possible. Always use good quality compost with adequate drainage in the bottom, and don't forget to feed and water on a regular basis. Large planters look good in isolation, but smaller ones are often better grouped together.

Lawn

When you're designing a garden, try and make the lawn a positive feature of your design. Long, sweeping curves can be used to direct your view around the garden. Circular lawns and square or rectangular lawns, which are set at an angle – say 45° or 60° – to the boundaries are an excellent way of disguising the shape of a small or narrow garden and of creating a greater feeling of space.

Brick paving

For a rather informal, rustic look in an area that is subject to only occasional or light use, you can lay bricks directly on a sand bed, butted tight against each other. For a more solid, heavily used path or paved area lay them on a bed of mortar on top of a hardcore base and leave joints between them of about 1cm (½in) filled with mortar. Traditionally, basket-weave and herringbone patterns are used, and they are ideal for square or straight runs of paving. However, you can use running bond – bricks laid end to end – to make long, sweeping curves.

Framing and creating views

Where you have identified a view that you would like to preserve and don't want to obscure with plants or garden structures, you will need to plan your garden layout to take account of this, so that you can appreciate it from the patio, from inside your house or maybe even from both.

It's important that you disguise the boundary in front of the 'view' to give the impression that the garden blends into the

Use arches, pergolas or even gaps in hedges to frame views and features.

space beyond. The ideal way to do this is to have no boundary at all, but this is not practicable for most gardens. However, if possible, keep your boundary walls or fences as low as possible – allowing for child safety and pet control – to maximize the view out.

Use trees to emphasize and frame the view, choosing species according to the type of view you're looking at. For example, trees with wide-spreading crowns can be used for low views that will be seen beneath the canopy. Where you want to look at something higher, choose narrow, upright trees, possibly conifers, set further apart.

You can use the same principles within your garden to highlight a particular feature or focal point. Trees and large shrubs or even tall grasses and bamboos are good for informal 'framing'. In a more formal setting, you can use arches and pergolas to create a picture-frame effect.

'Borrowing' trees, shrubs or even garden structures from neighbouring gardens is a useful trick to employ to improve the view from within your own garden and also make it appear larger. The essence of this idea is to plant your own beds and borders in such a way that your neighbour's trees and large shrubs appear to be part of it. Again, the success of this depends on your being able to hide the boundary fence or wall with soft planting. There is, however, an element of risk in this technique: you have no control over your neighbour's plants, and one day you could wake up to find them gone.

The far boundary of this garden is hidden by soft, low planting allowing a stunning, distant view to be seen, framed by trees.

Planting

The best plants for this garden

In this garden the planting functions in two very different ways: it masks the side boundaries to increase the feeling of spaciousness, and it frames a view beyond the far boundary. The borders are fairly generous to further emphasize the framing of the view, which is also captured from the patio by specimen evergreen shrubs on either side, and climbers on the walls surrounding the patio complete the greening of the garden.

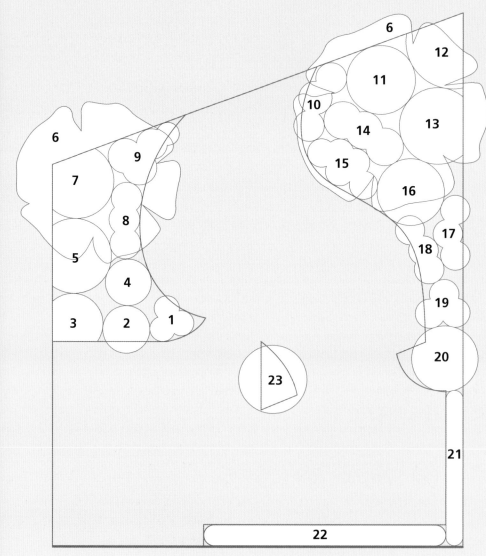

Planting key

1 *Iris* 'Braithwaite' (tall bearded)
2 *Hebe* 'Autumn Glory'
3 *Cytisus* 'Windlesham Ruby'
4 *Phormium* 'Bronze Baby'
5 *Hydrangea quercifolia*
6 *Sorbus aria* 'Lutescens'
7 *Ribes sanguineum* 'Tydeman's White'
8 *Hosta* 'Francee'
9 *Crocosmia* x *crocosmiiflora* 'Gerbe d'Or'
10 *Molinia caerulea* subsp. *caerulea* 'Variegata'
11 *Potentilla fruticosa* 'Katherine Dykes'
12 *Pyracantha* 'Teton'
13 *Rhododendron* 'Pink Pearl'
14 *Geum rivale* 'Leonard's Variety'
15 *Geranium* x *cantabrigiense* 'St Ola'
16 *Hypericum* x *inodorum* 'Elstead'
17 *Verbascum* 'Helen Johnson'
18 *Salvia* x *sylvestris* 'Blauhügel'
19 *Thalictrum flavum* subsp. *glaucum*
20 *Eucryphyia* x *nymansensis* 'Nymansay'
21 *Actinidia kolomikta*
22 *Rosa* 'Albertine' (rambler)
23 *Viburnum tinus* 'Gwenllian'

Despite their exotic appearance, many fuchsias are adaptable to windy situations, especially coastal.

Plants for windy situations

When you are choosing plants for your garden you are most likely to look for those that suit your soil type, the amount of sun or shade and whether the situation is dry or moist. In some gardens, however, you also need to be asking yourself how windy or exposed the site is. From time to time almost every garden is subject to a fierce wind, but some gardens are situated where strong winds are the norm rather than the exception. Roof gardens or balconies, especially those on tall buildings, are likely to be buffeted by strong winds, as are gardens near the coast, those on high ground and those in open countryside, where there is little or no shelter. In these situations, unsuitable plants will be subject to continuing damage and disfigurement, and they may even die. It's much better to choose plants that will tolerate these conditions and come through even the most serious gusts virtually unscathed.

Plants with smaller leaves, such as hebes, are less likely to be damaged than those with large, thin leaves like catalpas. Thick, leathery or hard leaves are also less likely to be affected, and good examples of these are *Elaeagnus* or evergreen viburnums, including *Viburnum tinus* and *V. davidii*. Large flowers are also likely to be bruised and battered in heavy winds, so try and choose plants on which individual flowers are small or set in tight heads – spiraeas, hebes and achilleas, for example. Try to avoid planting tall perennials with stiff stems, such as hollyhocks (*Alcea*) and delphiniums. Choose plants with flexible stems, especially grasses, or with low or more compact, bushy growth – dwarf asters, geraniums, heucheras and stachys are good examples.

Finally, when you are planting trees make sure they are adequately staked and supported until they are well established. Tease out the roots on container-grown specimens before planting to encourage even root growth and long-term stability.

Garden of illusion

If you have a tiny garden, your main aims when designing it will be to include everything essential for your gardening needs and to make it appear bigger than it really is, so that it won't seem cramped or claustrophobic. A good way to achieve this is to use mirrors that act as 'doors' or 'windows', suggesting that they lead to other parts of the garden, and by using climbers and taller plants to disguise your garden boundaries.

Why this works

✓ Careful positioning of a mirrored arch gives the impression of the brick path continuing through the boundary wall.

✓ Mirrored windows behind lightweight diamond trellis suggest holes in the walls, giving the impression of looking into the space beyond.

✓ Climbers and other plants are used to hide and soften the straight lines and angles of the boundary wall.

✓ A pool close to the patio reflects the sky and adds light.

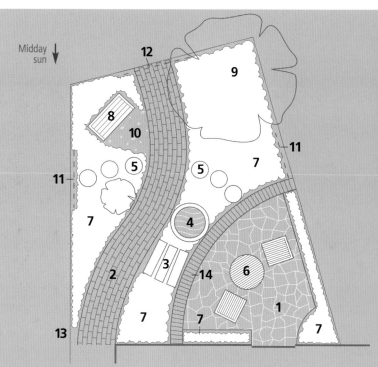

Garden elements key

1 Crazy paving patio
2 Brick path
3 Sleeper 'stepping stones'
4 Reflection pool

5 Random natural 'stepping stones'
6 Patio furniture
7 Planting
8 Seat or sitting area

9 Small tree

10 Gravel

11 Lattice mirror
'window'

12 Arched mirror 'door'

13 Boundary wall

14 Brick-on-edge step
up to patio

Mix and match
If you like this garden but would prefer
a different feature, see pages 250–51 for
possible variations.

Garden dimensions
6m x 5m (20ft x 16ft 6in) approx.

Key features

Mirror arch

This can be a central feature to make a small garden appear longer. By leading a path up to a wall-mounted mirror and framing this mirror with a trellis, an arch effect can be created – the reflection of the path and plants alongside it will give the effect of a gateway through the wall or fence into another part of the garden beyond.

Sleeper 'stepping stones'

Sleepers or other heavy baulks of timber can be set into the ground to act as stepping stones in place of more conventional natural stone or concrete slabs. Before laying them, make sure they are well treated with clear or coloured timber preservative. Don't forget to lay them on top of the ground first and practice stepping on them to make sure they are not too close together or too far apart before finally sinking them in.

Reflection pool

A pool like this can be set into the ground to act as a reflection for the sky. It shouldn't have any plants in it and therefore can be quite shallow. Building this type of pool doesn't have to be complicated – any durable, rigid container will do, such as a coldwater tank – but the critical point is to make sure it is absolutely level in all directions so the water can come right up to the lip.

Mirror arch or window

With a little care and some basic skills you can make your own mirror arch to give your garden the impression of being more spacious. Ideally, the arch needs to be mounted on a wall or solid fence, and you should make it of a size that you would expect a real gateway to be. Make sure that the mirror arch is positioned where it can be seen to greatest effect.

You will need

Mirrored glass or polished stainless steel to fit your chosen frame
Door or window frame
Long screws (for mounting on to wooden fence posts) and plugs or proprietary frame fixings (if mounting on a stone or brick wall)
Bitumastic or waterproof paint
Frame mastic or silicone sealant together with gun-type applicator
Hardwood, quadrant beading, 12–15mm (½–¾in) radius
Thin, small-headed nails or pins
2 trellis panels, 180cm x 30–45cm (72in x 12–18in)
Semicircular or arched trellis panel
Woodstain
6.5cm (2½in) galvanized nails
Lightweight, diamond cedar wood trellis (optional)

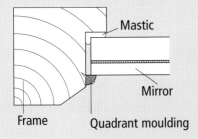

Mastic

Mirror

Frame

Quadrant moulding

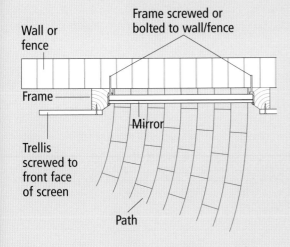

Wall or fence

Frame screwed or bolted to wall/fence

Frame

Trellis screwed to front face of screen

Mirror

Path

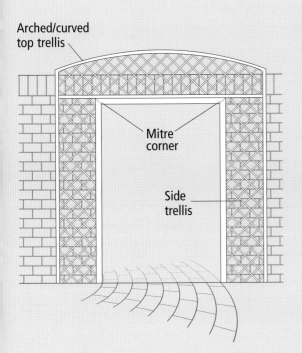

Arched/curved top trellis

Mitre corner

Side trellis

Step by step

1 Place the frame in the required position, making sure the uprights are vertical and the top cross-piece is level.

2 On a solid fence drill through the frame and screw into the fence behind with the long screws. If possible, make one of the frame edges coincide with a fence post for greater strength. For even greater security, concrete in a false fence post to go behind the other frame edge. For brick or stone walls use the screw and rawl plug or frame fixings.

3 Paint the back of the mirror with bitumastic paint and let this dry.

4 Using the applicator, squeeze out a continuous strip of the frame mastic along the rebated edge of the frame. Wearing heavy gloves for safety, lift the mirror and carefully press it into the mastic on the frame – ideally, this is a job for two people. You may need to temporarily tack a piece of thin scrap wood across the bottom of the frame under the lower edge of the mirror to prevent it from slipping while the mastic sets.

5 Apply a thin strip of mastic to the edge of the mirror. Cut the beading into three lengths to suit the angle between the frame and the mirror, cutting the ends at 45° (a mitre). Press the beading into the angle so that it is held by the mastic and nail through it into the frame with the small nails or pins.

6 Use the 6.5cm (2½in) nails to nail the two long trellis panels to each of the frame uprights and fix the semicircular or arched panel on top. (You may need to trim this to fit the overall width.)

7 For a really good effect, stain the trellis, frame and beading in the same colour to give the appearance of a complete gateway.

8 For a window effect, repeat steps 1–7 above but using a four-sided window frame. You can achieve a more attractive effect by cutting the piece of diamond trellis so that it exactly fits the mirror after it's mounted, and glue it to the face of the mirror with a few dabs of the mastic, making sure that this doesn't squeeze out on to the mirror's face.

Planting

25

28

33

The best plants for this garden

In this small plot plants have been used to mask the boundaries and corners so that the real shape and size of the garden are concealed. Climbers on the walls together with shrubs and bamboos especially selected for a limited space help to achieve this, while smaller shrubs and perennials add to the interest without making the garden claustrophobic.

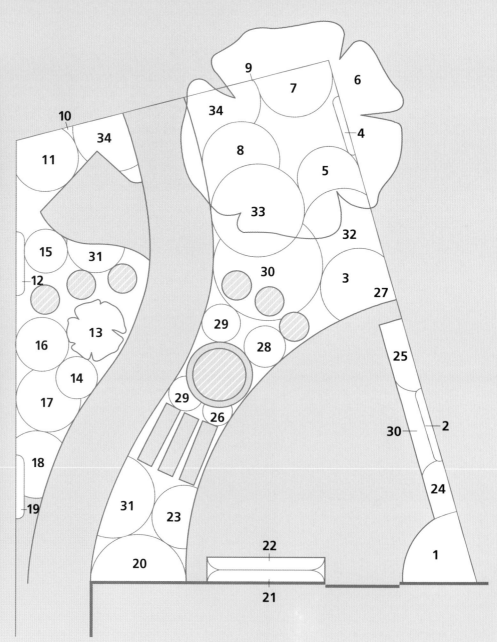

Planting key

1 *Abelia x grandiflora*
2 *Trachelospermum jasminoides*
3 *Perovskia atriplicifolia* 'Blue Spire'
4 *Lonicera periclymenum* 'Graham Thomas'
5 *Helleborus argutifolius*
6 *Acer negundo* var. *violaceum*
7 *Mahonia aquifolium* 'Apollo'
8 *Anemone hupehensis* var. *japonica* 'Bressingham Glow'
9 *Berberidopsis corallina*
10 *Clematis* 'Lincoln Star'
11 *Fargesia nitida*
12 *Clematis cirrhosa*
13 *Acer palmatum* var. *dissectum* Dissectum Viride Group
14 *Viola cornuta* Alba Group
15 *Aconitum* 'Ivorine'
16 *Phlox maculata* 'Omega'
17 *Hydrangea* 'Preziosa'
18 *Astilbe* 'Irrlicht'
19 *Hydrangea serratifolia*
20 *Osmanthus heterophyllus*
21 *Campsis radicans*
22 *Agapanthus* Blue Giant
23 *Lychnis chalcedonica*
24 *Bergenia* 'Silberlicht'
25 *Heuchera* 'Chocolate Ruffles'
26 *Thymus pulegioides* 'Archer's Gold'
27 *Rudbeckia fulgida* var. *sullivantii* 'Goldsturm'
28 *Yucca flaccida* 'Golden Sword'
29 *Diascia barberae* 'Ruby Field'
30 *Ajuga reptans* 'Pink Elf'
31 *Lamium galeobdolon* 'Hermann's Pride'
32 *Berberis thunbergii* f. *atropurpurea* 'Red Chief'
33 *Iris sibirica* 'Flight of Butterflies'
34 *Hosta* 'Frances Williams'

Garrya is an excellent evergreen wall shrub, even for a wall where sunlight can not reach.

Evergreen wall shrubs

Although you may want to plant and train climbers to hide bare boundary walls and fences as quickly as possible, species and cultivars that are vigorous enough to do this can then become a nuisance as you try to control them. Moreover, there are considerably more deciduous climbers to choose from than evergreen ones, so that the chances are that you'll lose some or all of the screening effect in winter. There are, however, many evergreen shrubs that can be trained flat against walls and fences to achieve the same effect, and these have the advantage that they require little support in the form of trellis and wires and are also much easier to keep under control.

Best evergreen wall shrubs for small gardens

- *Garrya elliptica* 'James Roof'
- *Piptanthus nepalensis*
- *Pyracantha* (most cvs.)
- *Euonymus fortunei* 'Silver Queen' (and other cvs. of *E. fortunei*)
- *Berberidopsis corrallina*
- *Crinodendron hookerianum*
- *Itea ilicifolia*
- *Osmanthus delavayi*
- *Rhaphiolepsis x delacourii*
- *Ribes speciosum*
- *Ceanothus impressus*
- *Viburnum japonicum*

First-time garden

As with all things in life, there's a first time for everything, and garden building is no exception. The key to making your success is to keep it straightforward: a simple, but imaginative layout with a few well-thought-out features and reliable plants will always beat a complicated design with lots of fussy details and temperamental planting.

Why this works

✓ The design has just a few features carefully positioned as focal points.

✓ Reliable plant cultivars will grow happily for many years with basic care and attention.

✓ The main sitting area is a deck obtained as a modular kit so that construction is straightforward and involves the minimum of excavation.

✓ There is no lawn: the area is covered in either gravel or bark laid on a geotextile membrane for easy construction, low long-term maintenance and modest cost.

✓ A simple pool, made by sinking a suitably sized container into the ground and incorporating a solar-powered pump and fountain, requires no electrical connection.

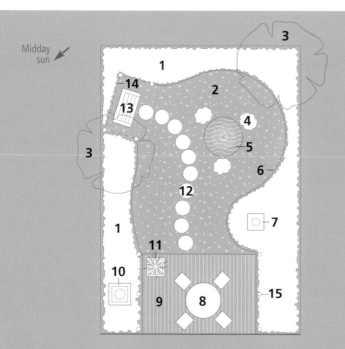

Garden elements key

1 Mixed border
2 Gravel mulch
3 Small tree
4 Spot planting

5 Pool with optional solar-powered fountain
6 Flexible edging
7 Obelisk and climber

8 Patio furniture
9 Modular deck
10 Statue or sculpture
11 Container or planter
12 Stepping stones

13 Seat
14 Trellis arbour
15 Solar-powered
   garden light

Mix and match
If you like this garden but would prefer
a different feature, see pages 250–51 for
possible variations.

Garden dimensions
5m x 7m (16ft 6in x 23ft) approx.

Key features

Deck

Decks are effective and relatively easy to construct. Most decking companies offer ready-to-build systems in a range of popular sizes, and all that is required for the most basic systems is to level the surface of the ground where you want to locate it, before following the assembly instructions, making it ideal for the first-time gardener.

Trellis arbour

A simple arbour made from upright posts with trellis panels fixed between them is a quick and easy way to create a cosy sitting area. To add an extra touch of class to your arbour, avoid cheap, basic square trellis and use a better quality type, possibly with a curved top, and a diamond pattern. Fix turned finials — spheres, acorns and so on — on top of the posts to finish them off and stain the whole structure to match your deck or boundary fence.

Stepping stones

These are an easy and inexpensive solution for making a path in your garden. Lay them out 'loose' first to achieve a shape or line that you are happy with, then walk on them to make sure they are at the right spacing. Mark out the shape of each stone, dig out the soil to the depth of the stone and then lay each one on a shallow bed of soft sand or, if your prefer, mortar. Leave the stones slightly proud, so that you can lay shingle in the spaces around them.

Planning and organizing

The planning and organizing of a garden project are as essential as the skill of the people carrying out the various tasks involved and the quality of the design, materials and products used. The following checklist will help you plan efficiently so that you end up with a finished garden with a minimum of snags or headaches.

This first-time garden design is very simple but the end result is strikingly effective.

Budget

From your design work out the cost of the materials of all the individual features: arbour, paving, water feature, plants, mulch and so on. You may need to allow for the disposal of surplus soil or existing plants and of any materials that are to be discarded. Don't forget to include an amount for any specialist work that you may be unable to carry out yourself, such as providing an electricity supply from the house to the garden and mechanical excavation. If you have a reasonably detailed design, reputable landscape contractors will be able to give you fairly reliable estimates.

Access and site storage

Because you have only limited space available, access into your garden and an area to stockpile spare products and materials are critical. Make sure the access is adequate for everything that needs to go in or out of the garden. You might, for example, need to leave out a fence panel or section of wall until the very end. Also try and ensure materials are delivered just in advance of when they'll be needed so that the site isn't cluttered up with plants that won't be required until the very end of the project.

Rubbish disposal

Consider how you are going to dispose of rubbish and surplus waste materials – particularly topsoil. You might need to arrange to have a skip or skips in which to collect the waste; remember that if the skip has to stand on the public highway outside your property you might need permission and a licence, which can take time, so make enquiries and book well ahead.

Construction

If necessary begin by clearing the site. You can then proceed with the groundworks – that is, excavating for patios, wall foundations and other structures, such as the post holes for new boundary fences. At this stage make provision for the electric and water supply throughout the garden by laying armoured cable or ducting to take cables and pipework. Once the groundwork is complete, continue with the hard landscaping – laying flags, building walls, fitting fence panels and erecting structures, such as pergolas, arches and summerhouses.

Planting

Only when all the hard elements are complete can you prepare the planting areas by digging, rotavating, adding organic matter, fertilizer and other soil improvers. Make sure you protect completed new work, such as your patio, with boards, sacking or polythene to keep it clean. Begin by planting trees and large shrubs, climbers on fences and garden structures, and then infill the remaining planting areas with the smaller shrubs, perennials, grasses and so on.

Lawns

Ideally, turf or seed the lawn right at the end of the project. If this is not possible or desirable, protect newly turfed or seeded areas with boards or planks if you need to walk on them, but move them regularly – say every day – to avoid killing the turf or young grass seedlings beneath the boards.

Ornaments and containers

As a final touch, place your chosen ornaments – sculpture, statue, bird bath, obelisk – in their positions, plant up any containers and mulch the planting areas with bark or other suitable mulch.

Phasing

You may find that the cost of your garden is going to exceed your agreed budget. If this happens you can either put the project on hold until you have sufficient finance or you can phase the work by completing it in stages over a longer period.

A simple way of doing this might be to carry out all the hard construction as phase 1; to put in the trees, large shrubs and, perhaps, lay the lawn as phase 2; and then complete the garden by putting in the small plants and adding the containers and any other final details as phase 3.

Alternatively, if you wanted to put in the plants as soon as possible so as not to lose any growing time, you could prepare the bases for your paved areas – patio, path – but not lay the flags or bricks. Instead, you could cover the areas with weed-suppressing mulch, possibly covered with bark or shingle that can eventually be used elsewhere in the garden.

Planting

The best plants for this garden

In this beginner's garden all the plants have been selected because of their healthy and reliable habits of growth, their undemanding nature as well as for their easy maintenance. They are mostly long-lived plants, as long,

that is, as they receive a minimum of regular care and attention. They are also readily available from most good nurseries and garden centres. In a relatively small space there is a good selection of plants that have a range of habits and shapes, and there is also colour or other interest at virtually any time of the year.

6

20

23

33

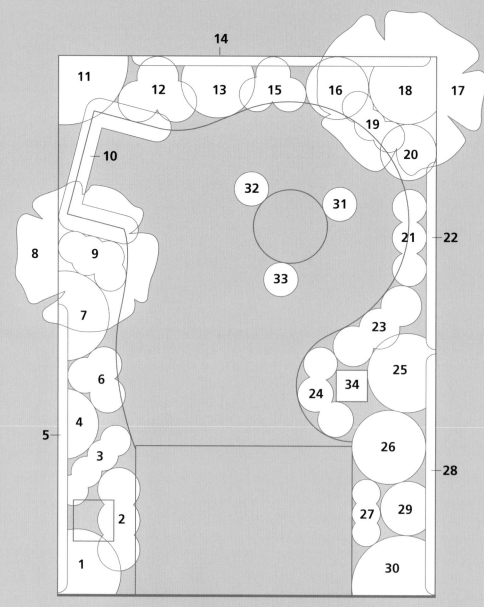

Planting key

1 *Ilex aquifolium* 'Ferox Argentea' (male)
2 *Euphorbia dulcis* 'Chameleon'
3 *Iris sibirica* 'Dreaming Yellow'
4 *Penstemon* 'Apple Blossom'
5 *Clematis* 'Elizabeth'
6 *Agapanthus* Headbourne hybrids
7 *Viburnum carlesii* 'Diana'
8 *Sorbus hupehensis* 'Pink Pagoda'
9 *Tradescantia* Andersoniana Group 'Innocence'
10 *Lonicera caprifolium*
11 *Escallonia rubra* 'Crimson Spire'
12 *Kniphofia* Ada
13 *Berberis candidula*
14 *Jasminum nudiflorum*
15 *Persicaria bistorta* 'Superba'
16 *Buxus sempervirens* 'Argenteo-variegata'
17 *Acer negundo* var. *violaceum*
18 *Skimmia laureola*
19 *Epimedium* x *rubrum*
20 *Viburnum davidii*
21 *Phlox paniculata* 'Mother of Pearl'
22 *Jasminum officinale* f. *affine*
23 *Liriope muscari*
24 *Geranium clarkei* 'Kashmir Pink'
25 *Cornus alba* 'Sibirica'
26 *Spiraea japonica* 'Gold Mound'
27 *Helleborus* x *hybridus* Ashwood Garden hybrids
28 *Akebia quinata*
29 *Miscanthus sinensis* 'Undine'
30 *Osmanthus delavayi*
31 *Hosta* 'Frances Williams'
32 *Caltha palustris* var. *palustris* 'Plena'
33 *Iris laevigata*
34 *Clematis* 'Betty Corning'

Bergenias are an excellent plant for first-time gardeners, being very robust and adaptable to many garden conditions.

Good starter plants

There's nothing worse in gardening than buying a choice plant, planting it and then watching as it fails to thrive and eventually dies. When you are working in your first garden this feeling must be even more acute, because you may have little or no idea why the plant has failed. It could, of course, be as simple as placing a shade- and moisture-loving plant, like a fern, in a hot, dry bed that is completely unsuitable for it. Fortunately, many plants are fairly tolerant and easy-going once they are established, and they will survive in a wide range of conditions without flinching, making them ideal for a beginner's garden.

Best starter trees
- *Betula pendula*
- *Sorbus aucuparia* cvs.
- *Prunus* x *subhirtella* 'Autumnalis'
- *Acer negundo* 'Kelly's Gold'
- *Pyrus salicifolia* 'Pendula'
- *Amelanchier lamarckii*
- *Corylus colurna*
- *Aralia elata*
- *Cotoneaster frigidus* 'Cornubia'
- *Crataegus laevigata* 'Paul's Scarlet'

Best starter shrubs
- *Euonymus fortunei* cvs.
- *Berberis thunbergii* cvs.
- *Spiraea nipponica* 'Snowmound'
- *Viburnum* x *burkwoodii*
- *Cornus alba* cvs.
- *Potentilla fruticosa* cvs.
- *Mahonia aquifolium*
- *Rosa* County Series (e.g., 'Hampshire', 'Suffolk')
- *Hypericum* x *moserianum* 'Tricolor'
- *Choisya ternata*

Best starter perennials
- *Persicaria affinis* 'Superba'
- *Viola riviniana* Purpurea Group
- *Tradescantia* hardy cvs.
- *Geranium* x *oxonianum* 'A.T. Johnson'
- *Euphorbia palustris*
- *Crocosmia* x *crocosmiiflora* 'Citronella'
- *Anemone* x *hybrida* cvs.
- *Alchemilla mollis*
- *Bergenia* cvs.
- *Pulmonaria longifolia*

Almost instant

What some people would like is a garden that takes little time to create and then, once it is built, looks mature. They want an 'instant' garden, and modern materials and techniques in the growing and handling of semi-mature or specimen plants now make this achievable.

Why this works

✓ Overlapping squares of shingle edged with old timbers make a quick, easy-to-build patio area.

✓ A small, ready-to-assemble gazebo is tucked into the corner as a more secluded sitting space.

✓ All the planting and paving areas are covered in a selection of shingle, stones and bark, which are easily and quickly laid.

✓ Box cubes are planted around the patio for immediate enclosure.

✓ Large, specimen-size trees and shrubs give an instant feeling of scale and maturity.

✓ The boundaries and the gazebo are planted with large climbers and wall shrubs, pre-trained on frames in the nursery, to soften and hide the surrounding walls from the start.

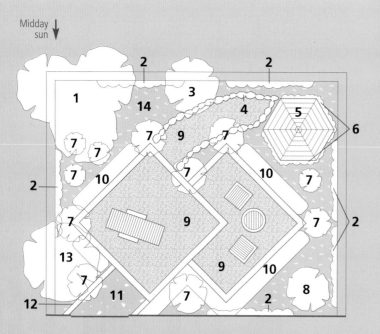

Midday sun ↓

Garden elements key

1 Semi-mature multi-stemmed small tree
2 Pre-trained climber or wall shrubs
3 Mop-head, semi-mature standard evergreen
4 Large, flat, stone edgings
5 Kit-form gazebo
6 Specimen size climbing roses on gazebo

7 Topiary

8 Specimen size shrub

9 Pea shingle patio
  areas

10 Low hedge of
  topiary box

11 Crushed slate path

12 Heavy timber edging

13 Semi-mature, slow-
  growing tree or
  large shrub

14 Crushed stone or
  ornamental grade
  bark mulch

Mix and match
If you like this garden but would prefer
a different feature, see pages 250–51 for
possible variations.

Garden dimensions
6m x 5m (20ft x 16ft 6in) approx.

Topiary

Topiary is a form of living sculpture, and in a small garden it can be effective, especially when it is included in a formal or geometric design. You may want to create and grow your own topiary from small, inexpensive plants. Alternatively, if you don't want to wait and cost is not critical, you can obtain ready-made, instant specimens from a specialist nursery.

Patio

Patios don't necessarily need to be made from solid stone, brick or concrete – use loose materials, such as shingle or finely crushed slate, for an interesting textured effect but make sure you enclose the space with a hard edging to stop the loose material from spreading into the adjacent beds and borders.

Specimen shrubs and trees

Ready-made specimen trees and shrubs are perfect for an instant effect, but do check the cost of these against your budget before you order. They will be delivered in large crates or containers or with a solid rootball secured with sacking and wire. Secure staking of trees is vital for at least the first couple of years, and you may need to do the same with large shrubs, especially evergreens, which can be susceptible to wind-rock, particularly in the winter before they have rooted into the surrounding soil.

Quick and easy paving ideas

If your 'paved' area is going to sustain only occasional or light use, or is even purely to be seen as a visual element in the garden, you can use a selection of loose materials, such as stone chippings, gravel, crushed slate or even graded bark, to create the surface, requiring significantly less cost, effort and time. You will also have less (or even no) surplus material in the form of topsoil or subsoil to dispose of, compared with the traditional excavations required for large unit or flag paving.

There is a wide range of loose materials or 'aggregates'

Pebbles and crushed stone or slate can be laid loose or pressed into wet concrete for a harder-wearing paving surface.

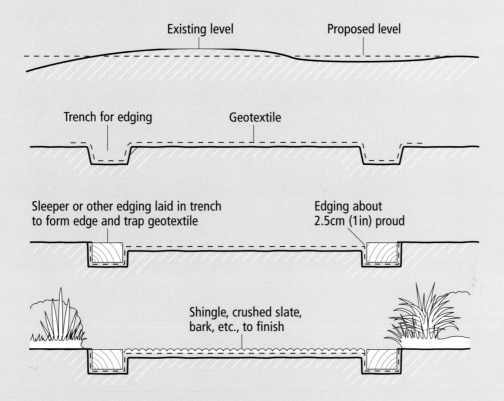

Existing level   Proposed level

Trench for edging   Geotextile

Sleeper or other edging laid in trench
to form edge and trap geotextile

Edging about
2.5cm (1in) proud

Shingle, crushed slate,
bark, etc., to finish

available, so your first step should be to select one that is in keeping with your garden. Look for colour – for example, do you want a single colour or a mixture that may be complementary or contrasting? Texture is important – smooth, naturally rounded aggregates will look and behave differently from crushed natural stone, which will be angled. Size or grade is also important, and you will need to select something that is comfortable to walk on. Remember, too, that smooth, rounded aggregates will move around more than sharp, angular ones, which tend to 'bind'.

For best results make sure that your chosen 'paved' area is smooth and firm, which may involve a certain amount of minor regrading with a spade and rake, followed by treading

down. If the soil is too soft or light to firm down solidly, rake cement thoroughly into the top 5–7.5cm (2–3in) – use 25kg (55lb) per 4–5 square metres (about 50 sq ft) – before treading and final levelling to stiffen the soil and create a shell or crust adequate to take the loose aggregate.

An edge is desirable, if not essential, both to retain the aggregate and to give a neat finish. Heavy timbers – 12.5 x 7.5cm (5 x 3in) or more thick – are an attractive and simple solution. All you need to do is excavate a trench around your chosen area to a depth slightly less than the depth of the timber and lay the timber in it, leaving about 2.5cm (1in) proud, which will allow for the thickness of aggregate. Since the usage of this area will be light, you

can set these on just sand or on a mixture of 1 part cement to 8 parts sand to get them level.

Where the base area is clean, firm hardcore, you can lay the final surface finish directly on top. However, if you are working over topsoil, firm the area and cover it with a piece of heavy-duty geotextile, which is widely available as mulching fabric. Use proprietary pegs to fix it down firmly around the edges and, especially, the corners. Put down the fabric before you fix your edging, and then lay the edging so that it traps the edge to give extra security before covering it with your chosen material. As a guide, the depth of stone or bark should be about twice the thickness of the individual pieces, but not more than three times, otherwise you'll sink into it as you walk.

Planting

The best plants for this garden

The 'instant' maturity of this garden is achieved largely by the use of specimen and semi-mature plants, with the emphasis being on the size, structure and scale of the planting rather than on bright or mixed colours. Trees and shrubs provide the garden with height, and climbers that have been grown on and trained in the nursery give an immediate impact on the walls around the garden. The patio is surrounded by rows of neat box cubes. Large topiary specimens of holly (*Ilex aquifolium* 'Handsworth New Silver') add the finishing touch with their neat, geometric shapes and splash of silver in the foliage.

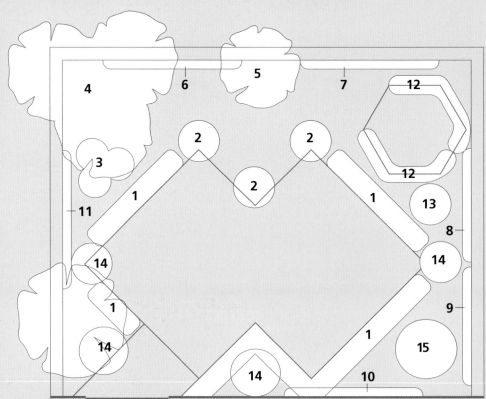

Make your own topiary

Training climbers

This method requires a wire mesh frame or former that has been made to your desired shape. Secure the frame in your chosen container and then plant one or more climbers around the edge of the frame. As the plants grow, all you need to do is to wind the new growths over the frame and tie them in loosely. Once your frame is covered it's simply a matter of trimming off new growths back to just above the surface of the frame. For this style of topiary the best plants are small-leaved ivies (*Hedera*), *Muehlenbeckia* spp., or *Rubus* 'Betty Ashburner'.

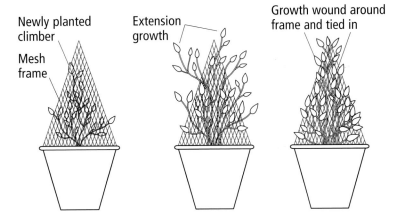

Newly planted climber · Mesh frame · Extension growth · Growth wound around frame and tied in

Clipping shrubs

This foolproof method requires a fairly open frame or former. You can make your own from something like chicken wire or you can buy a ready-made one. Plant a dwarf shrub inside the frame. As the plant grows, all you need to do is to trim back any new growths that project beyond the frame. This encourages more new shoots from within, and these will grow to fill up any spaces. Small-leaved plants are most suitable for this style of topiary: try box (*Buxus* spp.), junipers (*Juniperus* spp.) and dwarf berberis.

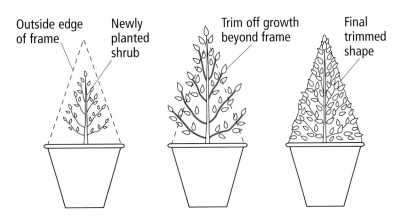

Outside edge of frame · Newly planted shrub · Trim off growth beyond frame · Final trimmed shape

Family-friendly garden

Mix and match
If you like this garden but would prefer a different feature, see pages 250–51 for possible variations.

Garden dimensions
8.5m x 11m (28ft 6in x 36ft) approx.

Small family gardens can be a challenge because you need to include a range of features to suit everyone in a limited space. The success of this design lies in the cohesive way in which the various elements are put together, so avoiding an unsatisfactory piecemeal effect and in the fact that all the space in the garden is put to good use with no dead areas that serve no purpose.

Why this works

✓ The well-placed lawn and patio give lots of room for children's play and adult relaxation.
✓ A summerhouse makes an elegant feature and also provides a handy outside play area in bad weather.
✓ Easy-to-maintain planting areas contain plenty of interesting, undemanding and durable plants.
✓ Simple benches on the patio double up as storage areas for small toys and garden tools.
✓ A shed, hidden from the patio with climbers on a trellis screen, acts as a store for larger equipment, such as a lawn mower and bicycles.
✓ The slender pergola and small water feature make an attractive focus and separate the patio from the play area.
✓ A raised bed, which can be used for growing a range of culinary herbs, is convenient for the kitchen and picking is easy.

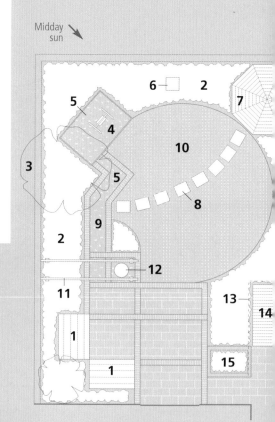

Midday sun

Garden elements key

1 Bench or store	**9** Path
2 Mixed border	**10** Lawn
3 Tree	**11** Narrow pergola
4 Play area	**12** Water feature
5 Bark	**13** Trellis
6 Obelisk or tripod	**14** Shed or store
7 Summerhouse	**15** Raised bed
8 Optional stepping stone path	

Key features

Summerhouse

Position a summerhouse in a far corner and create interest by making the doorway face the diagonally opposite corner, where you can balance it with a different feature – in this case the pergola and water feature. Don't forget to provide some form of all-weather access, whether it's basic stepping stones across the lawn or a more substantial brick-weave path.

Play area

Siting a play area in a small garden is not usually difficult because the options available will limit your choice to a place that can be most easily supervised from the house. However, try to link it to the lawn or patio – or both – so that the play can spill over when necessary and make sure that there is a simple path so that access is easy and clean.

Raised herb bed

Fresh herbs make a useful and enjoyable addition to the menu, and an easy way to grow them is in a raised bed. Position them in a sunny place close to the house so that it's convenient to nip outside and cut some when required. Make the walls of your raised bed from brick, stone or heavy, pressure-treated timber and fill it with good-quality, loam-based compost. If you make the walls about 45cm (18in) high and 20–25cm (8–10in) thick, the raised bed can be used for extra seating when you are entertaining outside.

Bench seat or store

Space for storing small outdoor toys, tools and other sundries, such as spare pots and garden canes, is always at a premium in any garden, especially a small one. One or more of these simple units will go a long way to solving the problem of lack of storage space, and if you put it on the edge of your patio it can be used as a bench seat or a display stand for containers and garden ornaments.

Use your bench seat or store to make a positive contribution to the garden's appearance.

Overhead plan view

1m (39in) long deckboard

Plan of levels

60cm (24in)
1.4m (4ft 6in)
60cm (24in)

Level 2

85cm (33½in)
1m (39in)
85cm (33½in)

Levels 1 and 3

35cm (14in)
1.4m (4ft 6in)

Level 4

Deckboard
Polythene or PVC
10cm (4in) overhang
2.5cm (1in) overhang
Bamboo matting
Tray
25cm x 12.5cm (10in x 5in) timber wall

4
3
2
1
Tray
25 x 12.5cm (10 x 5in) timber wall

You will need

25cm x 12.5cm (10in x 5in) pressure-treated timbers, total length at least 11m (36ft)

140cm x 85cm (55in x 33½in) heavy-duty black polythene or PVC pond liner

Thumb tacks or heavy staples

12.5cm x 1.5cm (5in x ¾in) grooved deck boards, total length at least 12m (40ft)

20 x 20cm (8in) self-tapping wood screws

4cm (1½in) deck screws

150cm x 45cm (59in x 18in) split bamboo or reed matting

Woodstain

Plastic trays to fit space 100cm x 60cm (40in x 24in) for storage

Step by step

1 Cut the 25cm x 12.5cm (10in x 5in) timber into the following lengths: three 140cm (55in), two 60cm (24in), four 85cm (33½in), two 1m (39in) and two 35cm (14in).

2 Lay one 1m (39in) length and two 85cm (33½in) lengths on your base in the selected position in a U-shape to form level 1.

3 Take one 140cm (55in) length and two 60cm (24in) lengths and lay them on top of level 1 to form level 2, so that the corners overlap as in the manner of bricks. Drill a 20cm (8in) screw through the end of each piece to secure it to the piece below.

4 Repeat step 2 to form level 3.

5 Take the remaining two 140cm (55in) lengths and the two 35cm (14in) lengths and lay them on top of level 3 to form a rectangle 140cm x 85cm (55in x 33½in). Screw through again to complete the frame.

6 Fix the polythene or PVC sheet to the top of the rectangle with thumb tacks or heavy staples. Ensure it is taut.

7 Cut the deck boards into 1m (39in) lengths and fix them to the top of the frame with the deck screws, leaving an overhang of 2.5cm (1in) at the back and sides, and about 10cm (4in) at the front.

8 Stain the completed unit.

9 Take the piece of bamboo or reed matting and fix one end horizontally beneath the 10cm (4in) overhang. Roll the matting up when access is required and secure with nylon tape or cord.

10 Fill trays with toys and tools and slide them under the bench before dropping the matting to conceal.

Planting

The best plants for this garden

In a family garden you will want to have plants that not only look good but that are also robust and easy to care for, so you should select those that aren't going to be terminally harmed by occasional damage and injudicious or untimely pruning. The trees, shrubs, perennials and climbers in this garden generally fall into this category. However, if you decide that you want to include one or two species that may be more susceptible, it is a good idea, and usually possible, to find an odd, protected corner where they can be cosseted a little.

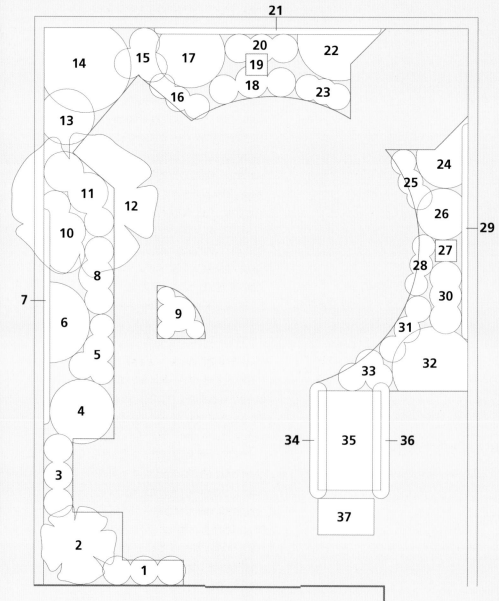

Planting key

1 *Perovskia atriplicifolia* 'Filigran'
2 *Laurus nobilis*
3 *Pleioblastus viridistriatus*
4 *Camellia japonica* 'Adolphe Audusson'
5 *Saxifraga umbrosa*
6 *Spiraea* x *vanhouttei* 'Pink Ice'
7 *Lonicera sempervirens* 'Dropmore Scarlet'
8 *Heuchera* 'Pewter Moon'
9 *Erica* x *darleyensis* 'Darley Dale'
10 *Filipendula palmata*
11 *Potentilla fruticosa* 'Manchu'
12 *Malus* 'John Downie'
13 *Skimmia japonica* 'Fragrans'
14 *Philadelphus* 'Avalanche'
15 *Anemone tomentosa*
16 *Geranium clarkei* (Purple-flowered Group) 'Kashmir Purple'
17 *Viburnum* x *burkwoodii*
18 *Aster amellus* 'King George'
19 *Lathyrus odoratus* (on obelisk)
20 *Phlox paniculata* 'Prospero'
21 *Clematis* 'Bill MacKenzie'
22 *Cornus alba* 'Elegantissima'
23 *Coreopsis verticillata* 'Golden Gain'
24 *Escallonia* 'Peach Blossom'
25 *Leucanthemum* x *superbum* 'Snowcap'
26 *Hebe* 'Great Orme'
27 *Lathyrus odoratus* (on obelisk)
28 *Potentilla* 'William Rollisson'
29 *Jasminum officinale*
30 *Hemerocallis* 'Pink Damask'
31 *Nepeta racemosa* 'Little Titch'
32 *Buddleja davidii* 'Nanho Purple'
33 *Carex elata* 'Aurea'
34 *Euonymus japonicus* 'Microphyllus'
35 Salad crops
36 Climbing (runner) beans on trellis
37 Herbs (in raised bed)

For robustness and durability, evergreen forms of euonymus such as *E. fortunei* 'Silver Queen' take some beating.

Robust plants

Indestructible plants that will grow anywhere with no care and attention would be ideal for most gardeners. As we all know, however, this can never be the case. There are, nevertheless, many plants that could be loosely described as robust, undemanding and generally easy to look after. These are ideal for a family garden, where they will not only be exposed to the odd bit of physical contact with bodies or objects but will also probably receive minimum attention because spare time is limited.

Best robust perennials

- *Hemerocallis* 'Stella de Oro'
- *Aster novi-belgii* 'Snowsprite'
- *Ajuga reptans* 'Catlin's Giant'
- *Vinca minor* 'Azurea Flore Pleno'
- *Phlox carolina* 'Miss Lingard'
- *Achillea* 'Taygetea'
- *Teucrium chamaedrys*
- *Potentilla* x *tonguei*
- *Melissa officinalis* 'All Gold'
- *Origanum laevigatum* 'Herrenhausen'

Best robust shrubs

- *Abelia* x *grandiflora*
- *Brachyglottis monroi*
- *Euonymus fortunei* cvs.
- *Diervilla* x *splendens*
- *Cornus alba* 'Kesselringii'
- *Spiraea japonica* 'Little Princess'
- *Viburnum farreri*
- *Olearia macrodonta*
- *Physocarpus opulifolius* 'Diabolo'
- *Pittosporum tenuifolium* cvs.

Easy-care garden

How you're going to look after your garden once it's completed should figure prominently at the design stage so that you can incorporate various ideas, features and plant types that will virtually eliminate the more mundane aspects of garden maintenance.

Why this works

✓ A simple layout makes effective use of space.

✓ The lawn is edged to make mowing easy.

✓ There is an interesting mix of plants with a range of qualities but none requires particularly lavish or complicated care and attention.

✓ All the plants are planted through a geotextile mulching fabric covered in ornamental bark to conserve moisture and suppress weed growth. The same textile is used to prevent weed invasion in the gravel path.

✓ An irrigation system for both lawn and borders can be used in times of drought. It can be run through an automatic timer programmed to suit your personal needs – when you're away on holiday, for example.

✓ The joints in the York stone paving are pointed with a mortar mix to provide a watertight and weedproof seal.

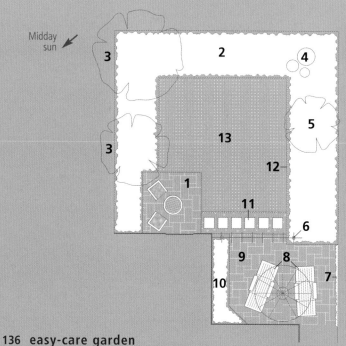

Garden elements key

1 Small patio	**6** Overheads
2 Mixed border	**7** Climber
3 Trees	**8** Patio furniture
4 Glazed ceramic	**9** Main patio
spheres	**10** Wall shrubs and
5 Small tree	climbers

11 Stepping stones in
    gravel

12 Lawn edging

13 Lawn

Mix and match

If you like this garden but would prefer
a different feature, see pages 250–51 for
possible variations.

Garden dimensions

7.5m x 9.5m (25ft x 31ft) approx.

Key features

Overheads

Overhead structures don't necessarily need to be planted heavily – nor indeed at all – to make a contribution to the garden. In this garden, a single, heavy oak beam spans from the house to an old brick pier, with a series of short lengths of oak on top. This makes an effective space divider between the main patio and the rest of the garden but does not block the view or sunlight.

Lawn

Cutting and generally looking after a lawn takes up a lot of time, but surrounding your lawn with a solid, firm edge can make mowing and cutting edges easier and quicker. Keep lawn shapes simple so that you can develop a simple, methodical mowing pattern – avoid awkward, fiddly shapes and don't plant individual shrubs or trees in the grass, which all adds to the time taken to cut it.

Weed-free borders

Many plants will act as natural weed-suppressors, but only when they are reasonably mature. In the meantime you will need to keep weeds at bay. Mulching clean, weed-free soil with bark, shingle or coco shells will do the same job and also conserve moisture. For ultimate weed prevention lay and pin down geotextile mulching fabric on your planting areas, and plant through it by cutting holes at the appropriate positions. Cover the fabric with a loose mulch for a natural look.

Personalized flagstones

If you are reasonably practical you could easily have a go at making some flagstones to your own unique design. You don't need to produce them on a grand scale – make, say, half a dozen to mix with plainer, bought-in flags or, perhaps, to lay in a lawn or a gravel area as stepping stones. If resources permit, try and make all your personalized flags at the same time from one large batch of concrete. This will make sure that the basic colour (with or without added pigment) is constant.

Personalized mosaic flagstones are more time-consuming to make than some, but the result is well worth the effort.

You will need

2.5 x 5cm (1 x 2in) planed wood for the sides of the moulds

38mm (1½in) wood screws

Form-releasing oil (to treat the inside of the mould before pouring the concrete) optional

Cement

All-in ballast (sand and aggregate premixed) or, for an exposed aggregate finish, use 4 parts of selected aggregate (river worn or rounded is more effective than crushed or angular) to 2 parts sand and 1 part cement

Soft, builders' sand

Stones, gravel, leaves and so on, depending on the style of flagstone

Colour pigment

Finish examples

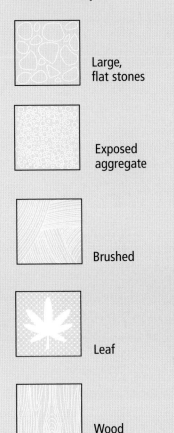

Large, flat stones

Exposed aggregate

Brushed

Leaf

Wood grain

Step by step

1 Cut the timber into lengths – for example, 45cm (18in) – and screw four pieces together to make a square box. Coat the inside with form oil.

2 On a hard, smooth, level area spread some soft sand at least 15mm (about ¾in) thick. Level it and tamp it down with a flat piece of wood or plasterer's steel float.

3 Press the mould lightly into the sand bed.

4 For inverted flags, place your desired objects – stones, leaves and so on – on the sand. With larger stones press them slightly into the sand.

5 Mix your concrete, with colour pigment if required, using 6 parts ballast to 1 part cement, or 4 parts aggregate (gravel) to 2 parts sand and 1 part cement. Make the mix fairly sloppy, pour carefully into the mould and level off.

6 Let the concrete go off for at least 36 hours before unscrewing the mould and prising off the timber edges. Leave for at least another 36 hours before laying the flags.

7 For non-inverted flags – exposed aggregate, brushed finish and the like – pour the concrete into the mould and level. While it's wet, press the stones into the surface or brush or comb it to form patterns. For a softer textured or exposed aggregate finish, let the concrete go green first – that is, set but not strong – before using the brush. Again you might need to make a trial flag to practise on.

Moulding or casting details

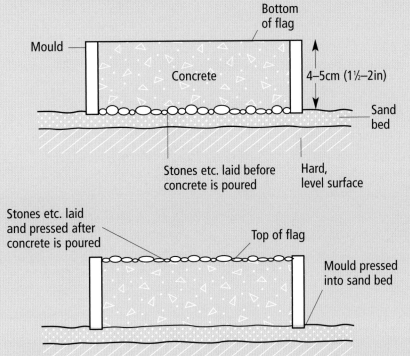

Planting

The best plants for this garden

Plants for an easy-care garden should not only look good but should be reliable, healthy and undemanding. The selection in this garden not only meets these criteria but makes an attractive backdrop to the geometric layout of lawn and paving. Many of the species are excellent groundcover plants in their own right, but here they are given an even better start by being mulched.

12

18

23

26

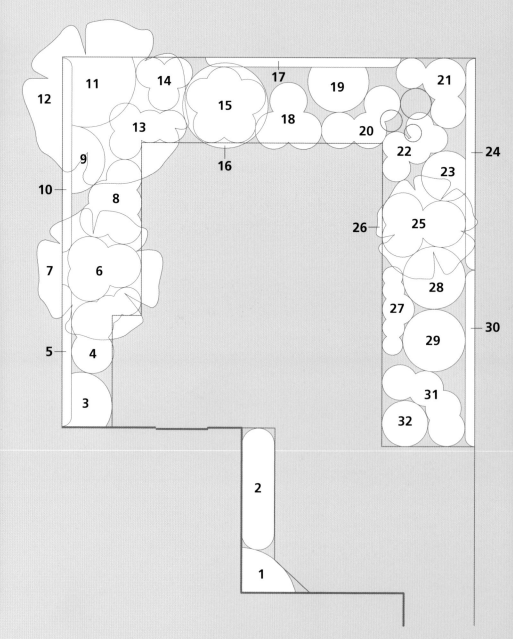

Planting key

1 *Aloysia citriodora*
2 *Euonymus fortunei* 'Silver Queen'
3 *Hebe* 'Mrs Winder'
4 *Agapanthus* 'Lilliput'
5 *Clematis* 'Princess Diana'
6 *Viburnum davidii*
7 *Prunus* 'Pandora'
8 *Heuchera* 'Plum Pudding'
9 *Prunus lusitanica* 'Variegata'
10 *Hydrangea anomala* subsp. *petiolaris*
11 *Rhododendron* 'Pink Pearl'
12 *Davidia involucrata*
13 *Aster novi-belgii* 'Heinz Richard'
14 *Geranium* x *monacense*
15 *Dicentra spectabilis*
16 *Hibiscus syriacus* 'Oiseau Bleu'
17 *Clematis* 'Alba Luxurians'
18 *Achillea* 'Moonshine'
19 *Weigela florida* 'Foliis Purpureis'
20 *Berberis buxifolia* 'Pygmaea'
21 *Arundo donax* var. *versicolor*
22 *Viola cornuta* Alba Group
23 *Pieris japonica* 'Mountain Fire'
24 *Hydrangea serratifolia*
25 *Polystichum polyblepharum*
26 *Acer griseum*
27 *Saxifraga* 'Wada'
28 *Fuchsia magellanica*
29 *Berberis* x *lologensis* 'Mystery Fire'
30 *Clematis* 'Etoile Violette'
31 *Hosta* 'Blue Angel'
32 *Taxus baccata* 'Semperaurea'

There are many dwarf grasses and grassy-leaved perennials to choose from that are really effective as groundcover.

Groundcover planting

If you ask a typical gardener to name some groundcover plants, they'll probably envisage low, flat drifts of perennials, such as periwinkle (*Vinca*), deadnettle (*Lamium*) and ivy (*Hedera*), or prostrate conifers, such as *Juniperus horizontalis*. These are all excellent plants, but there is more to groundcover than this. Many much larger perennials and shrubs are equally effective at covering ground and, of course, add the extra dimension of height to your planting scheme. Species that are naturally dense and bushy or that have large, overlapping leaves, especially evergreens, are all suitable for this purpose.

Medium and tall shrubs for groundcover

- *Potentilla fruticosa* 'Abbotswood'
- *Pittosporum tenuifolium* 'Tom Thumb'
- *Spiraea japonica* var. *albiflora*
- *Rosa* 'Swany'
- *Cotoneaster conspicuus* 'Decorus'
- *Brachyglottis* (Dunedin Group) 'Sunshine'
- *Berberis* x *media* 'Parkjuweel'
- *Viburnum opulus* 'Compactum'
- *Elaeagnus pungens* 'Goldrim'
- *Viburnum* x *hillieri* 'Winton'
- *Rhododendron* hybrids
- *Rosa* 'Buff Beauty'
- *Photinia* 'Redstart'
- *Choisya ternata*

Taller groundcover perennials and grasses

- *Achillea* 'Moonshine'
- *Carex comans* 'Frosted Curls'
- *Geranium psilostemon*
- *Deschampsia cespitosa* 'Bronzeschleier'
- *Rudbeckia fulgida* var. *sullivantii* 'Goldsturm'
- *Sedum* 'Indian Chief'
- *Miscanthus sinensis* 'Yakushima Dwarf'
- *Acanthus mollis* Latifolius Group
- *Persicaria amplexicaulis* 'Firetail'

Party place

Entertaining outdoors is a great way to relax and enjoy the good weather. Part of the challenge in designing a small garden for partying outside is to make sure that there is sufficient room to put out seats and tables and also to make sure you have enough furniture to accommodate all your guests.

Why this works

✓ The overlapping square theme gives lots of space for tables, chairs, barbecues and other essential party equipment.

✓ A mobile gas barbecue is clean and convenient.

✓ Three generous planting areas provide space for lots of plants yet still leave loads of space for the paved areas.

✓ Screen block or trellis walls and wooden overhead rails partially enclose the main square, giving a greater feeling of depth to the garden. In one corner they are covered in polycarbonate sheet to make a dry space behind that is ideal as a furniture and barbecue store.

✓ Simple cubes are ideal for extra chairs and tables and can be stored away when not required.

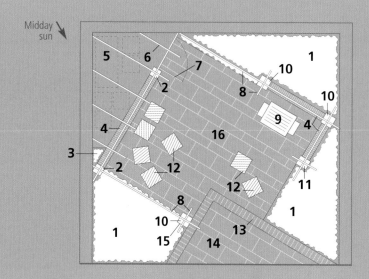

Garden elements key

1 Planting

2 Screen block pier

3 Climber to go on overheads

4 Screen block wall and trellis on top

5 'Cube' seats or barbecue store with polycarbonate roof

6 Overheads

7 Optional gate to store (lattice to match trellis)

8 Overhead rails

9 Barbecue

10 Pier

11 Pier and climbers

12 'Cube' seats or
   tables

13 Brick infill paving

14 Flag paving

15 Climber

16 Paving

Mix and match
If you like this garden but would prefer
a different feature, see pages 250–51 for
possible variations.

Garden dimensions
5m x 5.5m (16ft 6in x 18ft) approx.

Garden furniture

If you plan lots of regular outdoor entertaining you will need to make sure you have sufficient furniture to accommodate your guests. Furniture that can be stacked or folded when it is not in use takes up limited space and can be stored fairly easily. For larger, rigid chairs and tables you will need more storage space, in the house or garden, so make sure you plan for this in the early stages.

Screen block wall

Screen block walling is a quick and effective way to divide up a space, block an unsightly view and give height to a flat area without appearing too solid. There are different patterns available, and for a better finish you can colourwash the blocks using exterior-quality masonry paint. For extra effect, combine low walls with trellis or fencing panels on top, stained to match, to complement or to contrast.

Barbecue

Mobile barbecues are perfect for entertaining in a small garden as you can move them around to suit the weather and space available. Gas-fired examples, although more expensive than traditional types, are convenient and more controllable, with none of the drawbacks associated with firelighters and lighting fluid. With any mobile barbecue, don't forget to position it where the heat won't damage plants or other susceptible items.

Cube seats and tables

These cubes that can be used as seats or mini-tables are an ideal way to solve the problems of entertaining outside in a limited space. They are perfect for buffet-style parties and barbecues and take up little room when stored because they can be stacked vertically. You can personalize them with cut-out patterns in the sides, painting and staining in bright colours and topping them with vividly coloured cushions.

This fascinating wooden seat couldn't be easier to make – it is assembled with just four pieces of wood screwed together.

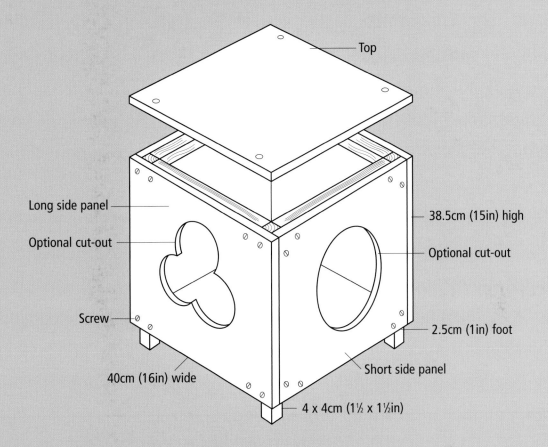

Top

Long side panel

Optional cut-out

Screw

40cm (16in) wide

38.5cm (15in) high

Optional cut-out

2.5cm (1in) foot

Short side panel

4 x 4cm (1½ x 1½in)

You will need

For each table or chair
125cm x 85cm (49in x 33½in) exterior-
    quality plywood 15mm (about ¾in)
    thick (this size allows a small
    amount of waste when cutting)
4 x 4cm (1½ x 1½in) planed
    softwood, at least 4m (13ft) long
36 x 4cm (1½in) countersunk wood
    screws
Stain or paint
Cushion

Step by step

1 Cut a square 40 x 40cm (16 x
16in) from the plywood sheet to
make the top.

2 Cut two rectangles, each 37 x
38.5cm (14½ x 15in), from the
plywood sheet for the short side
panels.

3 Cut two more rectangles, each
40cm x 38.5cm (16in x 15in), for the
long side panels.

4 Cut the 4cm x 4cm (1½in x 1½in)
softwood into four 41cm (16¼in)
lengths and eight 29cm (11½in)
lengths.

5 Take the four side panels and use a
jigsaw to cut out your chosen patterns.

6 Take a short side panel, 37cm x
38.5cm (14½in x 15in), and lay it
face down. Fix 41cm (16¼in) lengths
of softwood flush with both 38.5cm
(15in) edges with wood screws,
leaving a 2.5cm (1in) projection at
the bottom to form the feet. Fix a
29cm (11½in) length of softwood
flush to the remaining two edges so
that the panel is framed.

7 Repeat step 6 for the second short
side.

8 Take a long side panel and fix 29cm
(11½in) lengths of softwood to the
centre of the top and bottom edges.
Repeat for the other long side panel.

9 Fix the 40 x 40cm (16 x 16in) top
panel to the top edges of the two
short side panels using wood screws
and leaving a 15mm (about ¾in)
overhang at each end to form the top
and two opposite sides of the cube.

10 Take the two 40 x 38.5cm (16 x
15in) long side panels and fix them
to the legs of the other side panels to
complete the cube.

11 Stain or paint the cubes and finish
off with cushions.

Planting

The best plants for this garden

The emphasis in this garden is on entertaining, so the planting has been designed to be low maintenance as well as reliable. Arranging plants in simple blocks makes the result more effective visually and hides the corners, thereby helping to give a feeling of space. Climbers on the trellis or screen block wall and the overheads also help to add to this effect. Colours are harmonious and generally muted, and there is an emphasis on interesting foliage and shape. The low edge planting consists of species that are able to withstand a certain amount of traffic when the party spills over from the paved areas.

7

10

15

21

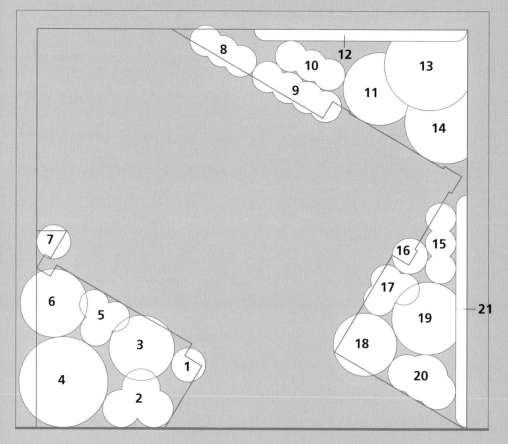

Planting key

1 *Trachelospermum jasminoides*
2 *Santolina chamaecyparissus* var. *nana*
3 *Potentilla fruticosa* 'Tilford Cream'
4 *Acer palmatum* 'Osakazuki'
5 *Carex oshimensis* 'Evergold'
6 *Pittosporum tenuifolium* 'Tom Thumb'
7 *Vitis coignetiae*
8 *Symphytum* 'Goldsmith'
9 *Vinca minor* 'Multiplex'
10 *Acanthus spinosus*
11 *Nandina domestica* 'Richmond'
12 *Lonicera hildebrandiana*
13 *Corylus maxima* 'Purpurea'
14 *Camellia japonica* 'Jupiter'
15 *Matteuccia struthiopteris*
16 *Hedera algeriensis* 'Gloire de Marengo'
17 *Geranium* x *magnificum*
18 *Juniperus horizontalis* 'Hughes'
19 *Viburnum tinus* 'Gwenllian'
20 *Rudbeckia fulgida* var. *sullivantii* 'Goldsturm'
21 *Clematis* 'Rouge Cardinal'

Clematis viticella 'Purpurea Plena Elegans' is worthy of a place in any garden, and is particularly striking when grown in a container.

Climbers

Climbers are an essential part of most gardens to grow on vertical surfaces, such as walls, fences or trellises, and on structures like arches and pergolas. In general in a small garden you will need to select climbers that are not too vigorous or invasive, because you don't want them to take over and become dominant or a nuisance. However, you could include fast-growing species, which can be hard pruned every year and so never exceed a certain size – some ornamental cultivars of the grape vine (*Vitis*) can be treated in this way. These plants are good for pergolas, where you want to provide some shade or screening. If you don't mind the extra work involved you can also try climbers like sweet peas (*Lathyrus odoratus*), nasturtium (*Tropaeolum*) or morning glory (*Ipomoea*), which are annuals and will not become invasive, but will need replacing each spring.

A great advantage of using climbing plants in a small garden is that they don't take up a lot of room on the ground, so where space is limited, you can still enjoy lots of flowers and foliage on your boundary walls and garden structures.

Best climbers for small gardens

- *Rosa* 'New Dawn'
- *Ampelopsis brevipedunculata* var. *maximowiczii* 'Elegans'
- *Schizophragma hydrangeoides*
- *Rubus henryi* var. *bambusarum*
- *Trachelospermum jasminoides* 'Variegatum'
- *Muehlenbeckia complexa* var. *trilobata*
- *Hedera helix* (small-leaved cvs., such as *H. helix* 'Goldchild')
- *Vitis vinifera* 'Ciotat'
- *Clematis viticella* cvs.
- *Rosa* 'Sombreuil'

Natural garden

A careful choice of native plants, including ornamental cultivars that look 'natural', will allow you to create a delightful garden with a quiet, relaxed feel. You can complement this style of garden with natural materials, such as wood and stone. One bonus is that you'll probably find that this type of garden becomes a magnet for wildlife, especially birds and insects.

Why this works

✓ It's an easy garden to maintain with no lawn, particularly if you mulch the borders.

✓ Planting is a well-balanced mixture of natives and plants that are either natural in appearance or are improved selections of a native species.

✓ The different garden features are built from natural materials to blend in and harmonize with the planting.

✓ Apart from the patio, where you may need some skilled help, it is not a difficult or expensive garden to build.

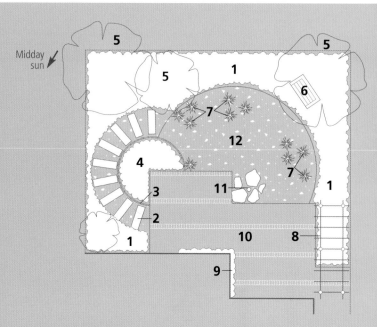

Garden elements key

1 Border planting
2 Sleeper 'stepping stones'
3 Slate edging
4 Grasses
5 Tree
6 Seat
7 Spot planting
8 Pergola
9 Wall shrub or climber

10 Patio

11 Water feature

12 Shingle and stone
mulch

Mix and match
If you like this garden but would prefer
a different feature, see pages 250–51 for
possible variations.

Garden dimensions
7.5m x 7m (25ft x 23ft) approx.

Key features

Grasses

Grasses add a distinctive, feathery quality to a garden. There are many sizes, from the lower growing ones that are particularly effective as groundcover or to soften the edge of paving to the taller, stronger growing varieties that make excellent accent plants in a mixed border.

Trees

Although many naturally occurring species are too large for this size of garden, there are some that are more commonly seen in the wild as large bushes, which can be carefully trained into modest, slow-growing trees that are ideally suited to the small garden, such as cornelian cherry (*Cornus mas*) and spindle (*Euonymus europaeus*).

Mulch

Mulches made from tree bark and other recycled organic materials are the most natural. Coarse (or ornamental) grades, which take a long time to break down and need only an occasional top up, are ideal, while finer grades are absorbed into the soil more quickly and have to be replaced more often. If a mulch is too fine the grains can prevent water from penetrating into the soil by absorbing it and holding it at the surface. Crushed stone and shingle mulches are particularly good for covering unplanted areas – you can spread the material directly on to a hardcore base or, if the base is soil, you can lay a geotextile mat first.

Roof garden variation

As with any other style of garden, you can take a design for a natural garden and adapt it so that it's suitable for a roof or large balcony. The same principles and restrictions apply, so you'll need to choose plants that are suited to the conditions that obtain at a higher level and that are suitable for growing in raised beds or containers.

Foliage planting can be equally striking whether it's in a large garden or, as here, on a roof.

Garden elements key

1 Deck board path
2 Raised bed
3 Crushed slate
4 Small tree in container
5 Underplanting
6 Pergola
7 Climber on pergola
8 Seat
9 Screen behind seat
10 Tiled paving
11 Fibreglass 'rocks'
12 Self-contained water feature
13 Climber on walls in container
14 Grasses in containers

Planting key

1 *Euphorbia polychroma*
2 *Tsuga canadensis* 'Jeddeloh'
3 *Hypericum x moserianum*
4 *Thymus vulgaris*
5 *Viburnum davidii*
6 *Euonymus alatus*
7 *Hedera helix* 'Ivalace'
8 *Viola cornuta* Alba Group
9 *Artemisia* 'Powis Castle'
10 *Cytisus x kewensis*
11 *Heuchera pulchella*
12 *Iris foetidissima*
13 *Clematis viticella*
14 *Lonicera periclymenum*
15 *Berberis candidula*
16 *Geranium sanguineum*
17 *Juniperus horizontalis* 'Prince of Wales'
18 *Clematis* 'White Columbine'
19 *Stipa gigantea*
20 *Festuca ovina*
21 *Carex comans*

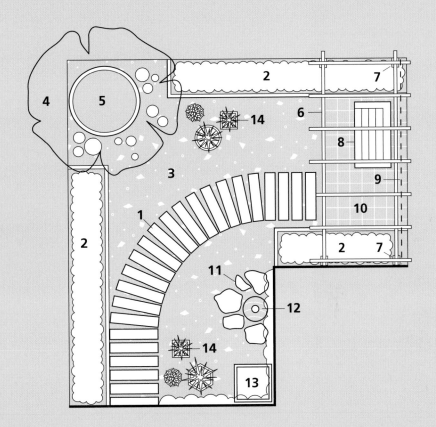

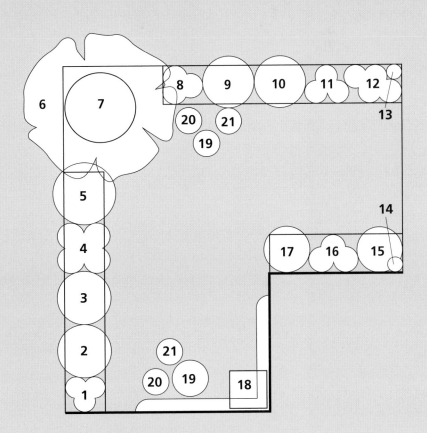

Planting

The best plants for this garden

Although native plants are the obvious choice for a natural garden, not all are suitable. In this garden there is a combination of native species that will do well in a small space and other plants that may strictly be classified as ornamental, yet associate perfectly well with the species. The colour palette in this garden is generally muted, and the style of planting fits in well with the natural materials used elsewhere in the natural garden.

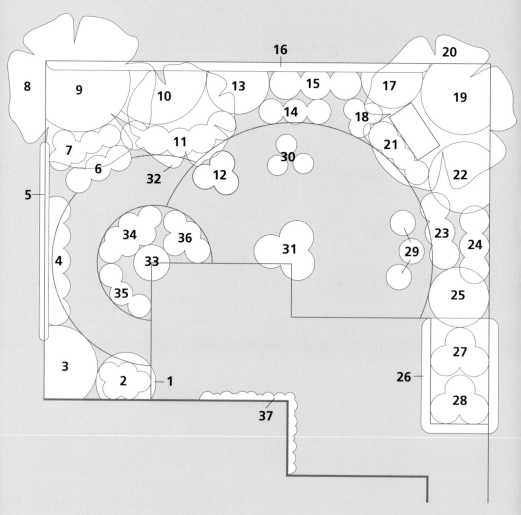

Planting key

1 *Rosa glauca*
2 *Primula vulgaris*
3 *Euonymus europaeus* 'Red Cascade'
4 *Digitalis purpurea* f. *albiflora*
5 *Lonicera periclymenum* 'Graham Thomas'
6 *Alchemilla mollis*
7 *Polygonatum multiflorum*
8 *Sorbus aucuparia*
9 *Prunus laurocerasus* 'Otto Luyken'
10 *Viburnum lantana*
11 *Geranium sylvaticum*
12 *Allium schoenoprasum*
13 *Cytisus* x *praecox*
14 *Nepeta* x *faassenii*
15 *Acanthus mollis*
16 *Hedera hibernica*
17 *Spiraea thunbergii*
18 *Pulsatilla vulgaris*
19 *Mahonia aquifolium*
20 *Betula pendula* 'Tristis'
21 *Viola cornuta*
22 *Cornus sanguinea*
23 *Geranium* 'Johnson's Blue'
24 *Verbascum* (Cotswold Group) 'Gainsborough'
25 *Hypericum androsaemum*
26 *Clematis flammula*
27 *Campanula latifolia*
28 *Filipendula ulmaria*
29 *Origanum vulgare*
30 *Iris pseudacorus*
31 *Daphne mezereum*
32 *Cornus mas* (standard)
33 *Deschampsia cespitosa* 'Goldschleier'
34 *Carex testacea*
35 *Hakonechloa macra*
36 *Briza media*
37 *Actinidia kolomikta*

Elegant white and cream tulips will harmonize perfectly with virtually any style of planting in your garden.

Bulbs

Where space for planting is limited, bulbs are an excellent way of bringing additional colour and interest to a small garden, especially in late winter and early spring, when flowers are scarce.

Best front-of-border bulbs

- *Galanthus* 'S. Arnott'
- *Tulipa humilis* 'Alba Coerulea Oculata'
- *Narcissus* 'Tête-à-tête'
- *Crocus tommasinianus* 'Whitewell Purple'
- *Anemone blanda* 'White Splendour'
- *Chionodoxa forbesii* 'Blue Giant'
- *Iris* 'Cantab'
- *Erythronium* 'Pagoda'
- *Scilla sibirica*
- *Muscari armeniacum* 'Dark Eyes'

Best mid- to back-of-border bulbs

- *Lilium regale* 'Album'
- *Allium cristophii*
- *Tulipa* 'Apricot Beauty'
- *Galtonia candicans*
- *Ornithogalum narbonense*
- *Bellevalia paradoxa*
- *Narcissus* 'Doctor Hugh'
- *Crinum* x *powellii* 'Album'
- *Nerine bowdenii* 'Pink Triumph'
- *Tritelia laxa* 'Koningin Fabiola'

Crops in pots

You don't need a large garden, or indeed a garden with soil, in order to grow and crop delicious fresh fruit, vegetables and salads. With a little care and attention, containers and raised beds can be made to perform the same job as a traditional kitchen garden. The only restriction is the space available, which will limit the amount of produce that can be achieved.

Why this works

✓ An efficient layout gives easy access to all the planted areas.
✓ The central frame, set in four planters, is not only an eye-catching feature but also makes a great support for climbing, edible plants.
✓ Large planters with fruit trees give height and structure to the design.
✓ The undercover potting bench and/or store cupboard accommodates seed sowing, potting-on, storing garden sundries.
✓ The space for additional individual pots and containers is ideal for short-term rotational crops and herbs.
✓ Decking tiles are easy to make and soft on the feet, and they can be lifted to allow the concrete base beneath to be swept and washed.

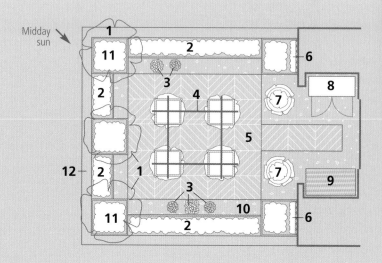

Garden elements key

1 Fruit tree
2 Trough
3 Mixed vegetables or annuals in containers

4 Frame for climbing plants; planter at each corner
5 Square decking tiles
6 Trellis on wall

7 Strawberry pot

8 Store cupboard and
work top

9 Potting bench with
shelves below

10 Shingle

11 Corner planter

12 Balustrade wall

Mix and match
If you like this garden but would prefer
a different feature, see pages 250–51 for
possible variations.

Garden dimensions
4m x 3.7m (13ft x 12ft) approx.

Key features

Frame

You can double up on features such as pergolas, arches and simple frames by using them to grow plants that will bear fruit or other crops, such as climbing beans or a grape vine. Even in the depths of winter they will provide some interest.

Fruit trees

Most top or tree fruits – apples, pears, plums and so on – are better suited to being grown directly in the ground. However, improved plant breeding and selection have led to an increasing range of trees that are relatively dwarf or slow growing and that can be grown in raised beds or even in large containers. Although they don't produce the same quantity of fruit as a conventionally grown tree, the size and quality should be the same as long as they are well cared for.

Troughs

Planting troughs to sit on the ground and against a low wall are easy to make and are ideal for seasonal vegetables and salad crops. Make sure you have enough troughs so that you can incorporate a crop rotation plan in your gardening programme. Because the nutrients are effectively removed from the growing medium every time you harvest a crop, pay extra attention to feeding and watering throughout the growing season and be prepared to replace the compost regularly.

Deck tiles

Making your own deck tiles is an easy and cost-effective way of covering a paved area, and they are also easier on the feet than standing for long periods on concrete or brick. You can choose a size that will exactly fit your own space, and, given regular care and attention, they should last for many years.

The beauty of deck tiles is that you can combine them in different ways to suit your own space.

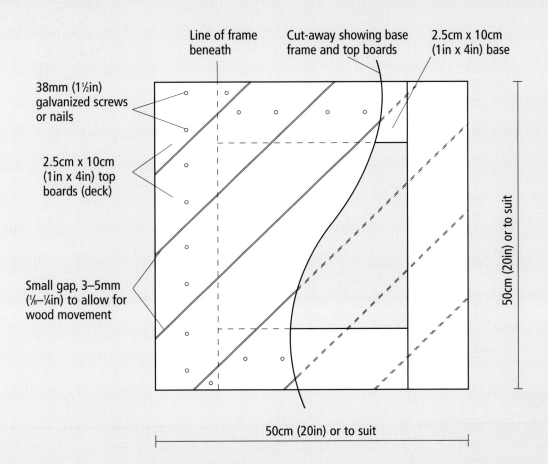

Line of frame
beneath

Cut-away showing base
frame and top boards

2.5cm x 10cm
(1in x 4in) base

38mm (1½in)
galvanized screws
or nails

2.5cm x 10cm
(1in x 4in) top
boards (deck)

Small gap, 3–5mm
(⅛–¼in) to allow for
wood movement

50cm (20in) or to suit

50cm (20in) or to suit

You will need

2.5cm x 10cm (1in x 4in) pressure-
treated sawn softwood boards;
allow about 5m (16ft 6in) per
50cm x 50cm (20in x 20in) tile
38mm (1½in) galvanized screws or
nails
Exterior-quality woodstain

Step by step

1 Cut two pieces of board each 50cm (20in) long and two pieces 30cm (12in)
long and lay them on a level piece of hard ground to form a 50cm (20in)
square. Measure the diagonals and adjust the wood so they are exactly equal
and thus a perfect square.

2 Carefully lay a section of board diagonally on top of the square so the centre
of the board aligns with the two opposite corners, screw or nail it to the boards
below and cut the projecting pieces flush with the square base to form a corner.

3 Cut one end of another section of board at 45° and lay it alongside the now-
fixed diagonal board, with the 45° end set flush to the edge of the square
below. Fix with screws and nails and trim off the overhanging end (which will
also be 45°). Continue to fill in the square, using the 45° cut ends to start each
row and avoid waste.

4 Once completed, apply two coats of stain, paying particular attention to newly
cut ends.

5 At least every other year, preferably every year, lift the tiles, brush off loose
dirt, wash down, dry and restain for a long life and to eliminate conditions that
might attract harmful pests and diseases.

Planting

The best plants for this garden

In this limited space there is a good selection of salad, soft and top fruits, and vegetables to give a general mix and provide something fresh for up to eight months of the year. You can fine-tune the plant selection to fit in with your own preferences and include unusual or hard-to-find crops that you especially like.

Planting key

1 Apple 'Greensleeves' (column/minarette or dwarf bush on M27 stock)

2 Apple 'Discovery' (column/minarette or dwarf bush on M27 stock)

3 Apple 'Grenadier' (column/minarette or dwarf bush on M27 stock)

4 Early potatoes followed by annuals for colour or winter cabbages or cauliflower

5 Japanese wineberry (trained on wires fixed to wall)

6 Blackberry 'Waldo' (trained on wires fixed to wall)

7 Strawberries (in strawberry pots)

8 Cherry tomatoes

9 Melon

10 Climbing (runner) beans (on frame)

11 Leaf salad crops – lettuce, rocket and so on

12 Spring onions, radish, early carrots

13 Courgette, summer cabbage

14 Blueberries

15 Mint and parsley (variegated mint illustrated)

16 Dwarf (French) beans or salsify or scorzonera

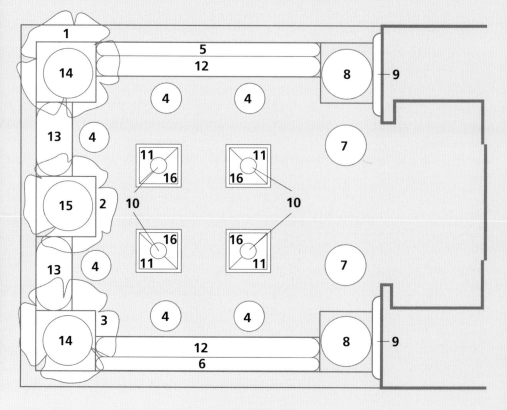

Fruit and vegetables in pots

Growing fruit and vegetables in pots, containers and raised beds can be as successful and rewarding as growing them in a traditional kitchen garden or allotment. In order to do this successfully, however, you must provide your crop plants with the best conditions possible, bearing in mind that space for root growth and the availability of moisture and nutrients will be limited. By following some simple procedures and advice, you will soon be able to enjoy the fruits of your labour.

Make raised beds as large as possible, or, if you're using containers, use the biggest ones you can find. Avoid tall, narrow containers and wide, shallow ones. A circular container will lose moisture more evenly than a square one, which will dry out more rapidly at the corners.

Containers and beds made from porous materials, such as terracotta (clay) or treated softwood, should be made less porous by lining the sides (but not the base) with polythene or by applying a coat of plant-friendly waterproof paint.

Use a good-quality compost or growing medium to backfill. Loam-based, sterilized soils, improved with some organic matter, are ideal, but these can be heavy, and you must be aware of this if you have a roof garden or balcony. Don't use ordinary garden soil, which may contain pests and diseases.

Watering

Make sure all containers, troughs and raised beds have drainage or weep holes to allow excess moisture to escape.

Regular watering is essential. If possible, install an irrigation system, preferably with an automatic timer, so that your plants can be watered even when you're away. Although periods of dryness at the root may not seriously harm or kill your plants, it can affect the ultimate quality of the crop or, in the case of fruit trees, cause the blossom or immature fruits to drop.

Feeding

Many food crops, such as potatoes and brassicas, require generous amounts of nutrients and will quickly deplete

Don't just grow vegetables and salad to eat – make them an attractive feature as well.

the food reserves in a limited volume of compost or soil. You will, therefore, have to replenish the nutrients in the growing medium once they have been exhausted. Choose a liquid fertilizer to suit the particular crop: different plants require different proportions of the main nutrients, nitrogen, phosphorus and potash. Look at the packaging of proprietary fertilizers to check not only the suitability of the produce but also the frequency of application.

Although a loam-based growing medium can be reused if you have followed a regular feeding regime, you will probably get better results in subsequent years if you replace all or at least a proportion of the growing medium every year with fresh.

Pests and diseases

Carry out regular checks for visible pests, such as caterpillars and aphids, and diseases, such as mildew or rust, and treat them with an appropriate remedy as soon as they are spotted. Aphids, in particular, will increase in numbers rapidly.

In addition, try to divide your planted areas into three sections so that you can practise crop rotation as you would in a normal kitchen or vegetable garden. This will contribute to the health of your plants by avoiding the build up of soil-borne pests and diseases, such as potato eelworm and clubroot in brassicas.

Remember, too, to sweep up and hose down paved areas around your raised beds and where pots are standing to remove detritus that can harbour diseases or provide ideal conditions for slugs, snails and millipedes.

Formal herb garden

The range of herbs available to the gardener nowadays is considerable. Many of the woodier species benefit from being regularly pruned or trimmed, and so they lend themselves particularly well to formal gardens, where the neat, uniform shapes of trimmed plants fit in perfectly with the overall design concept. Here, herbs form the backbone of the formal planting, with a few standard and climbing roses to add flower colour, structure and height.

Why this works

✓ A strong symmetrical design includes angled paving to create generous planting areas.

✓ Planting and paved areas are separated by trimmed woody herbs.

✓ Standard roses and bay laurels add to the formal, symmetrical effect and add vertical emphasis to the lower general planting.

✓ Sculptures against the walls add a dramatic touch.

✓ The central 'diamond' of the garden is sharply defined by barley-twist edging which encloses a central standard bay laurel.

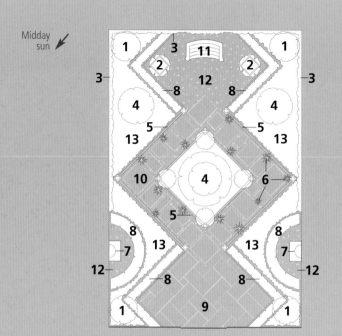

Garden elements key

1 Standard rose
2 Herbs in pots
3 Climber
4 Standard bay laurel
5 Barley-twist edging
6 Thymes in gravel
7 Wall sculpture or sta[?]
8 Herb hedge
9 York stone patio
10 York stone 'steppin[?] stones' in gravel
11 Bench seat

12 Gravel
13 Planting

Mix and match
If you like this garden but would prefer
a different feature, see pages 250–51 for
possible variations.

Garden dimensions
5.75m x 8.75m (19ft x 29ft) approx.

Key features

Herb hedge

Almost any woody herb – sage (*Salvia*), thyme (*Thymus*), rosemary (*Rosmarinus*), bay (*Laurus*) – can be used as a formal hedge, and in many cases the regular trimming helps to maintain the youth and vigour of the plants. If you want your hedge to flower don't trim it until after the flowers are finished. You can also make 'annual' hedges, using non-woody plants, such as parsley, basil or even coloured, ornamental lettuce.

Barley-twist edging

This traditional edging is becoming increasingly popular and is available in a range of colours and variations on the original theme. For a quick edge you can set them directly in the soil, but for a neater job lay them on a small foundation of mortar. Make use of the special finial pieces for the corners and ends of your main border edgings.

Wall sculpture

These sculptures make interesting and different focal points when they are mounted on a wall, as well as taking up less ground space than a traditional statue on a plinth. You can fix them in isolation on a blank wall or perhaps grow tall plants either side to act as a framework. Alternatively, encourage a climber to grow around the outside. Some combine a water spout, which adds to the attraction, and to maximize the effect use one or two side- or uplighters for night-time viewing.

Informal alternative design

With a little imagination you can use the same materials and plants to develop an informal layout. The introduction of curves and circles softens the layout, and by rotating the york stone patio, so that it is square to the building, you can create two alternative routes to the seating area at the end. Use the same plants but in an asymmetrical arrangement to lose the formality of a symmetrical layout.

Simple roof tiles are all that are needed here to formalize this herb garden.

Garden elements key

1 Stepping stones
2 Standard rose
3 Barley-twist edging
4 Thymes in gravel
5 Wall sculpture or statue
6 York stepping stones in gravel
7 Climber
8 Yorkstone patio
9 Herb edge
10 Standard bay laurel
11 Planting
12 Herbs in pots
13 Gravel
14 Bench seat

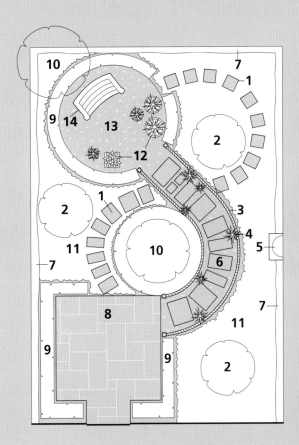

Planting key

1 *Rosa xanthina* 'Canary Bird' (standard)
2 *Pelargonium crispum*
3 *Foeniculum vulgare* 'Purpureum'
4 *Rosmarinus officinalis* 'Miss Jessopp's Upright'
5 *Salvia officinalis* 'Purpurascens' – hedge
6 *Laurus nobilis* (standard)
7 *Cichorium intybus* 'Roseum'
8 *Artemisia* 'Powis Castle' (hedge)
9 *Petroselinum crispum*
10 *Allium schoenoprasum* 'Forescate'
11 *Origanum vulgare* 'Aureum'
12 *Salvia officinalis* 'Tricolor'
13 *Chamaemelum nobile* 'Treneague'
14 *Monarda* 'Croftway Pink'
15 *Lavandula angustifolia* 'Hidcote'
16 *Rosa* 'Compassion' (climber)
17 *Clematis* 'Mrs P.B. Truax'
18 Mixed thymes (in gravel between flagstones)

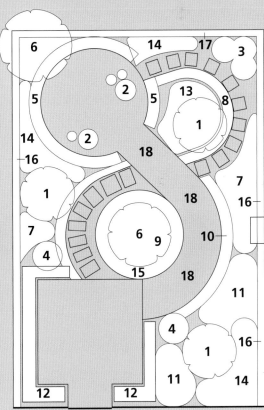

Planting

The best plants for this garden

The herbs for this design have been selected not only for their practical use in cooking and for herbal remedies but also for their appearance, both individually and in association with each other. Formality and symmetry are emphasized by the use of low herb hedges and the careful placing of standard roses and neatly trimmed bay laurel standard trees.

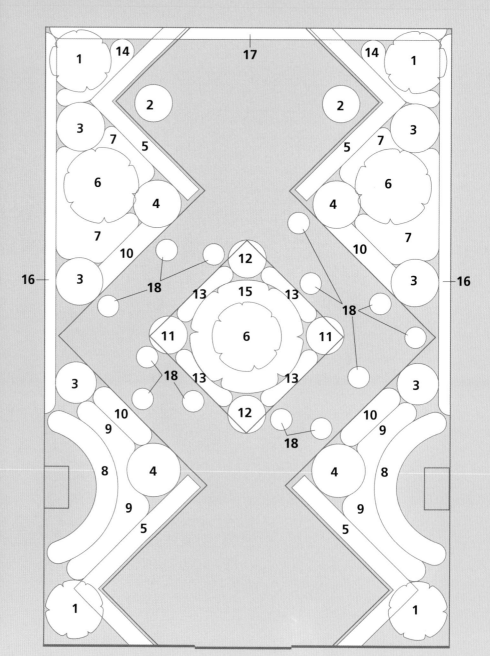

Prune your spring and early summer-flowering herbs straight after flowering in order to keep them fresh and young.

Pruning and storing herbs

Most woody herbs will benefit from being pruned at least once a year. This will encourage vigorous new growth, increase the plants' lifespan and health and generally keep them in good shape and looking attractive.

Most of these herbs bear flowers in spring, on growth made during the previous growing season. Unless the plant is old and neglected – in which case you will need to prune quite hard in winter – delay any trimming until flowering is finished. Premature pruning will result in a loss of blooms, unless, of course, you have no desire for the flowers. Woody herbs that flower from summer onwards should be pruned in the previous winter, preferably towards the end when the worst of the weather is over.

All herbs are best picked and used when fresh. If they are stored in a refrigerator in clean, dry, airtight containers many fresh herbs will remain in a good condition for several days.

Out of season, apart from evergreens, such as rosemary, thyme, sage and bay laurel, you will need to use herbs that have been dried or frozen. Alternatively, you can grow some more readily available herbs, such as chives and parsley, in small pots on your kitchen windowsill, although you may need to replace them from time to time.

You can dry herbs by placing them in shallow trays in a low oven or an airing cupboard. Depending on the type, it may take several days until the leaves are perfectly dry and brittle. If you have room, tie them in small bunches and hang them upside down in a dry, cool but well-ventilated space; this may take longer. Herbs dried in too much warmth may lose some of their flavour. Store dried herbs in a cool, dark place in small, airtight containers.

Some herbs – chives and dill, for example – do not dry well and should be frozen. Blanch them in boiling water for one minute and then refresh them by plunging them in ice-cold water before freezing them. When thawed, frozen herbs are best used as additives to sauces, stocks and dressings because they tend to lose their crispness in the freezing process and are not suitable as garnishes.

Winter interest garden

Planting up pots and urns with seasonal plants is a useful way of having something of interest all year round, and in the winter you can put in a selection of evergreens, plants with coloured stems or berries and even those that bear flowers at this time of year.

Why this works

✓ A well-thought out design provides an attractive year-round framework.
✓ The rather flat site has been split into two distinct levels with a simple curved step, accentuated by the third level of a raised bed.
✓ Distinctive wooden screens help to divide the garden into two parts, linking up with the raised bed and the step.
✓ An elegant and unusual summerhouse with a thatched roof and deck flooring offers an alternative sitting or entertaining area diagonally opposite the patio.
✓ Trees give height and structure to the garden, with the bonus of striking bark and stem colour in the depths of winter.
✓ Containers of early successionally flowering bulbs bring an extra splash of colour into the foreground for many weeks.

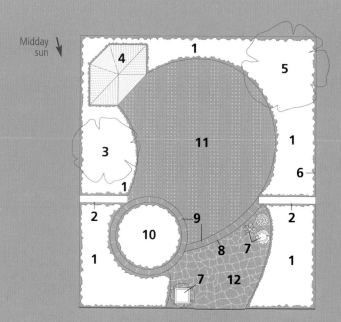

Garden elements key

1 Mixed border
2 Screen divider
3 Small tree for bark or stem effect

4 Thatched summerhouse or garden store
5 Multi-stemmed tree for bark effect

6 Boundary
7 Winter- and spring-flowering bulbs and bedding in containers
8 Step up
9 Stone edging
10 Winter heathers and dwarf conifers
11 Lawn
12 Crazy paving patio

Mix and match
If you like this garden but would prefer a different feature, see pages 250–51 for possible variations.

Garden dimensions
7m x 8m (23ft x 26ft) approx.

Key features

Winter heathers

The heathers *Erica carnea* and *E.* x *darleyensis* are among the most attractive and most reliable of winter-flowering plants and, depending on the cultivar you choose, you can have blooms for four or five months. Although they are ericaceous (acid-loving) plants, they will tolerate a small amount of lime in the soil, which extends their range of usefulness.

Multi-stemmed tree

Certain types of tree look particularly good when they are grown with three or more main trunks – forms with ornamental bark, such as birch (*Betula*) and the snake bark maples are especially attractive in winter. You can obtain them 'ready-made' or create them yourself by planting three young trees close together or by cutting back a single tree to just above ground level in winter one or two years after planting.

Screen divider

To make a garden more interesting try making a suggestion of division with some form of wooden screen, trellis or screen block walling. In a small garden this is more effective than completely dividing it into separate sections, when you might end up with two or three extremely small, claustrophobic spaces. Use 'open' screens or dividers, which let light through but are sufficiently solid to break up a direct view.

Screen or divider

You can buy a range of ready-made fence and trellis panels to use as a divider in your garden. Alternatively, you can design and make your own individual screen. This simple design can be easily modified to give you a range of heights and widths that will suit your personal needs. Stain it to match or complement other timber features in the garden and so develop a theme.

Individual posts can look like a fence or barrier, but let through light and air into the garden.

Side view

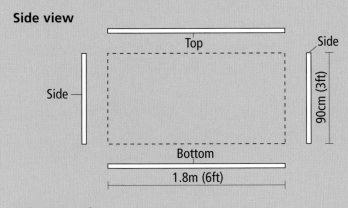

Side

Top

Side

90cm (3ft)

Side

Bottom

1.8m (6ft)

Side view of completed screen

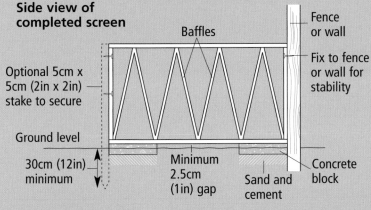

Baffles

Fence or wall

Fix to fence or wall for stability

Optional 5cm x 5cm (2in x 2in) stake to secure

Ground level

30cm (12in) minimum

Minimum 2.5cm (1in) gap

Sand and cement

Concrete block

Fixing detail

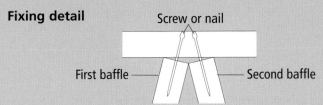

Screw or nail

First baffle

Second baffle

You will need

For a 180cm x 90cm (6in x 3ft) screen

2.5cm x 15cm (1in x 6in) pressure-treated sawn softwood boards

24 x 65mm (2½in) wood screws or nails

Coarse sandpaper

Stain

Concrete blocks

Sand and cement (optional)

Step by step

1 Cut two lengths of board, each 1.8m (6ft) long, to form the top and bottom and two lengths, each 90cm (3ft) long, to form each end.

2 Screw or nail the top and bottom of the frame to the ends to make a simple box shape, 180cm x 90cm (6ft x 3ft).

3 Cut eight lengths of board 90cm (3ft) long to form the angled baffles.

4 Lay the frame on its side on a smooth, level surface to make construction easier.

5 Take the first baffle, lay one end in the angle formed by the side and bottom of the frame and rotate the other end upwards until it butts up tight against the underside of the top.

6 Nail or screw downwards through the top of the frame into the end grain of the baffle to secure it in this position. Repeat at the lower end of the baffle, fixing upwards through the bottom of the frame. (Tip: to make screwing or nailing easier, drill narrow pilot holes through the top and bottom of the frame first.)

7 Take the second baffle and lay the top end into the wider angle formed by the first baffle and the top of the frame. Rotate the lower end downwards until it butts up right against the bottom of the frame. Secure as in step 6.

8 Repeat steps 6 and 7 for the remaining six baffles.

9 Stain the completed screen or divider in your chosen colour.

10 If the frame is to sit in a bed you will need to keep it a minimum of 2.5cm (1in) above the ground to prevent it becoming damp and rotting. To do this, lay a concrete block (or hard engineering brick) in the ground at each end of the screen divider, leaving 2.5cm (1in) proud. For a really solid job, lay the blocks on a mortar bed (one part cement to six parts sand).

11 To stabilize the screen, nail or screw one end to a fence or wall. If the screen is to be free standing or if there is no convenient fence or wall, fix it between two 5cm x 5cm (2in x 2in) treated stakes driven at least 30cm (12in) into the ground, one at each end. Stain the stakes to match the screen or divider.

Planting

18

19

The best plants for this garden

This garden has been designed to give maximum winter interest, using trees, shrubs, perennials and grasses, which make a striking combination of coloured and textured bark, stems, leaves and flowers for many months when most plants are dormant. The planting scheme includes rhododendrons and camellias, which require an acid soil; if you have alkaline soil you could substitute these with shrubs such as osmanthus and mahonia.

Planting key

1 *Yucca filamentosa* 'Bright Edge'
2 *Bergenia purpurescens* var. *delavayi*
3 *Iris foetidissima* 'Variegata'
4 *Pittosporum tobira* 'Nanum'
5 *Chimonanthus praecox*
6 *Clematis cirrhosa* 'Wisley Cream'
7 *Arum italicum* subsp. *italicum*
8 *Stipa tenuissima*
9 *Cornus alba* 'Sibirica'
10 *Cryptomeria japonica* 'Vilmoriniana'

21

42

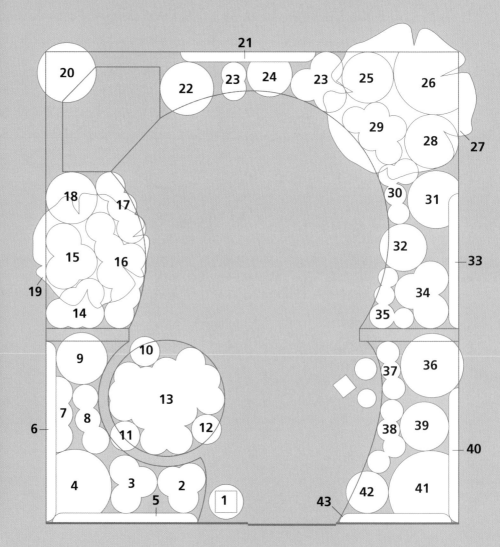

11 *Pinus mugo* 'Ophir'
12 *Juniperus squamata* 'Blue Star'
13 *Erica carnea* 'Myretoun Ruby'
14 *Acorus gramineus* 'Ogon'
15 *Polystichum polyblepharum*
16 *Persicaria affine* 'Donald Lowndes'
17 *Helleborus niger*
18 *Daphne odora*
19 *Acer palmatum* 'Sango-kaku'
20 *Fargesia nitida* 'Nymphenburg'
21 *Clematis* 'Apple Blossom'
22 *Euonymus japonicus* 'Aureus'
23 *Erica* x *darleyensis* 'Arthur Johnson'
24 *Berberis temolaica*
25 *Rhododendron* 'Praecox'
26 *Choisya* 'Aztec Pearl'
27 *Betula utilis* var. *jacquemontii* 'Jermyns'
28 *Euphorbia characias* subsp. *wulfenii*
29 *Geranium macrorrhizum* 'Czakor'
30 *Saxifraga* x *urbium* 'Variegata'
31 *Chaenomeles* x *superba* 'Rowallane'
32 *Erica arborea* 'Albert's Gold'
33 *Garrya elliptica* 'James Roof'
34 *Miscanthus sinensis* 'Morning Light'
35 *Epimedium* x *versicolor* 'Sulphureum'
36 *Hamamelis* x *intermedia* 'Jelena'
37 *Uncinia uncinata* f. *rubra*
38 *Iris unguicularis*
39 *Rubus thibetanus*
40 *Jasminum nudiflorum*
41 *Camellia* x *williamsii* 'Donation'
42 *Helleborus argutifolius*
43 *Abeliophyllum distichum*

A mature specimen of *Acer griseum* is perfect for the winter garden with its peeling bark.

Choosing the best plants for winter

In the quiet months of winter you are not likely to have the same bold, colourful displays of flowers that summer can bring. However, many plants actually look their best in winter becauce of their coloured bark or stems, dramatic or variegated foliage and even delicate, sometimes scented flowers. You may not wish to devote all of the planting areas in your garden to winter interest, but you could select, say, half a dozen plants that, if carefully placed in a prominent position where they can catch the low sun, will transform an otherwise dull outlook until the spring arrives.

Best trees and shrubs for stem or bark interest

- *Cornus alba* 'Sibirica Variegata'
- *Acer griseum*
- *Acer pensylvanicum* 'Erythrocladum'
- *Betula utilis* var. *jacquemontii*
- *Rubus cockburnianus* 'Goldenvale'
- *Cornus alba* 'Kesselringii'
- *Prunus serrula*
- *Berberis dictyophylla*
- *Rosa sericea* subsp. *omeiensis* f. *pteracantha*
- *Euonymus alatus* 'Compactus'

Minimalist impact

The adage 'less is more' can be applied as much to gardens as to other aspects of design. It allows you to appreciate line, shape and texture of both individual features and the garden as a whole. In this garden bold and bright colours are avoided and the planting is kept simple, purposely designed as secondary to the other elements of the scheme and being selected for form and texture to soften or contrast with the hard landscaping.

Why this works

✓ A strong geometric design is based on the overall shape of the garden.
✓ A simple and restrained choice of plants acts as a background to the architectural character of the garden.
✓ An interesting range of materials is used as ground finishes.
✓ Carefully selected and positioned features around the garden act as focal points.
✓ A spacious layout is contained within a modest plot.

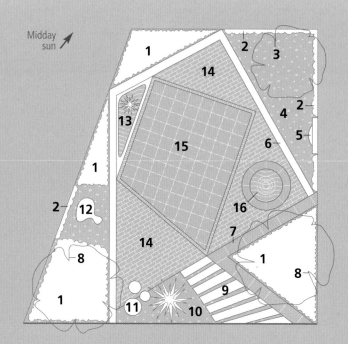

Garden elements key

1 Planting
2 Climber
3 Large shrub
4 Loose stone
5 Wall relief
6 Timber edging
7 Raised bed
8 Small tree
9 Timber insert
   stepping stones
10 Gravel
11 Ceramic globes

12 Sculpture
13 Pool
14 Sett paving
15 Flag paving
16 'Bell' fountain

Mix and match
If you like this garden but would prefer a different feature, see pages 250–51 for possible variations.

Garden dimensions
7m x 7m (23ft x 23ft) approx.

Key features

Timber insert paving

Use heavy, chunky timbers that have been treated against rot when you are setting them into the ground. These make a more solid paving and look better than thin flimsy pieces. If possible, locate your timber feature in a sunny, open position so that algae and mosses don't become a problem. Where this is not possible, clean the surface regularly with a stiff brush.

Flag and sett paving

Mixing large and small paving units, such as flags and setts, is an effective way to break up a large area. You can keep the two – or even more – types separate, as in this example, where the shape of the paved area reflects the shape of the garden, or you can mix them together. If possible, choose paving in modular sizes where the dimensions of the large units are an exact multiple of those of the smaller ones. This makes it easier to mix them together in a range of patterns with little or no fiddly cutting needed.

Sculpture

Sculpture and ornaments are what you might call the finishing touches in a garden design. Try and choose them to suit the mood or theme of your garden – here a very simple, but elegant, piece perfectly complements the minimalist design. Decide also whether they are to be prominently displayed or tucked away in subtle corners of soft planting.

Lighting

Putting lights into your garden will not only transform its appearance at night but will extend the time when you can be outside using it, especially in late spring, summer and early autumn. There are dozens of different types and specifications of light unit to choose from, each of which is suited to a particular purpose. Don't be tempted to install just one or two floodlights on the wall of your house: these add nothing to the quality or

Subtle, well-thought-out garden lighting can turn your garden into a night-time oasis.

appearance of your garden and will almost certainly be a nuisance to your neighbours and wildlife.

You will need to choose between a mains voltage lighting system or a low-voltage one. Mains voltage gives you more flexibility but with a slightly higher safety risk; low voltage is less flexible but safer, especially for self-installation. Solar-powered lighting is a useful supplement to either of the electrically powered systems, but it is not sufficiently powerful to replace them completely.

If you can, plan ahead for garden lighting, because you will save a lot of time, trouble and expense later on. There is no need to have an exact layout at the construction stage, but make sure you can get an electric supply beneath paths and paved areas at a later date by laying 2.5–5cm (1–2in) plastic conduit, such as low-density polythene cold water pipe, beneath them as they are built. Remember to include a drawstring to pull the cable through with.

Coloured lights should be used with care. It's all too easy to end up with a fairground effect if you overdo it. Stick to white, preferably daylight effect, light, which will pick up the natural colours of your plants and other features.

Some lighting systems allow you to add extra lights by way of a 'plug-in' system, and they are well worth considering if you're not quite sure how many lights you will need. Remember, though, that electricity is potentially dangerous if misused, so if you have any doubts seek expert help.

Lighting key

1 Mushroom downlighter
2 Downlighter built into wall of raised bed
3 Wide angle uplighter into crown of tree
4 Submersible uplighter beneath 'Bell' fountain in pool
5 Submersible diffused light in pool
6 Wide angle flood to light plain wall behind bamboo
7 Wall-mounted pencil spotlight down on to sculpture
8 Ground-mounted side light to wall relief

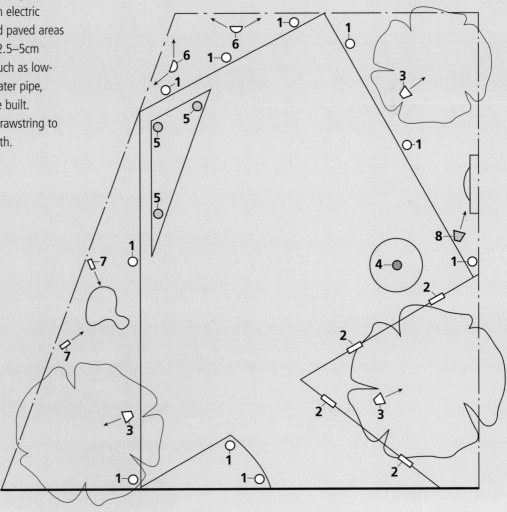

Planting

2

5

9

13

The best plants for this garden

Simplicity is the key to planting in this minimalist impact garden, with the emphasis being on the foliage and form of individual and drifts of plants. Flower interest is low key, being mostly incidental. Structure is provided by small, slow-growing trees, and a bamboo, *Hibanobambusa*, which is contained within a triangular bed to stop it spreading. Colour is generally muted with just a few carefully selected plants – *Phormium tenax* Purpureum Group and *Hedera helix* 'Buttercup' – providing relief against the green tones.

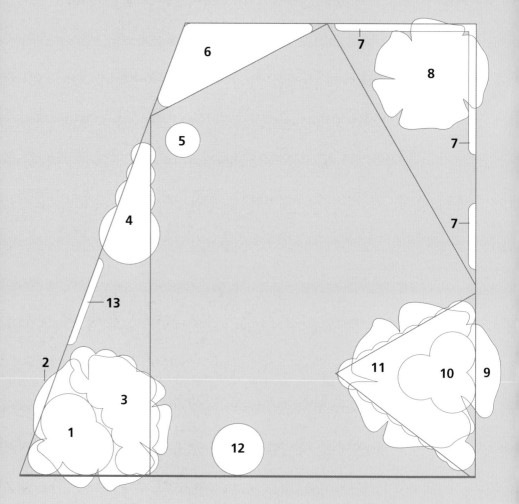

This mixed border demonstrates how colour, texture and shape can all contribute to visual impact.

Choosing plants for impact

In a small garden the number of plants you can fit in will naturally be limited by the size of space available. It's vital that you make the correct choice of plant for each position and that it makes the right impact in that position. Clearly, in a minimalist garden design your plant selection needs to be even more carefully thought out as you'll only be using a handful of cultivars. The 'impact' value of each one is therefore crucial, particularly as many of them will be seen in some isolation. The impact value of any plant is determined by one or more of several characteristics:

- The plant's overall shape or habit of growth – for example, weeping, fastigiate, prostrate.
- The colour, size or shape of leaf.
- The colour or texture of bark and stem.
- The size, shape and colour of flower and fruit.
- Whether the plant is best seen as an individual specimen or in a group of the same cultivar.

Plants for impact

- *Juniperus chinensis* 'Aurea' (fastigiate foliage conifer)
- *Catalpa erubescens* 'Purpurea' (tree, hard pruned for foliage)
- *Hosta* 'Big Daddy' (foliage perennial)
- *Mahonia* x *lomariifolia* (evergreen shrub for foliage)
- *Cornus alba* 'Sibirica' (shrub, hard prune for stem colour)
- *Darmera peltata* (foliage perennial)
- *Hydrangea aspera* Villosa Group (shrub for flower and foliage)
- *Cercis canadensis* 'Forest Pansy' (tree, hard prune for foliage)
- *Phormium* spp. (evergreen shrub)
- *Arundo donax* var. *versicolor* (foliage grass)
- *Pinus mugo* 'Ophir' (foliage conifer)
- *Rudbeckia fulgida* var. *sullivantii* 'Goldsturm' (flowering perennial)
- *Stipa gigantea* (flowering grass)

Drought-proof garden

Gardens that experience excessive dryness during the growing season, due either to the nature of the soil and ground conditions or because of climatic effects, can be challenging. However, by choosing your plants to suit the prevailing conditions and taking steps to improve the moisture retention of the soil you can still create a garden to be proud of.

Why this works

✓ Plants are carefully selected to be tolerant of hot, dry conditions.
✓ A pergola planted with climbers casts shade over part of the patio, creating a cool, refreshing sitting area during the heat of the day.
✓ A bark mulch over the planting areas conserves moisture.
✓ A stone obelisk and pool make a cool, refreshing feature on the edge of the patio.
✓ The rectangular patio is nicely balanced by a circle of crushed slate, edged with tiles and with a centrally placed sundial as a focal point.

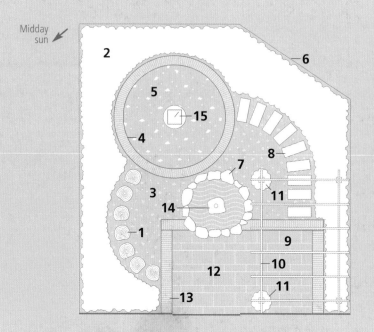

Midday sun

Garden elements key

1 Wood-effect stepping stones
2 Mixed border
3 Stone chippings
4 Tile edge to circle
5 Crushed slate
6 Boundary
7 Stone surround to water feature
8 Flags to match patio
9 Shade area beneath pergola

10 Pergola

11 Climber

12 Flagstone patio

13 Tile edge to patio

14 Obelisk water
feature

15 Sundial

Mix and match
If you like this garden but would prefer
a different feature, see pages 250–51 for
possible variations.

Garden dimensions
6.5m x 7m (21ft 6in x 23ft) approx.

Key features

Drought-tolerant plants

The selection of plants is one of the keys to a successful 'dry' garden. It is important, however, to understand that most of these plants will grow in conditions of limited moisture only once they are properly established. In the intervening period you may, therefore, need to do a limited amount of watering.

Obelisk water feature

An obelisk is essentially a tall, narrow piece of stone, and it can be drilled through the centre so that water can be pumped up, to cascade out of the top. These stones can be bought ready to install or you can go to a stone supplier, choose your own obelisk and ask a mason to drill it to your specifications. Large obelisks can be quite heavy, so check that your pool or water-retaining structure is strong enough to take its weight. They can look particularly stunning at night if lit from below.

Tile edging

Enclosing paving or beds with tiles laid on edge is a neat and effective way of defining areas in your garden and of separating different materials, such as bark from shingle or shingle from paving flagstones. You can make your own edgings from real tiles laid on edge in a bed of mortar, pointed with a dry sand-cement mix and then dampened with water from a watering can fitted with a fine rose.

Techniques for conserving moisture

At a time when there is increasing pressure on natural resources, reducing water usage in the garden makes a lot of sense, as well as saving money. There are various ways in which you can achieve this, and the methods can be applied to virtually any garden.

The first and most obvious step is to choose plants that are drought resistant. These plants require less water than non-drought-resistant plants such as hostas and astilbes.

Bark mulch is one of the simplest and effective ways of conserving moisture in any garden.

Incorporate lots of organic matter into the soil when you are preparing the planting areas. If possible, double dig and fork organic material into the upper layers of subsoil to encourage deeper rooting.

Mulch planting areas to prevent evaporation from the soil surface during hot, windy weather. Organic mulches look good and on cold, heavy soils will warm the soil quicker in early spring. Mulches of gravel, crushed slate or other inorganic materials are ideal for lighter, drier soils as they reflect heat and keep the soil cooler and therefore damper.

You will still need to water new plants and plants in containers, so save rainwater in butts attached to rainwater pipes. Don't forget to catch the water that runs off small outbuildings, such as sheds and glasshouses.

Waterproof the insides of containers, making sure there are drainage holes at the bottom, to minimize water loss through the sides.

When you put new plants in the ground, in addition to digging in extra organic matter into the planting hole, add some granules of water-retaining gel at the manufacturer's recommended rate. Add them also to containers and hanging baskets.

Identify windy areas in your garden and shelter them with fencing or trellis and screens or large drought-tolerant shrubs. Plants exposed to wind lose far more moisture through transpiration than they would in a sheltered spot.

Mulching spot plants

In a situation where you only want to spot-plant say a tree or large shrub — perhaps as a feature in the centre of a

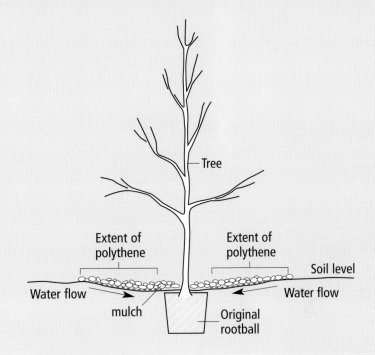

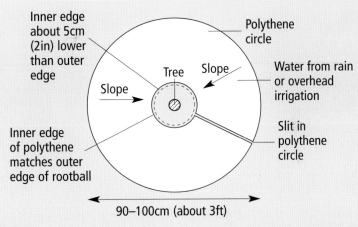

gravel circle — you can easily increase its potential water supply during its first critical growing season.

- Plant the tree or shrub in the chosen location. Create a shallow depression 90–100cm (about 3ft) across with the plant at the centre of the depression.
- Take a circle of heavy-duty black polythene or even inexpensive pond liner. Cut a circular hole in the centre to match the diameter of the plant's rootball, cut the circle from the outside to the inside and place it around the plant and in

the depression, with the plant in the centre.

- Cover the polythene and up to the trunk or stem with cobbles, gravel, crushed stone or bark.
- When it rains, the water falling in the polythened zone will drain back to the centre of the circle and penetrate the soil at the edge of the newly planted tree's rootball, exactly where the new root formation will occur.
- You can also use this method for treating selected new plants in a mixed or shrub border.

Planting

The best plants for this garden

Although this is predominantly a summer garden, the strength of the design coupled with a framework of garden features, evergreens and woody plants is still evident when most of the flowers are finished. There is plenty of contrast between different plant

forms and habits, such as the sharply spiky iris against the softer leaves of geraniums. The narrow, arching, strap-like leaves of agapanthus against the large, organized silver-grey of verbascums. Colours are generally restrained, with an emphasis on greens, silver, yellows and an occasional bright highlight of orange or cerise breaking through.

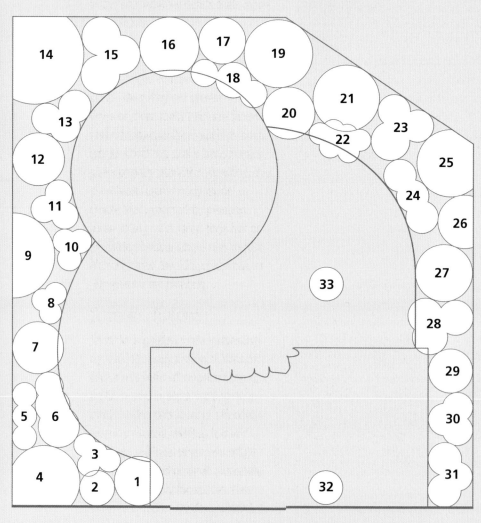

Planting key

1 *Genista lydia*
2 *Achillea millefolium* 'Cerise Queen'
3 *Festuca valesiaca* 'Silbersee'
4 *Griselinia littoralis* 'Variegata'
5 *Alcea rosea* double apricot-flowered
6 *Sedum telephium* 'Purple Emperor'
7 *Cistus* x *skanbergii*
8 *Santolina chamaecyparissus* var. nana
9 *Ribes speciosum*
10 *Salvia nemorosa* 'Ostfriesland'
11 *Oenothera fruticosa* 'Fyrverkeri'
12 *Caryopteris* x *clandonensis* 'Kew Blue'
13 *Agapanthus* white dwarf hybrids
14 *Elaeagnus pungens* 'Dicksonii'
15 *Verbascum chaixii* 'Album'
16 *Hibiscus syriacus* 'Woodbridge'
17 *Stipa gigantea*
18 *Eryngium variifolium*
19 *Choisya ternata*
20 *Cytisus* x *beanii*
21 *Ilex* x *altaclerensis* 'Belgica Aurea' (female)
22 *Sisyrinchium idahoense* var. macounii 'Album'
23 *Acanthus spinosus*
24 *Centaurea bella*
25 *Aucuba japonica* 'Rozannie'
26 *Verbena bonariensis*
27 *Fuchsia magellanica* var. *gracilis* 'Aurea'
28 *Euphorbia amygdaloides* 'Purpurea'
29 *Euonymus fortunei* 'Silver Queen'
30 *Iris foetidissima*
31 *Geranium phaeum* 'Album'
32 *Campsis* x *tagliabuana* 'Dancing Flame'
33 *Solanum laxum* 'Aureovariegatum'

Correct plant choice is always desirable, but especially so in a drought-proof garden.

Alternative planting for a shady garden

1 *Taxus baccata* 'Semperaurea'
2 *Geranium phaeum* var. *phaeum* 'Samobor'
3 *Polygonatum biflorum*
4 *Prunus lusitanica* 'Variegata'
5 *Anemone* x *hybrida* 'Königin Charlotte'
6 *Alchemilla mollis*
7 *Kerria japonica*
8 *Aegopodium podagraria* 'Variegatum'
9 *Ribes sanguineum* 'Brocklebankii'
10 *Geranium sanguineum* 'Max Frei'
11 *Arum italicum* 'Pictum'
12 *Prunus laurocerasus* 'Schipkaensis'
13 *Lamium maculatum* 'Roseum'
14 *Berberis darwinii*
15 *Digitalis lutea*
16 *Hypericum androsaemum*
17 *Taxus baccata* 'Standishii'
18 *Dryopteris affinis* Crispa Group
19 *Choisya* 'Aztec Pearl'
20 *Mahonia nervosa*
21 *Ilex* x *altaclerensis* 'Camelliifolia'
22 *Waldsteinia ternata*
23 *Acanthus mollis* Latifolius Group
24 *Millium effusum* 'Aureum'
25 *Chaenomeles speciosa* 'Geisha Girl'
26 *Ilex* x *altaclerensis* 'Purple Shaft' (female)
27 *Fuchsia magellanica* 'Versicolor'
28 *Liriope muscari*
29 *Euonymus fortunei* 'Emerald 'n' Gold'
30 *Tellima grandiflora* Rubra Group
31 *Convallaria majalis* 'Albostriata'
32 *Jasminum nudiflorum* 'Aureum'
33 *Hedera colchica* 'Sulphur Heart'

Gastro garden

The most efficient way of growing vegetables, salads and soft fruits is in uniform rows. However, this is not really practical in small gardens, where you have other equally important considerations. One way to overcome this dilemma is to use edible plants as part of the design, particularly fruit trees, fruit bushes and herbs, which can replace ornamental trees, shrubs, climbers and perennials.

Why this works

✓ A spacious and attractive layout combines roomy lawn and patio areas with generous borders.

✓ The arrangement of paths is practical, allowing access to beds.

✓ Height and structure are provided by the pergola and two fruit trees.

✓ The style of the borders matches that of any ornamental garden, and yet provides crops of salads, vegetables and herbs for much of the year.

✓ Containers and pots make a feature in their own right on the patio and provide an extra dimension when planted with soft fruit or herbs.

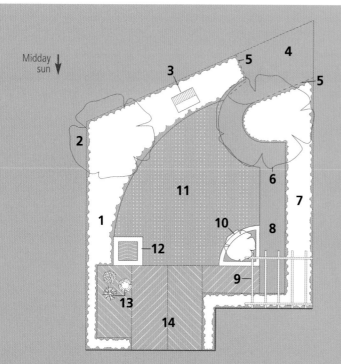

Garden elements key

1 Border

2 'Family' apple tree

3 Beehive

4 Chicken run

5 Trellis fence

6 'Family' pear tree

7 Border

8 Path

9 Pergola and vine

10 Raised bed

11 Lawn

12 Raised water feature

13 Ornamental pots
14 Patio

Mix and match
If you like this garden but would prefer a different feature, see pages 250–51 for possible variations.

Garden dimensions
6.5m x 9.5m (21ft 6in x 31ft) approx.

Key features

Ornamental pots

This is an easy way to grow a variety of edible crops in any garden. For ornamental cultivars of herbs, such as purple sage (*Salvia officinalis* 'Purpurescens'), you could use a plain container or one with a simple design. However, if your edible plants are not particularly exciting – a crop of early potatoes, for example – plant them in containers that are more colourful or unusual.

Family fruit trees

Family fruit trees are an ideal solution for a small 'edible' garden. They consist of three different cultivars of apple (or pear) growing on one tree. They are carefully selected and grafted in the nursery so that they cross-pollinate each other to produce good crops of fruit, avoiding the need for a second or third tree. The rootstock of the tree is specially selected so that the tree remains compact and slow-growing, making it ideal for the small garden.

Edible plants

Many edible plants, including potatoes, tomatoes and carrots are annuals so you need to include other forms of edible plants to give you some interest and shape during the winter months. Fruit trees, such as apples and pears, will give height; you can also train blackberries and loganberries on walls or fences as climbers; and woody herbs are evergreen and therefore especially useful in this type of garden.

Raised beds

Raised beds are an excellent feature for any garden, and they can be used for growing both ornamental and edible plants. Make them a positive feature of your design at the planning stage. They are particularly effective around patios or other paved areas or as a way of introducing a change of level in a flat garden.

When you want to plant an area where ground conditions are particularly difficult – perhaps on a heavy, sticky clay soil or even a pad of concrete or tarmac that can't be removed –

Raised beds don't need to dominate your garden – low-key ones like this are not intrusive.

a raised bed is a perfect and simple way of providing your plants with what they require for strong, healthy growth. You will need to provide a means of drainage at the bottom of the walls to allow excess water to escape sideways. Make weepholes by leaving several vertical joints unpointed in the lowest course of a brick or block wall, or by drilling large holes, about 2.5cm (1in) across, in a timber wall.

Around the edges of patios, raised beds can also be used as additional seating. You will need to build the walls thick enough to perch on – at least 20–25cm (8–10in) – and a convenient, comfortable height, about 40–45cm (16–18in).

If you are going to build your raised bed on a soft, topsoiled area you will need to dig out and provide a foundation for the walls. Once the walls are built, fork the trampled soil enclosed by the walls and dig in some garden compost and sharp grit to improve drainage if the original topsoil is on the heavy side. Once this is done, backfill the bed with good compost in layers of about 15cm (6in) at a time, gently firming each layer (especially in the corners and at the edges) before adding the next one. Once it's full, thoroughly water it to allow the soil to settle and top up with extra compost to bring it up to level before planting.

If the walls are particularly porous, line the insides (but not the base) with heavy-duty black polythene or even PVC pond liner, or paint them with waterproof bituminous paint before backfilling to reduce sideways moisture loss at the edges of the raised bed.

On soft ground

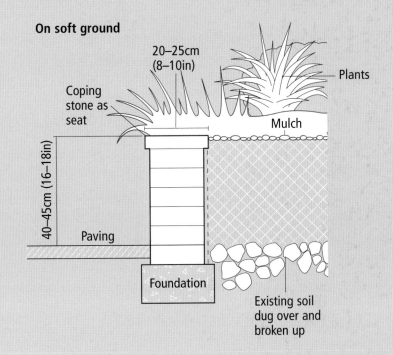

20–25cm (8–10in)

Coping stone as seat

Plants

Mulch

40–45cm (16–18in)

Paving

Foundation

Existing soil dug over and broken up

On existing hardstanding

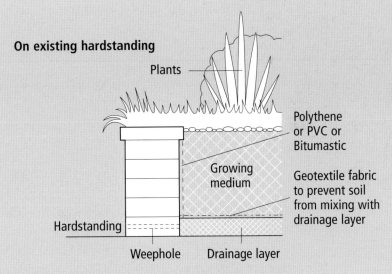

Plants

Polythene or PVC or Bitumastic

Growing medium

Geotextile fabric to prevent soil from mixing with drainage layer

Hardstanding

Weephole

Drainage layer

Drainage details for wood and brick walls

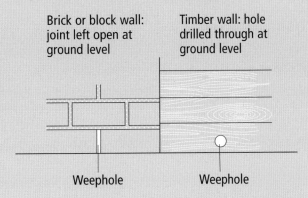

Brick or block wall: joint left open at ground level

Timber wall: hole drilled through at ground level

Weephole

Weephole

Planting

The best plants for this garden

Although the emphasis in this garden is on edible planting, there is still plenty of interest provided by woody plants, such as the fruit trees, herbs, fruit bushes and climbers, to keep the garden looking good for much of the year. Planting in the raised bed adds an extra dimension of change of level, and the containers on the patio introduce extra shape and colour. The family fruit trees on dwarfing rootstocks, cordon currants and fan-trained cherry 'Gisela' are ideally suited for growing in restricted conditions and are still able to produce good crops of delicious fruit.

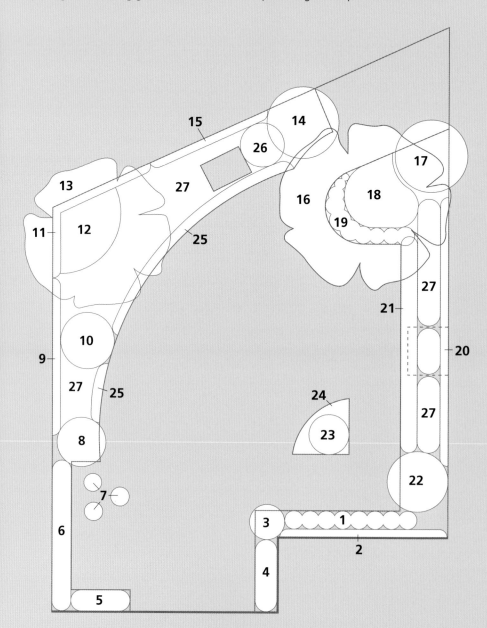

A well-grown, manicured lawn is the ideal way to set off any planting scheme.

Planting key

1 Ornamental lettuce etc.
2 Cordon red or white currants
3 *Salvia officinalis* 'Purpurescens'
4 Vine tomatoes
5 *Passiflora caerulea*
6 Fan-trained cherry 'Gisela'
7 Blueberries 'Bluetta' (2) plus 'Collins' (1)
8 *Salvia officinalis* 'Tricolor'
9 Thornless blackberry 'Merton Thornless'
10 *Rosmarinus officinalis* 'Miss Jessopp's Upright'
11 *Lonicera periclymenum* 'Belgica'
12 *Nandina domestica* 'Fire Power'
13 Family apple tree
14 *Laurus nobilis* (bay tree)
15 Climbing (runner) beans on fence
16 Family pear tree
17 Blackcurrant 'Ben Sarek'
18 *Melissa officinalis* 'All Gold'
19 Parsley edging
20 *Actinidia deliciosa* 'Jenny' plus mint in restricted root run
21 Step-over espalier apple
22 Rhubarb 'Timperley Early'
23 Standard gooseberry 'Invicta'
24 Strawberry 'Cambridge Favourite'
25 Low hedge of Thyme (*Thymus vulgaris*) and chives (*Allium schoenoprasum*), alternating
26 *Origanum vulgare* 'Thumbles Variety'
27 Areas set aside for rotating crops of dwarf beans, salad onions, early carrots, summer cabbage etc.

Lawns

A well-kept lawn is an asset to any garden, and by following some basic rules you can create your own green carpet.

Regular cutting during the growing season is an essential part of maintenance. The general rule is to set your mower blades low when the grass is growing vigorously and to raise them in hot, dry spells and early or late in the season when growth is slower.

Apply proprietary lawn feeds – use a combined one that kills weeds as well – in spring and autumn. During the growing season you should also feed once a month with a liquid feed that can be applied by spray or watering can.

A well-prepared and well-maintained lawn should suffer little from pests and diseases. In spring and autumn scarify the lawn with a rake or scarifier to remove moss and thatch, and spike it with a heavy garden fork or a purpose-made 'corer' to improve drainage and rooting. If you need or want to irrigate your lawn in dry periods, avoid doing it little and often, which encourages shallow rooting. Apply water more generously and less frequently – not more than once or twice a week in extremely dry weather – to encourage deeper rooting and therefore stronger grass.

Colour effect garden

Using a wide palette of colours, particularly strong ones, such as reds and oranges, can be overpowering in a small garden. By restricting your choice of colours to two or three at most, you can deliberately engineer a particular mood or atmosphere. In this garden, the dominant colours of white and blue bring a rather cool, elegant feeling into the space, and the use of dark timbers helps to emphasize this effect.

Why this works

✓ A bold, strong design incorporates alternative sitting areas to choose between sun and shade.

✓ The limited colour range of blue and white planting combines well with the greys and pale tones of the various garden features.

✓ A split-level pool provides a dramatic focal point both from the patio and from beneath the pergola.

✓ Planting is low maintenance, using reliable cultivars that will tolerate a range of conditions.

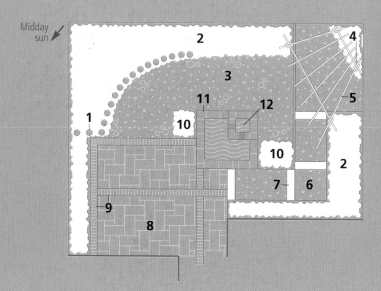

Garden elements key

1 Log palisade edging feature
2 Mixed border
3 Shingle and loose cobbles

4 Climber on pergola
5 Pergola and shady sitting area beneath
6 Gravel paving

7 Timber inserts in
    paving

8 York stone paving on
    patio

9 Brick inserts

10 Spot planting

11 York stone edging

12 Split-level pool with
    cascades

Mix and match

If you like this garden but would prefer
a different feature, see pages 250–51 for
possible variations.

Garden dimensions

7.5m x 6m (25ft x 20ft) approx.

Log palisade edging

In this design machine-rounded and pressure-treated logs of varying lengths are simply set into the planting to provide contrast and as a low key, informal edging. You could use three much taller logs set on end in a close group among the low planting as a feature in its own right. Alternatively, use just one on its own as a simple, basic obelisk on which you could grow a climber.

Colour

Blue is generally considered to be a cool, quiet colour, but if it is used to the exclusion of all other colours it can be monotonous. You can provide more interest, while keeping the same effect, by mixing it with white, grey and silver, or add some pale lemon yellow. For a warmer, more vibrant feel, choose plants with 'hot' coloured flowers – reds, oranges, rich yellows. These are strong colours, so you don't need to use them to the complete exclusion of others.

Cascade

Cascades are a neat and effective way of transferring water from a high level to a low level, especially in a small water feature. Remember that the 'lip' of your cascade must be made from thin material, such as stainless steel, aluminium sheet or roofing slate, or, if it's made from a thickish piece of flat stone, you must grind the front edge to give a 'chisel' point.

Variation for a rectangular garden

You can easily adapt this design to suit a long, narrow garden yet still retain all the main features with just a few minor variations.

- The patio and paths are rotated so that they're now at an angle to the boundaries and house. This technique is effective for any long, narrow garden space.

This 'fence' of variable height log palisades makes an attractive backdrop that doesn't need covering in climbers.

- Instead of being a low-key feature, the palisade edging is much taller – from 90cm to 1.8m (3–6ft) – and is split into two sections where it makes a more obvious division to the garden.
- The space between the path and the pergola sitting area is planted with taller plants, and a bamboo or large shrub is located immediately behind the pool. This planting gives more privacy to the pergola area, and again gives a suggestion of division without completely blocking off the view to the far end of the garden.

Garden elements key

1 Shingle and loose cobbles
2 Climber on pergola
3 Mixed border
4 Spot planting: tall shrub or bamboo
5 Split-level pool with cascades
6 York stone edging
7 Log palisade edging feature
8 York stone paving on patio
9 Brick inserts
10 Timber inserts in paving
11 Gravel paving
12 Tall planting
13 Pergola with shady sitting area beneath

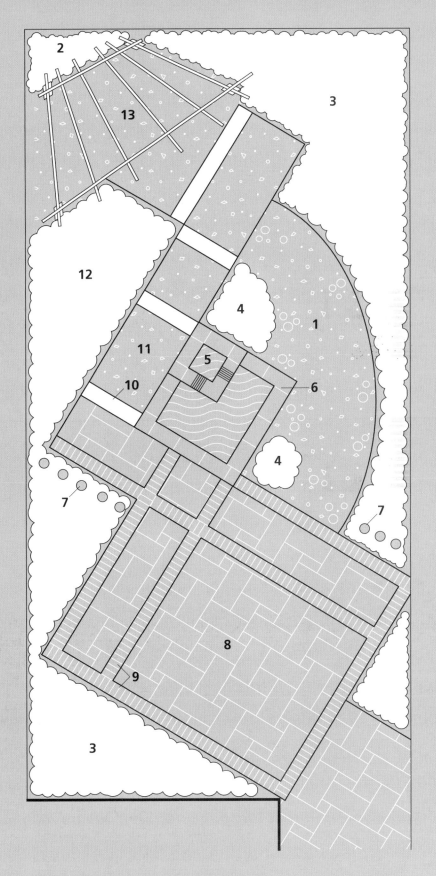

Planting

The best plants for this garden

Blue, white, silver and grey are the predominant plant colours, set off by varying tones of green foliage and the underlying subdued greys and creams of the fixed garden features.

Planting key

1 *Clematis* 'Frances Rivis'
2 *Stachys byzantina*
3 *Agapanthus* 'Bressingham Blue'
4 *Geranium sanguineum* 'Album'
5 *Lavandula angustifolia* 'Beechwood Blue'
6 *Aconitum carmichaelii* Arendsii Group 'Arendsii'
7 *Aralia elata* 'Argenteovariegata'

8 *Juncus patens* 'Carman's Grey'
9 *Convolvulus cneorum*
10 *Hydrangea macrophylla* 'Mariesii Perfecta'
11 *Scabiosa caucasica* 'Clive Greaves'
12 *Miscanthus sinensis* 'Silberfeder'
13 *Solanum laxum* 'Album'
14 *Phlox paniculata* 'White Admiral'
15 *Tradescantia* Andersoniana Group 'Isis'
16 *Enkianthus campanulatus*
17 *Veronica gentianoides*
18 *Sarcococca hookeriana* var. *digyna*
19 *Vitis vinifera* 'Incana'
20 *Clematis* 'John Huxtable'
21 *Geranium ibericum*
22 *Exochorda* x *macrantha* 'The Bride'
23 *Aruncus dioicus* 'Kneiffii'
24 *Hibiscus syriacus* 'Oiseau Bleu'
25 *Iris sibirica* 'White Swirl'

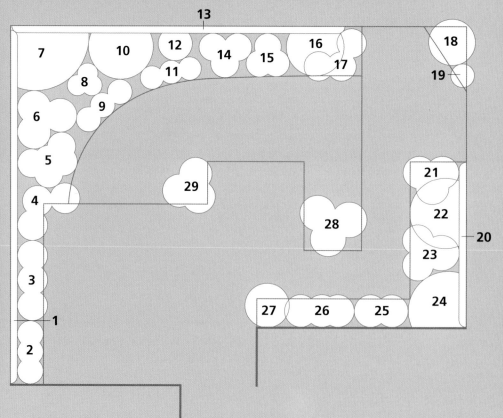

26 *Ceratostigma plumbaginoides*

27 x *Halimiocistus sahucii*

28 *Artemisia* 'Powis Castle'

29 *Iris* 'Blue Rhythm' (tall bearded)

Alternative hot, vibrant planting

1 *Clematis* 'Bill MacKenzie'

2 *Dierama* 'Fairy Bells'

3 *Kniphofia* 'Jenny Bloom'

4 *Geranium psilostemon*

5 *Lavandula angustifolia* 'Nana Alba'

6 *Phlox paniculata* 'Prince of Orange'

7 *Luma apiculata* 'Glanleam Gold'

8 *Imperata cylindrica* 'Rubra'

9 *Geum* 'Borisii'

10 *Hydrangea macrophylla* 'Forever Pink'

11 *Scabiosa caucasica* 'Miss Willmott'

12 *Miscanthus sinensis* 'Ferner Osten'

13 *Clematis* 'Madame Julia Correvon'

14 *Oenothera* 'Summer Sun'

15 *Tradescantia* Andersoniana Group 'Charlotte'

16 *Rhododendron* 'Fireball'

17 *Astrantia major* 'Claret'

18 *Aucuba japonica* 'Picturata'

19 *Lonicera implexa*

20 *Clematis* 'Gravetye Beauty'

21 *Geranium* x *oxonianum* 'Wargrave Pink'

22 *Camellia japonica* subsp. *rusticana* 'Beni-arajishi'

23 *Leucanthemum* x *superbum* 'T.E. Killin'

24 *Hibiscus syriacus* 'Red Heart'

25 *Iris sibirica* 'Dreaming Yellow'

26 *Zantedeschia* 'Kiwi Blush'

27 *Ozothamnus rosmarinifolius*

28 *Euphorbia griffithii* 'Fireglow'

29 *Hemerocallis* 'Stafford'

Yellow is a good choice for a colour theme, especially if you introduce some white or silver to balance.

Different colour schemes

Using colour in the garden is no different from using colour in the house: your aim is to try to bring together a combination that is pleasing on the eye and comfortable to live with. In the garden the usual plan is to harmonize the colours so that a restful or eye-catching image is created, allowing the eye to drift easily from one group of colours to the next, perhaps resting occasionally on an accent plant of a different or contrasting colour. Not all schemes are mixed, however, and many extremely successful schemes have been developed by using a single colour.

If you want to have a go at a single colour theme, choose your plants with care, as sometimes such planting can be a bit overpowering. Go for the less intensive forms of your colour – pale or light blues, lemon and pale yellows – and avoid flowers of your chosen colour that are not pure. For example, blues erring on the purple side or strong yellows with a hint of orange. Also add a little white, grey or silver to add interest.

In practice, of course, there is no such thing as a single-colour bed. The flowers you have chosen may be all of one colour, but the foliage may be every possible shade of green. This is no bad thing, because an unrelenting stretch of red or blue or orange would be too much to take in and live with. The foliage provides a background against which the colour stands out, and it also creates a buffer between areas of slightly different colours that would not work if they were next to each other.

Borders and beds based on two colours are an extension of the single-colour scheme. Two sympathetic colours can be chosen to harmonize, or two contrasting colours can be used to create some excitement. Popular schemes include white and yellow and blue and yellow. Sometimes one colour is allowed to predominate, while the other is used sparingly for emphasis. Sometimes the two colours are used in equal proportions.

Multicoloured borders can still be selective. Soft pastel colours create a gentle, romantic atmosphere that is restful to look at. A border of vibrant reds, oranges and yellows, on the other hand, will have the opposite effect.

Scented sanctuary

A great advantage of a small garden over a large one is that, as long as it is reasonably enclosed by walls or fences, the fragrance of flowers and aromatic foliage is more likely to hang around for your pleasure. This compact garden is designed around scented plants that will provide delicious smells virtually all year round.

Why this works

✓ A striking design combines circular and octagonal shapes in a small space.

✓ There are lots of opportunities to grow scented climbers on boundaries, trellis and arches.

✓ A neat, enclosed patio is surrounded by fragrant plants set in the sunniest corner of the garden.

✓ Plants with fragrance at different times of the year are adjacent to the house, allowing them to be appreciated indoors as well as out.

✓ A central fountain adds the sensation of gently running water to the pervading scents around the garden.

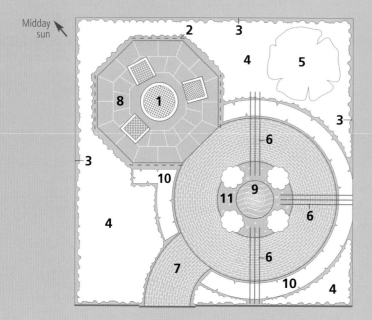

Midday sun

Garden elements key

1 Garden furniture
2 Trellis screen
3 Climber on wall
4 Planting
5 Dwarf tree
6 Arch and climber
7 Brick paving
8 Octagonal patio
9 Fountain
10 Dwarf hedge
11 Gravel

Mix and match
If you like this garden but would prefer a different feature, see pages 250–51 for possible variations.

Garden dimensions
6m x 6m (20ft x 20ft) approx.

Key features

Patio

Reproduction stone can be extremely convincing and is more cost effective than real stone, and prefabrication and moulding techniques mean you can now buy complete patios in kit form in many shapes, especially octagonal or circular, which require only a modest amount of do-it-yourself skills to lay. Alternatively, you could make an informal patio in an amorphous shape by laying a course of bricks, setts or tiles around the wandering curved edge and infill with crazy paving or even just gravel.

Dwarf hedge

Dwarf hedges are an excellent way to define different areas in a small garden and to accentuate boundaries, for example between planting and paving. Evergreens, such as dwarf hebes, *Euonymus fortunei* cvs. and dwarf box (*Buxus sempervirens* 'Suffruticosa'), are especially useful. If you prefer flowering shrubs lavenders (*Lavandula* spp.) and dwarf fuchsias, such as 'Tom Thumb', are equally effective in a small garden.

Arch

Arches take up little room, so you should include them in your garden when you want to create height and structure in a small space. Apart from their obvious function as supports for climbers, use them to frame a focal point or view within your garden or as a link or separation between two different areas, such as your lawn and patio.

Roof garden variation

Scented and aromatic plants can make a valuable contribution to a roof or balcony garden, especially as you will be in close contact with them in such a limited space. Select them as you would any other plants, bearing in mind the possible climatic extremes they may have to contend with, particularly strong wind, and make sure they are suitable for growing in positions where the root zone might be restricted because they are in containers or small raised beds. Try to position your key scented plants in the most sheltered corners of your balcony or roof garden where the fragrance can linger and not be carried away on the breeze.

Many aromatic plants are ideally suited to the more open, fresher environment of a roof garden.

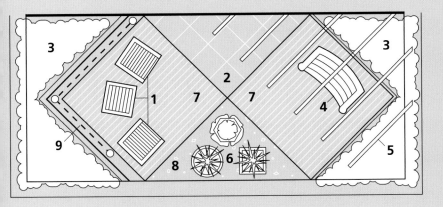

Garden elements key

1 Patio furniture
2 Tiled paving
3 Mixed planting in raised bed
4 Bench seat
5 Overheads and climber
6 Plants in containers
7 Deck boards
8 Gravel mulch
9 Ornamental trellis screen and climber

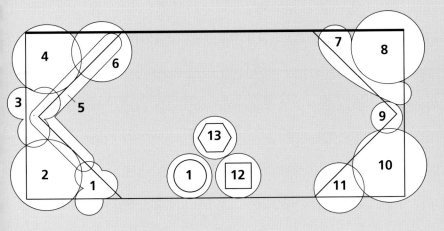

Planting key

1 *Iris graminea*
2 *Yucca filamentosa*
3 *Viola odorata*
4 *Philadelphus* 'Manteau d'Hermine'
5 *Clematis recta* (on trellis)
6 *Skimmia japonica* 'Fragrans'
7 *Geranium macrorrhizum* 'Ingwersen's Variety'
8 *Hebe* 'Midsummer Beauty'
9 *Rosa* 'Albertine' (rambler; on overheads)
10 *Mahonia aquifolium* 'Apollo'
11 *Lavandula angustifolia* 'Munstead'
12 *Genista lydia*
13 *Dianthus* 'Doris'

Planting

The best plants for this garden

The shrubs, climbers and perennials in this small, enclosed garden have been selected because they all possess fragrant or aromatic flowers or foliage or both. Climbers on the boundary walls, the small trellis screens around the patio and on the arches over the circular brick path provide high-level scent as you sit in or move around the garden, with other shrubs and perennials making their contribution at a lower level. The inclusion of one or two early- and late-flowering species makes sure that there is scent in the garden at virtually all times of the year.

10

11

14

15

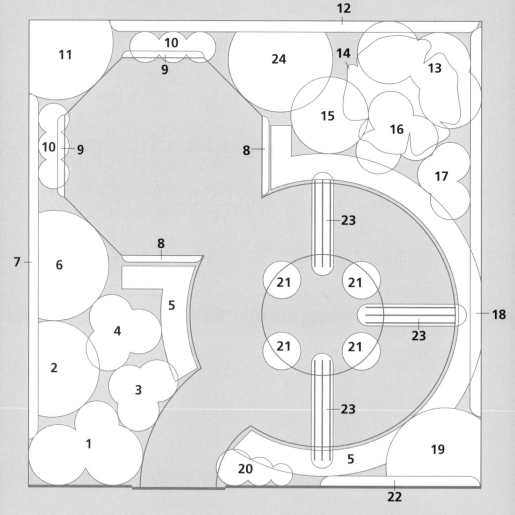

Planting key

1 *Clematis recta* 'Purpurea'
2 *Jasminum humile* 'Revolutum'
3 *Iris pallida* 'Argentea Variegata'
4 *Phlox paniculata* 'David'
5 *Lavandula angustifolia* 'Miss Muffet'
6 *Osmanthus* x *burkwoodii*
7 *Jasminum officinale* 'Fiona Sunrise'
8 *Clematis* 'Betty Corning'
9 *Trachelospermum asiaticum*
10 *Convallaria majalis*
11 *Azara serrata*
12 *Clematis terniflora*
13 *Mahonia aquifolium* 'Apollo'
14 *Cytisus battandieri* (standard)
15 *Paeonia lactiflora* 'Sarah Bernhardt'
16 *Geranium macrorrhizum* 'Pindus'
17 *Hosta* 'Honeybells'
18 *Lonicera periclymenum* 'Harlequin'
19 *Viburnum* 'Eskimo'
20 *Filipendula ulmaria* 'Flore Pleno'
21 *Origanum vulgare* 'Aureum'
22 *Akebia quinata*
23 *Rosa* 'New Dawn' (climber)
24 *Viburnum* x *bodnantense* 'Deben'

When choosing plants for scent, try and select several that flower at different times to extend the period of interest and appeal.

Plants for scent

Scented climbing plants, such as honeysuckle (*Lonicera* spp.) and jasmine (*Jasminum* spp.), are well known and are an essential part of many gardens. Similarly, there are also lots of shrubs that are equally well known for their aromatic qualities – mock orange (*Philadelphus*), lilac (*Syringa* spp.), lavender (*Lavandula* spp.) and, of course, roses (*Rosa* spp.). There are also perennials and bulbs that have perfumed flowers and aromatic foliage.

Best scented shrub roses for the small garden

- 'Gruss an Aachen' (pink-cream)
- 'Alexander Hill Gray' (lemon-yellow)
- 'Angele Pernet' (orange-yellow)
- 'Papa Meilland' (red)
- 'Cosimo Ridolfi' (lilac)
- 'La Reine' (deep pink)
- 'Madame Abel Chatenay' (soft pink)
- 'Michèle Meilland' (pink-salmon)
- 'Glamis Castle' (white)
- 'Camayeux' (pale pink-crimson)

Best scented and aromatic perennials and bulbs

- *Tulipa* 'Prinses Irene'
- *Albuca shawii*
- *Iris histrioides* 'George'
- *Lilium candidum*
- *Artemisia* 'Powis Castle'
- *Dianthus* 'Mrs Sinkins'
- *Clematis heracleifolia* 'Cassandra'
- *Hemerocallis* 'Hyperion'
- *Nepeta* x *faassenii*
- *Lilium regale*
- *Narcissus* 'Cheerfulness'

Water garden

There are few gardens that won't benefit from having a water feature included in the design, usually as one of several focal points. In this example, however, water is the main feature and focal point of the small garden, and it is linked to the paved and decking areas as a major, central attraction.

Why this works

✓ The angled layout of the bodies of water and sitting areas helps to disguise the squareness of the plot and creates relatively generous spaces in the corners for planting.

✓ Three different water levels allow the water to flow around the garden, providing movement, sound and reflections.

✓ Over the lowest pool is a decking bridge, which links the two main sitting areas.

✓ The edges of the central raised pool double up as extra seating when space is at a premium for barbecues and entertaining.

✓ Planting is lush and dense, surrounding the water and paving arrangement and highlighting it as a central feature.

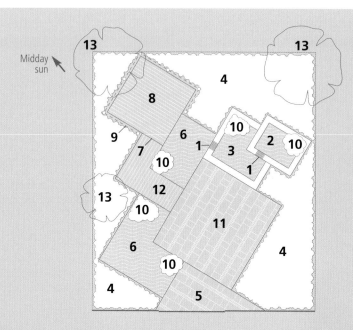

Garden elements key

1 Cascade	**7** Step up
2 Upper pool	**8** Raised deck
3 Middle pool	**9** Balustrade around
4 Mixed planting	deck
5 Paving	**10** Marginals
6 Lower pool	**11** Patio

12 Deck 'bridge'
13 Small tree

Mix and match
If you like this garden but would prefer
a different feature, see pages 250–51 for
possible variations.

Garden dimensions
6m x 7.5m (20ft x 25ft) approx.

Key features

Deck bridge

A bridge over a body of water always brings extra interest to a garden design. Simple structures, such as this decking arrangement, or perhaps just three or four simple, heavy oak planks side by side, are invariably more satisfactory than any over-ornamented, exaggerated designs. A single handrail is usually enough to satisfy both the needs of safety and the desire to lean on it to peer into the depths of the pool below.

Marginal planting

Planting in the shallows or margins of a pool or stream gives a more natural feel to the water feature and introduces interesting reflections as well as providing a habitat for small pond life. Put your plants in aquatic planters set on shelves 15–20cm (6–8in) below the water level. These will be easier to manage than planting directly in the pond itself.

Raised pools

Split-level pools with water flowing down cascades or waterfalls from higher to lower levels bring lots of life to a garden. They're especially useful where you want to give some flow to a water feature but don't have room for a longer stream. Build them from brick, stone, blocks or even heavy timbers, perhaps combining the feature with raised beds to the side or back of the pool, allowing leafy perennials, like hostas and astilbes, to hang over the water's edge.

Creating a water garden

Putting to one side the aesthetic considerations of your water feature, there are a number of more practical details that you must consider early on in the design and construction processes if your water garden is to be successful.

For a natural-looking water feature, cover the shallows with stones and gravel so that the pond liner is hidden from view.

Location

Position your water feature where it can be properly appreciated, preferably in an open situation or at least away from overhanging trees.

Excavation

Remember that the bigger the pond, the more soil you will have to dispose of. Plan in advance what you're going to do with this surplus material, because although you may be able to spread the topsoil over the beds and borders, subsoil and stones will probably have to be taken away in a skip.

Pond liners

Line the excavated hole with proprietary matting or soft sand to protect your liner from being punctured. Lay it on a warm day when the liner will be more pliable, and at least one extra pair of hands will make it easier to manoeuvre. Keep pond shapes simple, with smooth flowing curves.

Power

Arrange the provision of electricity to your water feature at an early stage, before you build surrounding paths and patios. Always use a competent electrician to check the arrangements and make the final connection. You will need the power for the submersible pump, optional filtration system and, if used, underwater lighting. Always test the pumps, fountains and cascades before finally burying the pipework to save time and trouble if there are teething problems.

Pumps

Choose a pump with more capacity or power than you think you might need. The manufacturer's recommendations are for ideal conditions, and increasing the length of your pond hose or making waterfalls higher will reduce the potential flow. Remember, too, that the pump must be readily accessible for regular cleaning and maintenance.

Safety

Even tiny pools are a potential hazard for small children. Plan your feature to be 'safe' – a millstone fountain, for example – or make sure that it can be fenced off, if only for a temporary time.

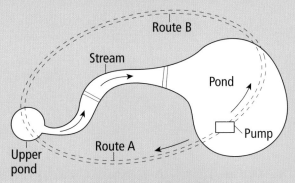

Keep pond hose runs short

Route B is longer than route A, resulting in reduced flow

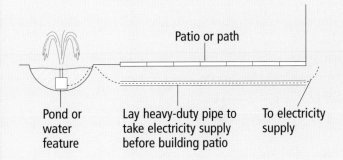

Planning for electric supply

Pond or water feature

Lay heavy-duty pipe to take electricity supply before building patio

To electricity supply

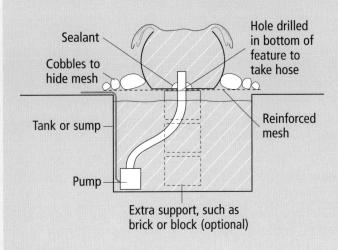

A self-contained (safe) water feature

Sealant

Cobbles to hide mesh

Hole drilled in bottom of feature to take hose

Tank or sump

Reinforced mesh

Pump

Extra support, such as brick or block (optional)

Planting

1

13

18

19

The best plants for this garden

Planting in this water garden is fairly lush and dense to hide the boundaries and to provide a bold backdrop to the central feature. There is a strong framework of shrubs, complemented by perennials that add colour and texture in contrast to the squareness of the deck, paving and pools.

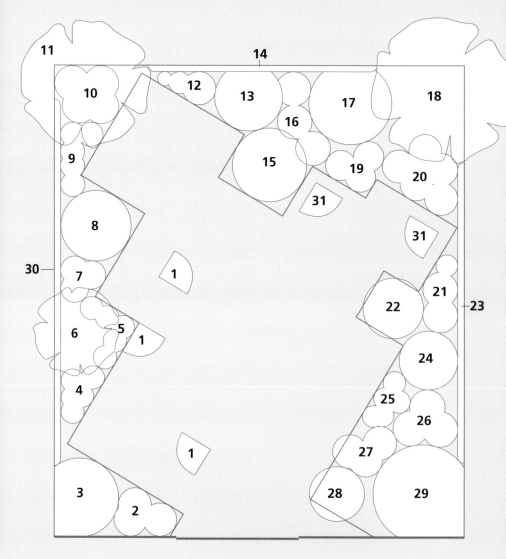

Planting key

1 *Iris ensata*
2 *Hosta* 'Francee'
3 *Rhododendron* 'Brigitte'
4 *Astilbe* 'Fanal'
5 *Carex flagellifera*
6 *Acer palmatum* 'Katsura'
7 *Iris graminea*
8 *Ceanothus* 'Blue Mound'
9 *Trollius* x *cultorum* 'Earliest of All'
10 *Persicaria microcephala* 'Red Dragon'
11 *Cercidiphyllum japonicum*
12 *Stipa gigantea*
13 *Carpenteria californica*
14 *Parthenocissus tricuspidata* 'Veitchii'
15 *Juniperus chinensis* 'Kaizuka'
16 *Miscanthus* 'Purpurescens'
17 *Cornus alba* 'Aurea'
18 *Magnolia* x *soulangeana* 'Lennei'
19 *Verbascum* (Cotswold Group) 'Pink Domino'
20 *Actaea simplex* Atropurpurea Group 'James Compton'
21 *Lythrum salicaria* 'Robert'
22 *Pinus mugo* 'Mops'
23 *Clematis* 'Hagley Hybrid'
24 *Skimmia japonica* 'Veitchii'
25 *Libertia grandiflora*
26 *Eupatorium purpureum*
27 *Hosta* 'Krossa Regal'
28 *Skimmia japonica* 'Rubella'
29 *Cornus kousa* var. *chinensis*
30 *Actinidia kolomikta*
31 *Caltha palustris*

Plants that produce fruits and berries such as callicarpa are an excellent way of extending autumn colour.

Berries and fruit

In a small garden your choice of plants is naturally going to be limited by the space available. Every plant has got to earn its place, and species that provide colour and interest outside their normal flowering period are worth including. For many plants, that additional colour and interest can be provided by fruits and berries, many of which will appear and be retained for part or all of the winter months when the garden is at its quietest.

Most berrying shrubs and trees flower and then subsequently produce fruit on growth made in the previous season. These plants tend to flower in spring and early summer, so you will need to be careful not to prune them hard before they flower, apart from removing one or two complete older and dead or weak branches to improve the overall shape and appearance. A good way to keep these plants reasonably tidy and restrained without losing flowering wood is to wait until the berries or fruit are set and then remove any new extension growth beyond the bunches of berries. This not only encourages more flowering spurs on the older wood but also improves the appearance of the fruits themselves. Pyracanthas and cotoneasters are particularly suitable for this type of spur pruning.

Best plants for fruit and berries
- *Sorbus aucuparia*
- *Malus* 'John Downie'
- *Callicarpa bodinieri* var. *giraldii* 'Profusion'
- *Pyracantha* 'Orange Glow'
- *Rosa rugosa*
- *Cotoneaster frigidus* 'Cornubia'
- *Viburnum opulus* 'Notcutt's Variety'
- *Euonymus planipes*
- *Ilex aquifolium* (female cvs. requiring male to pollinate)
- *Skimmia japonica* subsp. *reevesiana* (no male required)

Circular garden

Incorporating a theme – a colour, material, shape, style – is a good way to unify a garden, especially a small one where it can be tempting to introduce too many different and diverse elements, making it feel cramped and busy. In this garden a circular theme features strongly, not only on the ground with lawn and paving but also in the garden features, and even some of the plants themselves. The result is a striking and elegant design.

Why this works

✓ The circular lawn, paving and path link neatly together and are both eye-catching and practical.

✓ The circular nature of the sunken lawn is highlighted and emphasized by the crisp stone mowing edge and step.

✓ Selected trees and shrubs are trimmed regularly into spherical or hemispherical shapes for a three-dimensional circular effect.

✓ The circular theme is repeated in the 'sun' trellis feature, the gazebo and the raised pool.

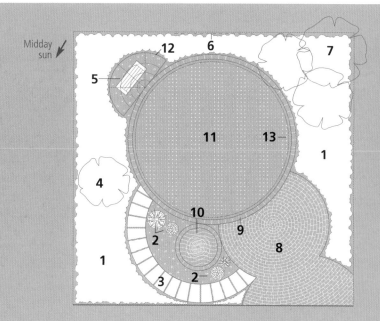

Garden elements key

1 Mixed border
2 Containers
3 Path
4 Trimmed conifer
5 Seat
6 'Sun' trellis
7 Trimmed 'lollipop' trees
8 Circular sett paving
9 Step up
10 Raised pool and fountain

11 Sunken lawn
12 Gazebo
13 Mowing edge

Mix and match
If you like this garden but would prefer
a different feature, see pages 250–51 for
possible variations.

Garden dimensions
7.5m x 7m (25ft x 23ft) approx.

Key features

Trimmed conifer

Many conifers are excellent subjects for trimming into formal shapes and topiary. Try to select a cultivar whose natural shape closely resembles the one you want to achieve to minimize pruning. To keep your trimmed conifers looking good, pay close attention to regular feeding, mulching and watering, and remember that each time you cut them you're effectively removing nutrients from the soil.

Sunken lawn

Introducing a sunken area into your garden – a lawn or patio, for example – adds extra interest to your design. A single step down is often all that is necessary, but bear in mind that a lowered, enclosed area can act as a water trap, so make sure that the drainage is adequate before embarking on the work. Put a mowing edge around your lawn, regardless of its shape, because it will not only make the lawn easier to cut and edge but will also protect the edge from damage or erosion and emphasize the shape of the lawn, in the same way a frame does a painting.

Gazebo

Gazebos are simple and easy features to incorporate in a garden. Site your gazebo where it will not only look good from the house but will also have an attractive or interesting outlook when you're sitting in it.

Making small gardens seem spacious

There are a number of techniques you can employ when you design a garden to increase the feeling of spaciousness within it. These are clearly of particular interest to anyone who has a small garden where physical space is limited to start.

Some of the most effective techniques are quite straightforward and can be incorporated at the planning stage of your garden and therefore don't require any specialist skills or knowledge. Others may need a certain level of expertise and creative talent.

Circular lawns are a classic and very effective way of making small gardens appear more spacious.

Boundaries

Being able to see the boundaries of your garden immediately tells you how big (or small) it is. Disguise the boundaries with a mixture of climbers, small trees and large shrubs. Don't just use climbers with no taller plants in front, or you will end up with straight green walls instead of terracotta ones. Also, avoid wall shrubs that need regular, neat trimming, which again will accentuate the geometry of the boundaries. Loose, informal planting is best.

Colour

Light colours are less oppressive and enclosing than dark ones. Consider this when you are choosing both your paving and planting. You might find it better to have a square area of white limestone chippings rather than a green lawn, for example. Apply the same rules to any garden structures, especially arches, pergolas, gazebos and summerhouses. Using brightly coloured plants or garden ornaments in dark corners will make them seem less gloomy.

Angles

At the planning stage avoid straight lines and rectangular or square spaces that run parallel to the boundary or the building. Angle them at, say, 45° or 60°, which diverts your eye away from the boundaries and creates generous areas for planting.

Curves

For a more informal design use multi-directional curves for paths, paving and lawns. Go for long, sweeping curves rather than lots of small, in-and-out squiggles. Designs incorporating a circular theme are especially effective.

Focal points

Use plants, statues, fountains and other elements as focal points to draw your attention. Try and tuck one or two of them out of sight so that you see them only as you proceed down the garden.

Mirrors

Although it requires a certain amount of skill, you can incorporate mirrors into your garden design by mounting them on heavy frames on walls to give the appearance of gateways or windows. Design the path so that it leads up to the gateway and the reflection will make it appear to go straight through the wall into another part of the garden beyond (see Garden of Illusion on page 112). Well-filled pools can also have a similar effect by reflecting the sky in the water.

Trompe l'oeil

This phrase roughly translates as 'fooling the eye', and it involves the same principle as mirror doorways or windows. In this case, however, the 'view' through is painted on the wall or fence. You'll need a fair amount of skill and artistic ability for this. Alternatively, ask a talented friend to help.

Colour recession

'Warm' colours, such as red, orange and deep yellow, tend to come forward, while 'cooler' ones, like blue and purple, recede. Think about this characteristic when you decide on your planting and position warmer ones near the house and around the patio, and the cool ones towards the far end of the garden.

False perspective

This is a fairly specialized technique, which is particularly suited to formal gardens. It involves exaggerating the effects of perspective by, for example, planting a row of the same cultivar of trees or shrubs but pruning each successive one so that it is slightly smaller than the one before. In a similar way, a straight path down the centre of the garden is actually made narrower at the far end, making it appear to be longer than it really is. The disadvantage of this technique is that it works only when viewed from one end of the garden — that is, from nearest the house.

Planting

8

19

20

30

The best plants for this garden

For a small garden there is a substantial amount of planting here in order to mask the boundary fence and thereby emphasize the strong, central, circular theme. Three trees are grouped together in one corner and make a striking feature, with their crowns regularly pruned to maintain a spherical or 'lollipop' shape. Similarly, the yew (*Taxus* spp.) is trimmed tightly to make a hemisphere that reflects the overall theme of the garden.

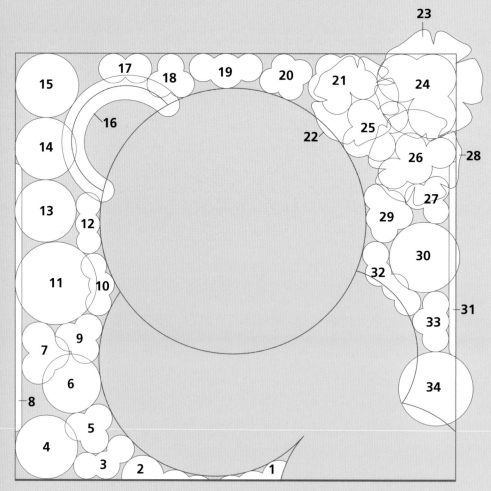

Planting key

1 *Elymus magellanicus*
2 *Achillea* 'Martina'
3 *Kniphofia* 'Nancy's Red'
4 *Myrtus communis* subsp. *tarentina*
5 *Artemisia ludoviciana* 'Valerie Finnis'
6 *Juniperus chinensis* 'Blaauw'
7 *Perovskia atriplicifolia* 'Filigran'
8 *Rosa* 'Zéphirine Drouhin'
9 *Schizostylis coccinea* 'Maiden's Blush'
10 *Limonium platyphyllum* 'Violetta'
11 *Taxus baccata* (trimmed to hemisphere)
12 *Eryngium bourgatii* 'Oxford Blue'
13 *Phormium* 'Sundowner'
14 *Hibiscus syriacus* 'Hamabo'
15 *Buddleja davidii* 'Empire Blue'
16 *Solanum laxum* 'Album'
17 *Macleaya microcarpa* 'Kelway's Coral Plume'
18 *Iris sibirica* 'Tycoon'
19 *Meconopsis betonicifolia*
20 *Polygonatum odoratum*
21 *Tricyrtis hirta*
22 *Ilex aquifolium* 'Pyramidalis' (female)
23 *Acer platanoides* 'Schwedleri'
24 *Prunus laurocerasus* 'Zabeliana'
25 *Dicentra eximia*
26 *Darmera peltata*
27 *Campanula persicifolia*
28 *Cupressus macrocarpa* 'Goldcrest'
29 *Primula bulleyana*
30 *Cordyline australis*
31 *Clematis* 'Fuji-musume'
32 *Pulmonaria angustifolia* 'Munstead Blue'
33 *Lysimachia ciliata* 'Firecracker'
34 *Syringa* x *persica*

Perennial borders

Perennials are good value in any garden. They are relatively inexpensive and don't take long to establish and make an impact, unlike some shrubs. They make good fillers and edge plants in mixed plantings, and they can be especially striking when planted in a purely herbaceous border. They are best appreciated if planted in groups of three, sometimes five, of each cultivar, although in the smallest of gardens you might get away with single plants.

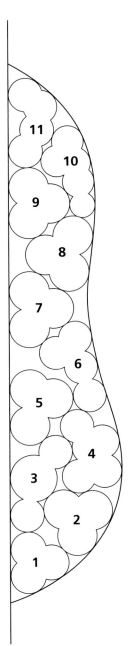

1 *Bergenia* 'Abendglut'
2 *Oenothera macrocarpa*
3 *Aster novae-angliae* 'Purple Dome'
4 *Dianthus* 'Devon Dove'
5 *Iris sibirica* 'White Swirl'
6 *Heuchera* 'Plum Pudding'
7 *Rudbeckia fulgida* var. *deamii*
8 *Geranium himalayense* 'Plenum'
9 *Phlox maculata* 'Alpha'
10 *Euphorbia polychroma*
11 *Anemone hupehensis* var. *japonica* 'Bressingham Glow'

Urban hideaway

Privacy and seclusion are welcome in any garden, even if it's only in a tiny corner where you can sit in isolation from what's going on around you. Hedges, solid fences and walls are obviously effective at providing privacy at a level, but there are other equally good solutions, which are particularly suitable for using in small gardens.

Why this works

✓ A generous paved area has plenty of room for garden furniture and space for general relaxation.

✓ Lots of planting disguises the shape of the garden and adds to the feeling of seclusion.

✓ Extra privacy is provided by the stilted hedge, hit-and-miss screen and a pergola.

✓ Taller plants, particularly the tree, are carefully placed to block unsightly views out of the garden.

✓ The planting and screening features not only give privacy but also help to shelter the garden from strong, gusty winds, making it a comfortable place to sit.

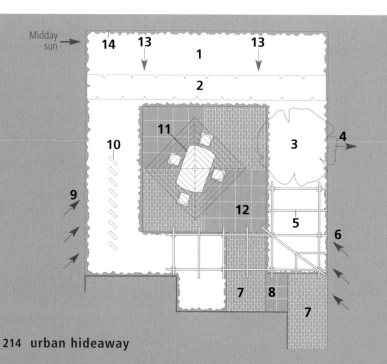

Garden elements key

1 Mixed border
2 Stilted hedge
3 Tree
4 Tree blocks unsightly views
5 Pergola
6 View into garden blocked by pergola
7 Brick path
8 Flag paving insert

9 View into garden
blocked by hit-and-
miss screen

10 Hit-and-miss screen

11 Garden furniture

12 Patio

13 View into garden
screened by stilted
hedge

14 Boundary

Mix and match
If you like this garden but would prefer
a different feature, see pages 250–51 for
possible variations.

Garden dimensions
7m x 7.5m (23ft x 25ft) approx.

Key features

Pergola

Pergolas can be used to block and screen, either by heavily planting them with leafy climbers or, when they are more lightly planted, by filling in the spaces between adjacent uprights with trellis panels or reed or bamboo screens. Plant with deciduous climbers if you need privacy in summer but want to let sun and light through in winter, when you are less likely to sit out.

Hit-and-miss screen

A hit-and-miss screen is a classic way to obscure a view both into and out of a space but without blocking out too much light. Depending on its location, you could stain it a strong colour so that it becomes a positive design feature. or leave it as natural wood or stain it in a subdued colour so that it blends into the planting and becomes less obvious. Because each individual post or board is set vertically in the ground you can make the screen follow any shape you like, curved, straight or angled.

Stilted hedge

Use a stilted hedge where you need to block out a particular high-level view but don't want to obscure too much of your garden. Because of the amount of light stilted hedges allow to pass through underneath them, you can place them nearer to your patio or sitting area where a traditional solid hedge would be too much of a barrier.

Creating a secluded patio

To make your patio private and secluded you will need to enclose it completely or partially with plants, garden structures or a combination of both. In order to avoid creating a dark, airless space, however, you will need to make sure that you avoid creating completely solid barriers on all sides.

Try and use climbers or wall shrubs to soften the appearance of walls and fences around your patio for a softer, secluded feeling.

Open structures

On a patio that is more likely to be used in summer, you might want to put the emphasis on planting predominantly deciduous plants, particularly taller shrubs, on the basis that in summer – when they are in leaf – they will create welcome shade but in winter will let more light through the bare stems.

However, if your patio is going to be put to use throughout the year, you will want to use more large evergreen shrubs, perhaps in combination with open structures, such as hit-and-miss screens or fences and different types of trellis work. You can use plants, especially shrubs, in the same way as a hit-and-miss screen for a more natural, softer look.

Trees as screens

Small trees or individual large shrubs can be used to break up or screen unsightly views out of your garden where a more uniform barrier, such as a hedge or fence, is undesirable or inappropriate. Small and slow-growing trees are advisable for small gardens, and you should position them where they are going to be most effective. Use a tall garden cane pushed into the soil to see where the optimum site for your tree will be before you actually plant it. It's not always necessary to plant the tree right at the boundary: remember the basic principle that the nearer to the viewer you place your screening tree or shrub, the smaller it can be. So, where you might need a 5m (16ft 6in) tall tree if it were planted on the boundary, by moving its position, say, 3m (10ft) nearer to you, the viewer, it might only need to reach 3m (10ft) to do the same job.

Overhead view of hit-and-miss screen

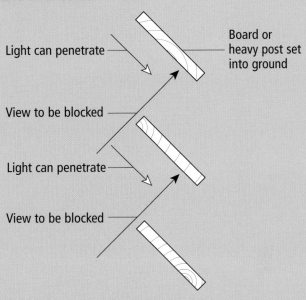

Light can penetrate

Board or heavy post set into ground

View to be blocked

Light can penetrate

View to be blocked

Side view of hit-and-miss screen

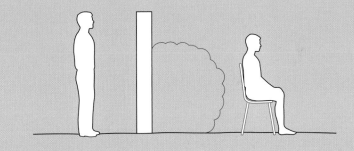

Screen size

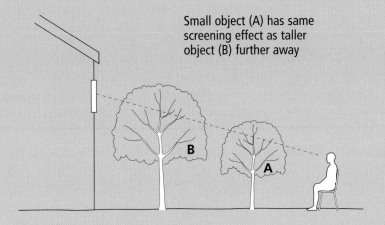

Small object (A) has same screening effect as taller object (B) further away

B

A

Planting

The best plants for this garden

The stilted hedge is the major planting feature in this garden, and it is trimmed squarely to echo the shapes of the patio, paving and pergola. Shrub planting is also a key element to balance the scale of the hedge, to mask the boundaries and to increase the feeling of privacy and seclusion. Lower perennials at the front of the borders provide additional flower colour and soften the straight edges of the paved areas.

Planting key

1 *Crinodendron hookerianum*
2 *Leucothoe fontanesiana*
3 *Dryopteris erythrosora*
4 *Hedera algeriensis* 'Marginomaculata'
5 *Pulmonaria angustifolia* 'Munstead Blue'
6 *Astilboides tabularis*
7 *Molinia caerulea* subsp. *caerulea* 'Strahlenquelle'

10

11

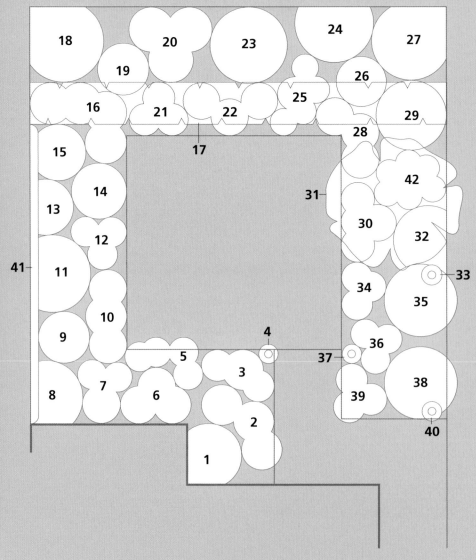

15

28

Stilted hedges

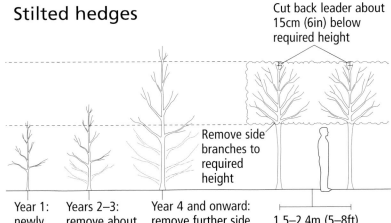

Cut back leader about 15cm (6in) below required height

Remove side branches to required height

Year 1: newly planted

Years 2–3: remove about one-third of the lowest side branches

Year 4 and onward: remove further side branches each year until the desired height is reached

1.5–2.4m (5–8ft) depending on vigour and habit of chosen trees

Stilted hedges are exactly what the name suggests: hedges on stilts. In this case the 'stilts' are the trunk or stem of each individual plant, which has been stripped of side branches, usually up to a height of 1.8–2m (about 6ft). The great advantage of this type of raised hedge is that it can be used to provide screening at a high level but will still allow light (and views) to penetrate beneath the solid 'hedge' section, so that you can plant both behind and in front of it. It's particularly effective at the back of a patio, where it can be planted quite close to the paved area without blocking the sun, and doesn't need to be so tall, making maintenance easier.

To grow a stilted hedge you should plant an appropriate species, usually evergreen, that can grow on a single main stem, as for a hedge, but further apart. As the plants grow, you need to progressively trim off side branches until the clear stems or 'stilts' have reached the chosen height. Once they are at this stage you should trim and maintain exactly as you would an ordinary hedge.

Alternatively, for a more instant effect, you can plant standard trees or mophead shrubs that have already been clean-stemmed to the required height in the nursery.

Best plants for an evergreen 'stilted' hedge

- *Quercus ilex*
- *Ilex aquifolium* cvs.
- *Photinia* x *fraseri*
- *Taxus baccata*
- *Cupressus macrocarpa*
- *Cotoneaster frigidus* 'Cornubia'
- *Viburnum tinus*
- *Laurus nobilis*
- *Prunus lusitanica*
- *Osmanthus* x *burkwoodii*

Eco-friendly garden

As demands on raw materials and natural resources, such as water, increase, we should all be considering ways in which we can make a small contribution to reducing this pressure by constructing and managing our own garden in a thoughtful, eco-friendly way. As with all gardens, a little forward planning makes the process smoother and will help you achieve an attractive end result.

Why this works

✓ The patio is built from reclaimed granite setts and old, exposed aggregate flagstones.
✓ Rainwater is saved for use in the garden with water butts.
✓ A kitchen garden is based on organic principles, and there are compost bins for recycling garden and vegetable waste and a wormery.
✓ The ornamental planting areas are mulched with bark, which is a by-product of the softwood (conifers) forestry industry.
✓ Solar-powered lights around the patio and a solar-powered pump for the pond reduce the need for mains electricity.

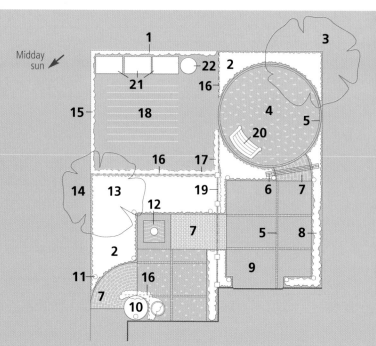

Garden elements key

1 Climber
2 Mixed planting
3 Pollarded tree
4 Bark
5 Reclaimed sett edging
6 Arch
7 Sett paving
8 Wall shrubs or climbers
9 Reclaimed exposed aggregate paving
10 Water butt

11 Solar-powered
    lighting
12 Water feature
13 Tall shrubs
14 Small tree
15 Cordon fruit
16 Trellis and climber

17 Beans and other
    vegetables on trellis
18 Kitchen garden
19 Rope swag
20 Bench seat
21 Compost bins
22 Wormery

Mix and match
If you like this garden but would prefer
a different feature, see pages 250–51 for
possible variations.

Garden dimensions
6.5m x 7.5m (21ft 6in x 25ft) approx.

Pollarded tree

Pollarding – that is, pruning a tree hard back at about 2m (6ft) above ground every year – is a way of controlling growth and producing good winter stem colour. A bonus of this is that the stems produced are generally straight and long, which makes them ideal material for anywhere you might need canes: for example, as supports for climbing beans. Ideally, cut them several months before they are needed because otherwise they might root when you push them into the ground.

Reclaimed paving

Use reclaimed paving materials for your patio if possible to reduce the need for mining and quarrying of new stone and building aggregates. If you can't find enough of one type of flag, mix them with inserts of a salvaged old brick or granite sett for a more random, patchwork effect.

Wormery

Worms are to be encouraged in any garden since they are excellent at recycling soft, vegetable waste – kitchen peelings, grass clippings, shredded newspaper – and converting it into healthy organic compost. There are plenty of ready-made wormerys on the market but you can easily make a simple one yourself from a large, plastic container. Make sure there is lots of drainage, and don't stand it in full sun or the inside temperature may rise rapidly and cook your worms.

Bin screen

In a small garden there is often insufficient room to tuck away less attractive features, such as bins, water butts and compost heaps. You will, therefore, need to provide some sort of screening device that takes up little room. A simple timber frame will provide you with a basic support to which you can attach your screening material.

Make your bin screen or store match other elements in the garden to reduce its impact.

You will need

4 posts, 1.2–1.5m (4–5ft) long, from 7.5cm x 7.5cm (3in x 3in) second-hand or recycled timber

6 rails, from 7.5cm x 4cm (3in x 1½in) second-hand or recycled timber; you will need 4 for the chosen width of your screen and 2 to fit the length

Nickel-chrome screws or galvanized nails

Water-based woodstain or preservative

Screening material

Step by step

1 If your posts are not pressure-treated, stand the bottom 30–40cm (12–16in) in a pot of preservative overnight and allow to dry.

2 Mark the four corners of the 'frame' on the ground. In undisturbed ground you can cut a point on the end of the posts (before step 1) and drive them directly into the soil with a sledgehammer or post-driver. Otherwise fix them into holes about 20cm x 20cm (8in x 8in) by 30–40cm (12–16in) deep with a

Basic frame
End view

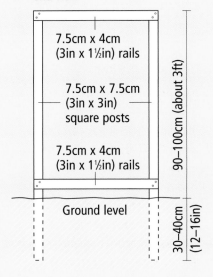

7.5cm x 4cm (3in x 1½in) rails

7.5cm x 7.5cm (3in x 3in) square posts

7.5cm x 4cm (3in x 1½in) rails

Ground level

90–100cm (about 3ft)

30–40cm (12–16in)

Plan view

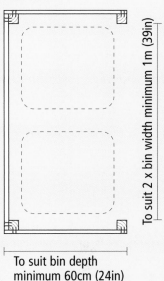

To suit 2 x bin width minimum 1m (39in)

To suit bin depth minimum 60cm (24in)

mixture of crushed brick, small stones and soil rammed tight.

3 Screw or nail the rails to the top and bottom of the posts, leaving a gap of about 5cm (2in) between the bottom rail and ground level.

4 Stain the completed frame with preservative if required. Use a water-based product, which is more environmentally friendly.

5 Fix your chosen screen material to the frame, making sure that the lower edge is not in direct contact with the ground. Again, try to incorporate recycled or salvaged material, especially wood: even the boards off pallets or wooden crates can be roughly sanded, cut to size and stained to give a more than acceptable appearance.

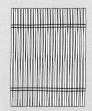

Bamboo or reed

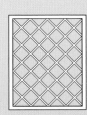

Diamond trellis (climber optional)

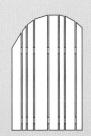

Multi-width board with shaped top

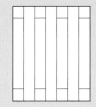

Vertical 'hit-and-miss'

Horizontal 'hit-and-miss'

Mesh with climber

Planting

The best plants for this garden

Tall and medium-sized shrubs, climbers and perennials are used to divide the garden into several distinct but linked areas, with the kitchen garden being well screened from the ornamental, leisure areas nearer to the house. The lower planting, such as French lavender (*Lavandula stoechas*) and valerian (*Centranthus ruber*), is used to break up the rigid geometric lines of the different paved areas, while climbers and wall shrubs, such as clematis and *Forsythia suspensa*, soften the boundaries.

Planting key

1 *Lonicera sempervirens*
2 *Ilex verticillata* 'Winter Red' (female)
3 *Anemone* x *hybrida* 'September Charm'
4 *Hosta* 'Frances Williams'
5 *Dryopteris erythrosora*
6 *Salix alba* var. *vitellina* 'Britzensis' (pollarded)

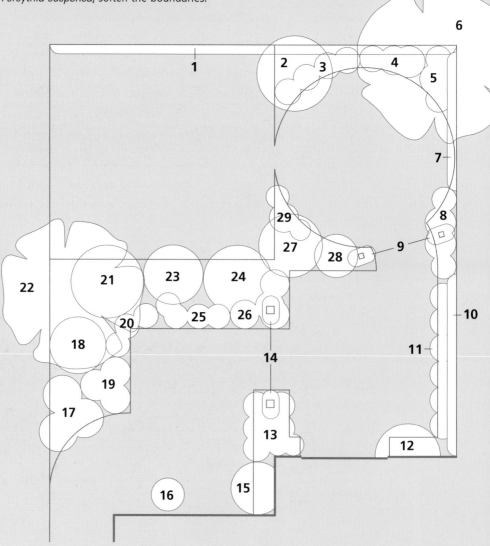

Growing your own plants from seed is not only eco-friendly, but also cheap and fun.

Eco-friendly gardening

Almost everything we do has an environmental consequence to some degree, and if you were to analyse your lifestyle closely to see how you could reduce this impact you would probably be overwhelmed. However, you can achieve a lot by adopting a few basic principles in the way you garden that will not leave your head spinning.

- Look for second-hand tools in auctions, car boot sales and local advertisements. If you have to buy new, try to find brands that can be repaired rather than be thrown away, and don't acquire more tools than you'll actually need.
- If possible, grow your own vegetable and salad plants from seed, using peat-free seed compost. If you have to buy plants, see if you can find locally grown ones (thereby saving on transport) that are in peat-free compost or that are rootballed or bare root.
- Improve your soil with home-produced organic matter from the compost bin and wormery or use locally obtained, well-rotted manure.
- Mulch soil in ornamental beds with composted bark chippings to preserve moisture and reduce the competition from weeds. If you need to carry out additional feeding during the growing season use organic or natural fertilizers.
- Avoid having to use chemical treatments by keeping your plants well fed and watered, and don't cram plants into beds and borders so that they are struggling for light and air.
- Encourage beneficial insects to your garden, such as ladybirds, bees and hoverflies, by providing suitable overwintering quarters and some desirable food plants.
- There are many safe ways to catch slugs and snails, including upside-down citrus fruit halves and beer traps. Hedgehogs eat slugs, too, but their favourite food is lobworms, which are good for improving heavy soil: this is a dilemma!

Garden squared

As a shape, the square lends itself perfectly to the design of gardens: you can use it in an abstract way to create a geometric layout or symmetrically for a formal effect. In this example, the latter arrangement has been created by taking a perfectly square lawn and combining it with square paving. The effect is underlined with screen and trellis panels in the same style.

Why this works

✓ The garden is defined by overlapping square shapes of lawn and patio, which consists of square flags.

✓ A dwarf hedge is trimmed into a formal shape to define the edge of the patio and link it to the lawn.

✓ The square theme is repeated in the screen and trellis panels, which are rotated to create square diamond shapes.

✓ A small ground-level water feature acts as a focal point and also as a division between lawn and patio.

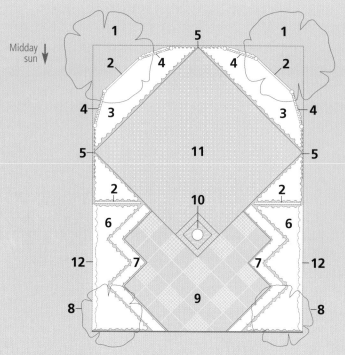

Midday sun ↓

Garden elements key

1 Tree
2 Ornamental screen
3 Mixed low planting
4 Rope swag
5 Ornamental trellis on fence or wall
6 Mixed border
7 Dwarf hedge
8 Formal small tree or large shrub
9 Patio
10 Water feature

11 Lawn
12 Climber

Mix and match
If you like this garden but would prefer
a different feature, see pages 250–51 for
possible variations.

Garden dimensions
5.5m x 7m (18ft x 23ft) approx.

Key features

Square lawn

Rotating a square or rectangular lawn or patio through 45° or 60° doesn't create extra planting space, but it does make the areas deeper from front to back and therefore allows you to plant taller, larger subjects at the back or apex of the triangular areas formed. This is a useful technique in small gardens, where you need extra planting height to mask boundaries, corners and even garden stores or compost heaps.

Rope swag

Rope swags are an easy way to provide simple support for many climbers, most notably roses (*Rosa* spp.) and clematis, where an arch or pergola is too heavy or formal. Use a heavy rope for best effect – natural fibres look good with unstained wood posts such as oak. Man-made fibre is longer lasting, and white rope can be used effectively with white-painted posts.

Water feature

Water features – such as this drilled, glazed sphere – where the main body of water supplying the 'bubble' or 'geyser' is contained in a sump or tank below the feature are excellent for two reasons. Firstly they are ideal for small children who can get thoroughly wet in complete safety, and secondly they collect far less rubbish in the form of leaves and wind-blown debris, making them virtually maintenance free.

Simple screen

There may be occasions when you want to give a suggestion of screening in your garden without using a solid barrier, such as a wall, fence or hedge.

You will need

For a single panel
2 pressure-treated or hardwood posts, 7.5cm x 7.5cm (3in x 3in), at least 2.1m (7ft) long
1.2m x 1.2m (4ft x 4ft) trellis panel
5cm x 2.5cm (2in x 1in) treated softwood, such as roofing batten, about 8m (26ft) in length
12 x 60mm (2¼in) screws or nails
Woodstain
Cement
Ballast

Take a little extra time and effort to make your screen a bold feature.

Step by step

1 Cut the batten into two lengths, each 1.7m (5ft 6in), and two lengths, each 1.6m (5ft 3in). Lay the four lengths of batten on their edges on a smooth, level area to form a square. Make the 1.7m (5ft 6in) lengths form the top and bottom of the square, with the shorter lengths set between them to form the sides.

2 Screw or nail through the ends of the top and bottom battens into the end grain of the shorter side battens to fix the square.

3 Rotate the trellis panel through 45° and place it on top of your square frame, nailing or screwing it to the frame so that the corners of the trellis panel are fixed to the midpoints of the square side to form a diamond.

4 Excavate two holes, with centres 1.8m (6ft) apart, to take the posts, about 30cm (12in) wide and at least 30cm (12in) deep. Put the posts in the holes and backfill with concrete of 1 part cement to 6 parts ballast. At least 30cm (12in) of the posts need to be below ground.

5 When the concrete is set screw or nail the trellis frame through the sides on to the inside face of the posts.

6 Stain the finished screen panel.

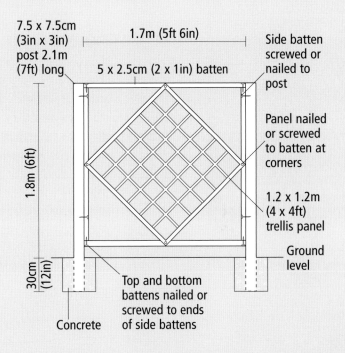

7.5 x 7.5cm (3in x 3in) post 2.1m (7ft) long

1.7m (5ft 6in)

5 x 2.5cm (2 x 1in) batten

Side batten screwed or nailed to post

Panel nailed or screwed to batten at corners

1.2 x 1.2m (4 x 4ft) trellis panel

Ground level

1.8m (6ft)

30cm (12in)

Concrete

Top and bottom battens nailed or screwed to ends of side battens

Different shapes

Designing a garden to incorporate lines of symmetry – creating mirror images on either side of these lines or axes – results in a formal arrangement. The same basic shapes can be used in a different, random or abstract way to make an equally attractive garden, which you might call asymmetric. You don't have to limit your choice to just one shape, such as a circle, square or rectangle, in order to do this; sometimes a combination of different individual shapes can be just as attractive, resulting in a geometric design.

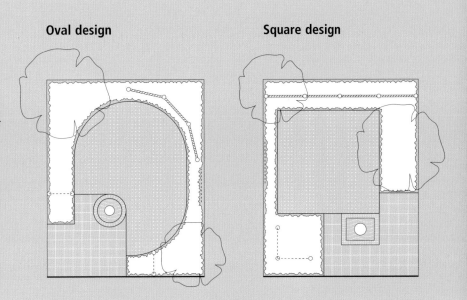

Oval design

Square design

Planting

The best plants for this garden

Emphasizing the symmetry of this design, the planting in the left-hand half of the garden is a mirror image of that on the right-hand side. There is a combination of low perennials, that help to soften the hard edges of the lawn, and paving, plus taller, more upright trees, shrubs, perennials and grasses that provide more height. The paving is divided from the beds by a neat hedge of squarely trimmed dwarf box (*Buxus sempervirens* 'Suffruticosa').

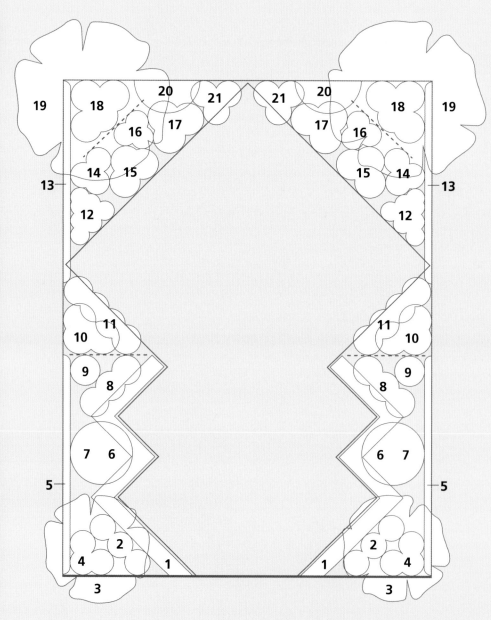

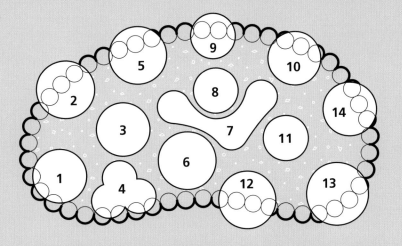

Planting key

1 *Buxus sempervirens* 'Suffruticosa' (dwarf hegde)
2 *Asphodeline lutea*
3 *Acer griseum*
4 *Aster lateriflorus* var. *horizontalis*
5 *Jasminum officinale* 'Argenteovariegatum'
6 *Rosa glauca*
7 *Anemone sylvestris* (underplanting)
8 *Lilium regale*
9 *Miscanthus sinensis* 'Kleine Fontäne'
10 *Verbascum* (Cotswold Group) 'Cotswold Queen'
11 *Coreopsis* 'Tequila Sunrise'
12 *Allium schubertii*
13 *Lonicera* x *brownii* 'Dropmore Scarlet'
14 *Phlox paniculata* 'Sandringham'
15 *Stokesia laevis* 'Blue Star'
16 *Iris sibirica* 'Sparkling Rosé'
17 *Ranunculus acris*
18 *Actaea simplex* Atropurpurea Group 'Brunette'
19 *Koelreuteria paniculata*
20 *Euphorbia mellifera*
21 *Carex oshimensis* 'Evergold'

Alpine raised bed

A ground-level pool could be regarded as a potential danger if you have children, and the space could be used instead for alpine plants.

By definition, alpines are plants that thrive in alpine conditons, where the main factors contributing to their continued health are good drainage and sunlight. Nowadays, many dwarf shrubs and perennials that form mats or rosettes can be included in the general term 'alpines', and others, such as dwarf conifers and heathers, associate well with them.

Some of the more vigorous alpines or alpine-like plants, such as *Helianthemum* and *Acaena*, can be used as edging in mixed borders or around paved areas. The less vigorous forms, however, are best displayed where they won't be swamped by larger, more robust perennials and shrubs. Rock gardens are a popular and traditional way of growing alpines, and they they can be combined with one or two miniature or dwarf conifers, such as *Juniperus communis* 'Compressa', and small, neat grasses, such as *Festuca glauca* 'Blauglut'.

1 *Iberis* 'Dick Self'
2 *Saponaria* 'Bressingham'
3 *Chamaecyparis lawsoniana* 'Pygmaea Argentea'
4 *Sempervivum* 'Othello'
5 *Diascia barberae* 'Blackthorn Apricot'
6 *Artemisia schmidtiana* 'Nana'
7 *Dianthus deltoides* 'Leuchtfunk'
8 *Berberis thunbergii* f. *atropurpurea* 'Bagatelle'
9 *Crepis incana*
10 *Thymus pulegioides* 'Bertram Anderson'
11 *Juniperus communis* 'Compressa'
12 *Campanula* 'Birch Hybrid'
13 *Helianthemum* 'The Bride'
14 *Phlox subulata* 'Emerald Cushion Blue'

Flower garden

While many gardens are designed to provide as much year-round colour and interest as possible, in this example the emphasis is on masses of flowers from spring through to autumn, while a shrubby framework provides some structure to carry the garden through the winter. The summer effect is heightened by the use of seed-sown annuals in drifts, and you can change the species or cultivars from year to year to suit your own preferences.

Why this works

✓ A bold geometric theme, dominated by a striking circular path, maximizes the available space for planting in a modestly sized plot.

✓ There are three alternative sitting areas to choose from.

✓ A mixed border of shrubs and perennials gives sustained interest from early spring to late summer.

✓ Drifts of annuals provide extra impact at the height of the growing season and more flowers for cutting.

✓ Troughs and a bubble fountain, gazebo and bench act as focal points.

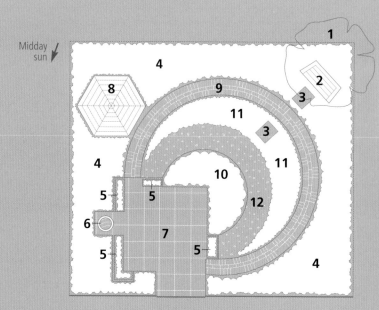

Garden elements key

1 Small tree
2 Bench
3 Stepping stone
4 Mixed planting
5 Trough
6 Bubble fountain

7 Patio
8 Gazebo and seats
9 Brick and stone path
10 Perennials
11 Annuals
12 Stone chippings

Mix and match
If you like this garden but would prefer
a different feature, see pages 250–51 for
possible variations.

Garden dimensions
8m x 7m (26ft x 23ft) approx.

Key features

Brick and stone path

Combining two complementary materials in a random pattern creates an exciting path. Making the path weave its way through planted areas adds to its attractive quality, particularly if you use soft, low plants along the edges. Keep the level of the path 2–3cm (about 1in) above the level of the surrounding beds so that soil cannot wash on to the path in heavy rain and to give space for an organic mulch if you wish.

Bench

The placing of a relatively simple feature such as a bench can add greatly to a garden's attraction. Make a positive design statement by placing it at the end of a path – where it might be backed by a formal, yew hedge – or by siting it more discreetly among lush planting or under a shady tree in a quiet location waiting to be 'discovered'.

Bubble fountain

Small, compact, self-contained water features like this are perfect for modest gardens where large bodies of water would look out of place and out of scale. Set the feature at the edge or corner of your patio or among low planting so that you can enjoy the sound of the splashing water when you are sitting and relaxing outside. Avoid models with vigorous jets of water, and instead choose one with a gently gurgling, bubbling outlet that will soothe and calm you.

Gazebos and arbours

As design features in a garden both gazebos and arbours offer good value. They are relatively simple to build, and you can even buy some models in kit form, which are not overly expensive compared to a solid garden building and which will give virtually instant impact, with or without climbing plants.

However, you can really make the best of these structures by a little advanced planning rather

Stain or paint your gazebo or arbour to connect it with any colour theme in your garden design.

than just going out, buying a style that appeals to you and then erecting it in the most convenient spot in your garden.

Choose a gazebo design that is in keeping with the rest of the garden in terms of style, colour, material and, of course, scale.

The location is important. Your gazebo must serve a purpose within the garden, whether it is at the end of a path, is seen framed through an arch or between two trees or is set in a corner backed by two or three large evergreen shrubs to create a quiet, contemplative sun trap. Decide if you want your gazebo to be prominent or if it will be tucked away in a corner of your garden, perhaps half-hidden by soft planting.

Choose a size that suits its purpose. If you want a gazebo purely as a visual feature, then a small, elegant design will probably be sufficient. However, if you would like to create an alternative sitting area – perhaps in a sunny corner of the garden – it must be large enough to accommodate garden chairs and perhaps a table but without dominating the rest of the garden.

The visual effect of your gazebo can be modified by what you plant around and over it. Low surrounding planting and perhaps just one light, delicate climber will let your gazebo stand out. However, taller plants around it and vigorous, leafy climbers over it will help it blend into the background to create a more secret, surprise retreat.

Always provide some kind of paved link to your gazebo, whether it is a few simple stepping stones through creeping alpines and groundcover or a wide gravel sweep edged in lavender or box for a grander entrance.

Frame your garden building with plants to make it seem an integral part of your design, not an afterthought.

Planting

The best plants for this garden

With an emphasis on seasonal colour, perennials are a major element in the planting of this garden. The plants selected not only look good in association with each other but also include many that can be used as cut flowers or for arranging. Annuals are used in a bold, crescent-shaped bed for extra impact. For an organized look you could plant out individual cell- or pot-grown plants, but for a more natural effect sow seeds of different varieties and thin them out by hand as they develop.

Planting key

1 *Cistus* x *pulverulentus* 'Sunset'
2 *Abutilon megapotamicum* (on wall)
3 *Aster amellus* 'Rosa Erfüllung'
4 *Deutzia* x *elegantissima* 'Rosealind'
5 *Ceanothus* 'Burkwoodii' (trained on wall)
6 *Lavandula angustifolia* 'Loddon Blue'
7 *Kniphofia* 'Jenny Bloom'
8 *Echinacea purpurea* 'White Swan'
9 *Limonium platiphyllum* 'Violetta'

11

22

23

53

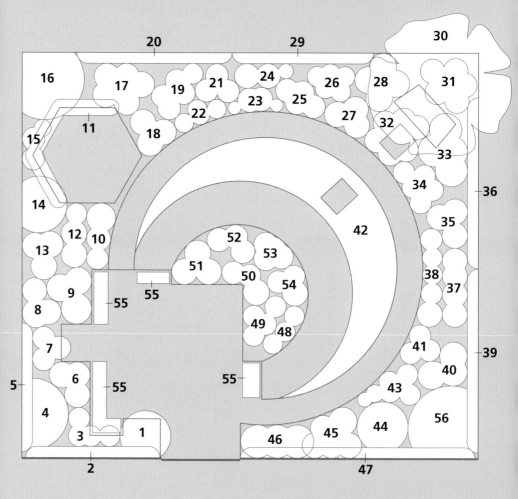

10 *Anthemis* 'Susanna Mitchell'
11 *Clematis* 'Jackmanii' (on gazebo)
12 *Tanacetum coccineum* 'James Kelway'
13 *Delphinium* Black Knight Group
14 *Hydrangea* 'Preziosa'
15 *Campanula persicifolia* 'Chettle Charm'
16 *Viburnum* x *bodnantense* 'Charles Lamont'
17 *Tricyrtis* 'White Towers'
18 *Zantedeschia aethiopica* 'White Sail'
19 *Aconitum* 'Spark's Variety'
20 *Crinodendron hookerianum* (against wall)
21 *Solidago* 'Ledsham'
22 *Schizostylis coccinea* 'Major'
23 *Primula denticulata* var. *alba*
24 *Chelone obliqua*
25 *Omphalodes cappadocica*
26 *Meconopsis* Fertile Blue Group 'Lingholm'
27 *Salvia* x *sylvestris* 'Viola Klose'
28 *Rodgersia pinnata* 'Superba'
29 *Chaenomeles* x *superba* 'Crimson and Gold' (against wall)
30 *Prunus* 'Pandora'
31 *Polygonatum odoratum* var. *pluriflorum* 'Variegatum'
32 *Viola sororia* 'Albiflora'
33 *Astilbe* 'Rheinland'
34 *Veronica gentianoides* 'Robusta'
35 *Phlox paniculata* 'Eventide'
36 *Berberidopsis corallina*
37 *Macleaya microcarpa* 'Kelway's Coral Plume'
38 *Scabiosa atropurpurea* 'Chile Black'
39 *Rosa* 'Apple Blossom'
40 *Hymenoxys hoopesii*
41 *Leucanthemum* x *superbum* 'Esther Read'
42 Annuals (in drifts of same variety)
43 *Eryngium* x *zabelii* 'Jos Eijking'
44 *Rosa* 'Sweet Juliet'
45 *Crocosmia* x *crocosmiiflora* 'Solfatare'
46 *Achillea* 'Inca Globe'
47 *Wisteria sinensis* 'Blue Sapphire'
48 *Dianthus* 'Doris'
49 *Sedum spectabile* 'Iceberg'
50 *Agapanthus* 'Golden Rule'
51 *Campanula alliariifolia*
52 *Scabiosa caucasica* 'Clive Greaves'
53 *Liatris spicata*
54 *Coreopsis verticillata* 'Moonbeam'
55 Annuals
56 *Osmanthus delavayi*

Achilleas are excellent for cutting and look good for many weeks in the garden.

Flowers

The range of flowering plants available is extensive, but where you have limited space some cultivars provide extra value and are therefore worthwhile including.

Best low–medium plants for the flower garden

- *Dianthus* (border types)
- *Doronicum columnae* 'Miss Mason'
- *Leucanthemum* x *superburm* 'Snowcap'
- *Limonium*
- *Scabiosa* (scabious)
- *Astilbe*
- *Calendula*
- *Heuchera* (purple-leaved forms)
- *Helichrysum*
- *Trollius*

Best medium–tall plants for the flower garden

- *Agapanthus*
- *Digitalis*
- *Rudbeckia*
- *Leucanthemum* x *superbum* 'Esther Read'
- *Helenium*
- *Delphinium*
- *Iris*
- *Tanacetum* (syn. *Pyrethrum*)
- *Achillea*
- *Eryngium*

Cottage-style garden

The key features of a cottage garden are included in this contemporary, small-scale interpretation of a traditional style. Although the garden has a distinctly rustic feel, it is a more manageable layout than the old-fashioned cottage garden, and it is, therefore, well suited to a modern family, who perhaps don't have a great deal of spare time for the more mundane tasks of regular garden maintenance.

Why this works

✓ A traditional, small kitchen garden is concealed at the far end, supplying small quantities of fresh, choice vegetables, fruit and salad.

✓ The rustic gazebo, built in brick, oak and cedar shingles, is in keeping with the style of garden and makes a delightful focal point.

✓ Planting is confined to a simple, bold perimeter border incorporating cottage-style planting in a modern, easy-to-maintain layout.

✓ There are two sitting areas of old-fashioned stone crazy paving linked by a gently meandering, brick-edged, stone path.

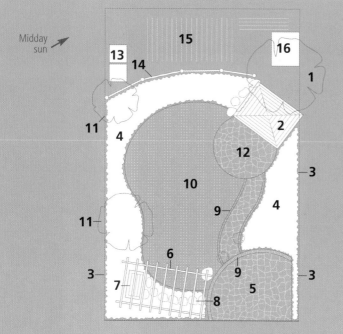

Garden elements key

1 Tree	**7** Seat
2 Rustic gazebo	**8** Stepping stones
3 Climbers on fence	**9** Brick edge
4 Mixed border	**10** Lawn
5 Crazy paving patio	**11** Small tree
6 Rustic pergola	**12** Crazy paving

13 Compost bins
14 Rustic screen
15 Vegetable garden
16 Garden store

Mix and match
If you like this garden but would prefer a different feature, see pages 250–51 for possible variations.

Garden dimensions
7m x 11.5m (23ft x 38ft) approx.

Stepping stones

Use stepping stones where you need only occasional access to an area of your garden or where a solid path might appear too intrusive. When they are set in lawns always make sure the top of each stepping stone is set slightly below the level of the grass to make mowing easier. On the other hand, you should keep them slightly above, by 15–20mm (about ¾in), loose materials, which might otherwise spread over the stones.

Crazy paving

This style of paving is suited to old-fashioned, romantic, types of design. Its great advantage is that it can be used to make almost any shape, formal or informal. Although it is quite labour intensive, the material costs are modest compared with rectangular stone flags, and the random nature of the paving means that you can mix in highlights of different coloured stone or leave spaces unpaved to make small planting pockets.

Rustic screen

Screens made from prefabricated lengths of natural materials make ideal dividers. They are quite easy to erect, and as long as they are attached to a strong framework and do not come into direct contact with the ground they will last for many years. Use them also for making sheltered spots – fix lengths between the posts along the back and sides of a pergola for an enclosed effect.

Patio patterns

When you're looking for ideas for paving in a small garden, don't get too carried away and feel that you want to include all sorts and sizes of different materials. You will probably have plenty of additional features to add later on, such as furniture, pots and ornaments, and you could end up with a busy area that is not as relaxing as you first imagined.

Instead, restrict your choice to just one or two materials in a limited range of sizes and colours. It's surprising how many variations you can achieve with, for example, standard bricks and 45cm x 45cm (18in x 18in) flags. The illustrations show several ways in which to use these, but with a little imagination you can probably come up with more.

Even in contemporary gardens, herringbone brick paving always looks good.

Square-butted flags

Square-butted flags with brick inserts

Alternative brick patterns

'Windmill' flags around two-brick square

Soldier brick course

Soldier brick course as patio edge

Soldier or stretcher brick course as separating band between flag courses

Broken bond (staggered) flags

Broken bond with brick inserts

Edge detail for broken bond to avoid cutting flags

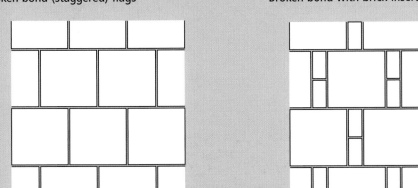

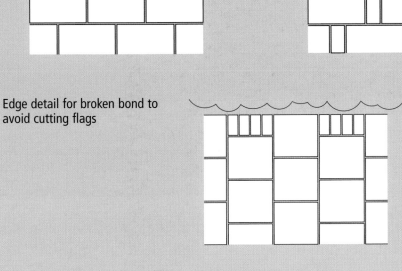

Planting

The best plants for this garden

Plants in keeping with a traditional cottage garden are used here with an emphasis on a shrubby framework and infilling of perennials for mid-season flower and colour. Climbers on the fence and pergola add an extra degree of height and softness to the boundaries, and the effect is completed with the edible plants in the small kitchen garden.

Planting key

1 *Rosa* 'Casino'
2 *Clematis florida* var. *sieboldiana*
3 *Helleborus orientalis*
4 *Matteuccia struthiopteris*
5 *Anemone sylvestris*
6 *Filipendula ulmaria* 'Aurea'
7 *Rhododendron* 'Nancy Evans'
8 *Clematis* 'The President'
9 *Daphne odora* 'Aureomarginata'

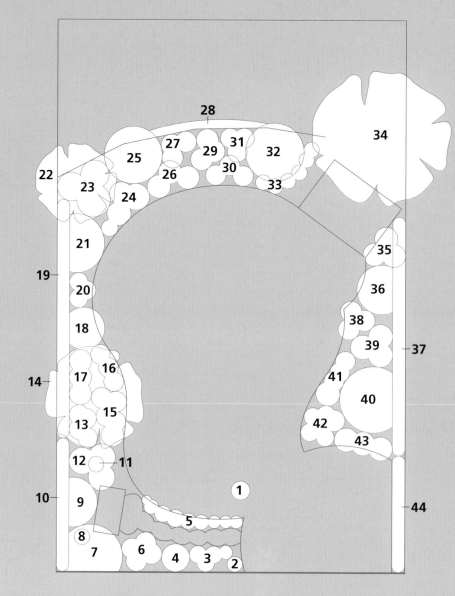

Alternative edible planting

Where you don't have sufficient space for a separate kitchen garden, you can include edible plants, particularly herbs and fruit, in an ornamental way within the main design.

10 *Jasminum officinale*
11 *Clematis* 'Niobe'
12 *Hosta sieboldiana* var. *elegans*
13 *Astilbe* 'Deutschland'
14 *Sorbus* 'Kirsten Pink'
15 *Primula* polyanthus
16 *Geranium sylvaticum* 'Mayflower'
17 *Tricyrtis hirta* 'Albomarginata'
18 *Rosa* 'Graham Thomas'
19 *Rosa* 'Albertine' (rambler)
20 *Digitalis grandiflora*
21 *Rhododendron* 'Berryrose'
22 *Malus* 'Evereste'
23 *Ligularia veitchiana*
24 *Heuchera* 'Rachel'
25 *Rosa glauca* underplanted with *Dicentra spectabilis* (illustrated)
26 *Hemerocallis* 'Penelope Vestey'
27 *Phlox maculata* 'Omega'
28 *Clematis* 'Purpurea Plena Elegans'
29 *Helenium* 'Biedermeier'
30 *Sedum telephium* 'Purple Emperor'
31 *Thalictrum delavayi* 'Hewitt's Double'
32 *Weigela* 'Florida Variegata'
33 *Viola riviniana* Purpurea Group
34 *Acer pseudoplatanus* 'Simon-Louis Frères'
35 *Monarda* 'Snow Queen'
36 *Rosa* 'Bonica'
37 *Lonicera periclymenum*
38 *Achillea* 'Anthea'
39 *Delphinium* Summer Skies Group
40 *Buddleja davidii* 'Nanho Purple'
41 *Dianthus* 'Haytor White'
42 *Iris* 'Kent Pride' (tall bearded)
43 *Echinacea purpurea* 'Baby White Swan'
44 *Rosa* 'Aloha'

1 Climbing beans
2 Mint (in container)
3 Parsley
4 Gooseberry 'Keepsake'
5 Oregano
6 Basil
7 Blackcurrant 'Ben Sarek'
8 *Actinidia deliciosa* 'Bruno' (for fruit)
9 Rhubarb
10 *Actinidia deliciosa* 'Matua' (pollinator for *A. deliciosa* 'Bruno')
11 Melon (trained up pergola)
12 Blueberry 'Chandler'
13 Raspberry 'Glen Clova'
14 Apple 'Discovery' (pollinator for 'Greensleeves')
15 Dwarf French kidney beans
16 Spinach
17 *Melissa officinalis* 'Aurea'
18 Redcurrant 'Laxton No.1'
19 Climbing beans on fence
20 Florence fennel
21 Rhubarb
22 *Malus* 'John Downie'
23 Asparagus
24 Cut-and-come-again lettuce – e.g., 'Valmaine'
25 *Rosmarinus officinalis* 'Miss Jessopp's Upright'
26 Shallots
27 Sweetcorn
28 Climbing beans
29 Purple sprouting
30 *Salvia officinalis* 'Tricolor'
31 Autumn-fruiting raspberry 'Sceptre'
32 Globe artichoke
33 Strawberry 'Cambridge Favourite'

34 Family pear tree
35 Jerusalem artichokes
36 Gooseberry 'White Eagle'
37 Thornless Blackberry 'Merton Thornless'
38 Tomato 'Tumbler'
39 Tree onion (*Allium cepa* Proliferum Group)
40 *Laurus nobilis* 'Aurea'
41 Chives
42 Asparagus pea
43 Thyme
44 Fan-trained apple 'Greensleeves' (pollinator for 'Discovery')

The bold leaves of edible climbing plants, such as melons and thornless blackberries, can be every bit as striking as ornamental climbers.

Vertical garden

One of the main conflicts that occurs in many small gardens is that of balancing the need for adequate uncluttered space – paving – against the room taken up by plants. The best approach to tackling this dilemma is a two-pronged one: first, select climbers and other wall plants that can naturally be grown up vertical features without using up lots of space; second, use plants that have a naturally vertical or fastigiate habit.

Why this works

✓ All the walls are clothed in climbers, hanging pots and wall shrubs to give maximum planting while taking the minimum of floor space.
✓ A corner overhead structure makes a shady optional sitting area and additional support for more climbers.
✓ Small, triangular corner beds add depth to the planting by using taller upright shrubs and perennials.
✓ The geometric use of bricks and square flagstones provides an attractive link between the two arms of this L-shaped plot.

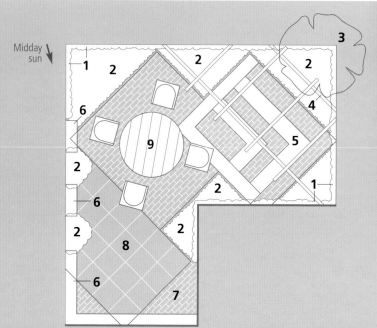

Garden elements key

1 Climbers on wall
2 Upright planting in beds
3 Fastigiate tree
4 Optional overheads
5 Optional shady sitting area
6 Wall-mounted containers
7 Brick paving

8 Flag paving
9 Patio furniture

Mix and match
If you like this garden but would prefer
a different feature, see pages 250–51 for
possible variations.

Garden dimensions
5m x 5m (16ft 6in x 16ft 6in) approx.

Wall-mounted containers

Sometimes you have a blank wall to be softened but it is not possible to plant a climber directly in the ground and there may not even be enough space for a large pot or urn. In these circumstances you can hang containers on to the wall. Remember that wall-mounted containers will need regular watering and feeding during the growing season.

Fastigiate tree

Many of the most popular trees, including birch (*Betula*), cherry (*Prunus*) and rowan (*Sorbus*), have fastigiate forms – that is, they are tall and narrow, often columnar. These are ideal for gardens where space is limited and where you need something to plant for permanent height and framework. Some of these fastigiate forms can still be too vigorous for a small garden, however, so check with your supplier before making a final choice.

Climbers

These are the perfect solution for bringing height and softness to a small space. Try to select climbing plants that won't take over your garden, unless you are deliberately trying to create a jungle effect. Alternatively, you can choose rampant forms that should be cut hard back every year if you don't mind some extra spring pruning or that are herbaceous and that will reshoot each spring from ground level.

Personalized trellis

There are many types of trellis available in a range of styles and shapes. However, they are not always suitable for everyone's needs – for example, if you want to cover an awkwardly shaped piece of wall without major, time-consuming modification. In these circumstances you would be better off making your own tailor-made trellis that will not only fit the space perfectly but will also look attractive. You can even make your own 'artistic' trellis design to create a feature – with or without a climber – on a blank wall.

Personalized trellis that are made to fit a space exactly can often look much more elegant than 'off-the-peg' types.

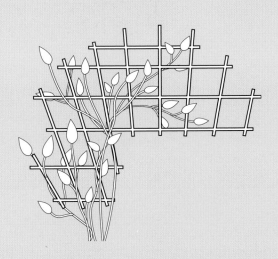

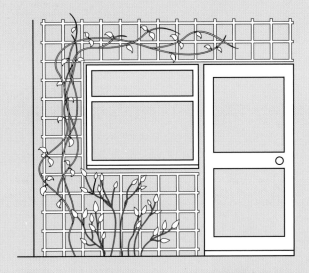

Trellis made as a feature (with or without climber)

Trellis tailor-made to fit exact spaces

You will need

Sufficient laths for your chosen
design (draw a large or
complicated trellis on some graph
paper to calculate how much you
need); roofing battens are ideal
and they are usually 25–38 x
38–50mm (1–1½ x 1½–2in)

7.5cm (3in) wood screws and wall
plugs

60mm (2¼in) wood screws or
galvanized nails

Woodstain

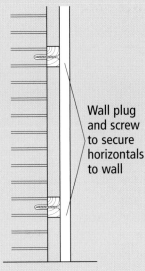

Wall plug
and screw
to secure
horizontals
to wall

Detailed section

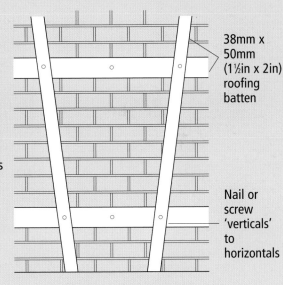

38mm x
50mm
(1½in x 2in)
roofing
batten

Nail or
screw
'verticals'
to
horizontals

Detailed elevation

Step by step

1 Cut the battens to lengths
according to your design. Stain them
(using two coats if required) and
leave them to dry.

2 Fix the horizontal lengths to the
wall using 7.5cm (3in) wood screws
and wall plugs, spacing them
according to your design but ideally

not more than 25–30cm (10–12in)
apart, roughly equivalent to four
courses of bricks, down to as little as
10–15cm (4–6in) apart for a denser,
chequerboard effect.

3 Take the vertical lengths of batten
and fix them to the faces of the
horizontal battens to match your
design. If you are going to nail them

on, don't drive the nails fully home
until you're happy that the verticals
are all in the correct position, so that
you can remove and reposition them
if you make a mistake.

4 Plant your climbers and tie them in
to the trellis panel (optional).

Planting

The best plants for this garden

Space for planting in this tiny courtyard is limited, so the emphasis is on climbers that will grow on the walls and the overhead structure, on shrubs and perennials that are naturally more upright and on a fastigiate tree that will provide some permanent height to break up the horizontal line of the boundary. Additional seasonal colour and hotspots are provided by using wall-hanging containers of annuals, alpines and dwarf trailing perennials.

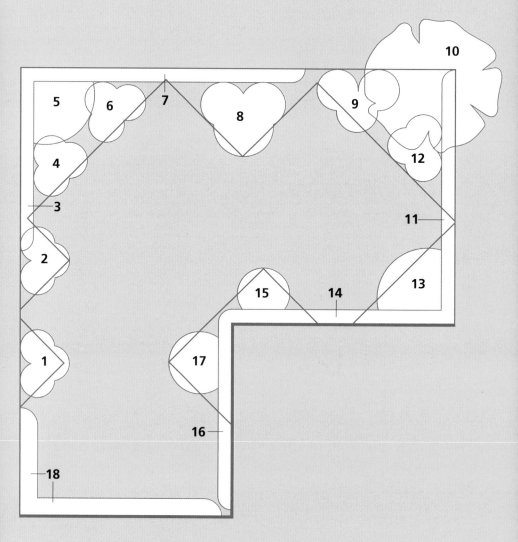

Upright-growing perennials with narrow leaves, like this crocosmia, are perfect where space is very limited.

Plants for limited space

Although there are many woody plants that you can trim to keep within bounds, this obviously requires regular pruning, and in the process you quite often lose the benefit of both flowers and the beauty of the plant's natural shape or habit. Where planting space is limited using trees and shrubs that are naturally narrow and upright will mean that you won't have to spend time on pruning and you will still be able to admire the plant's natural habit of growth. In addition, you will have some space for lower, smaller plants – particularly perennials – both in between the trees and shrubs and in front of them.

Similarly, many perennials, such as irises and crocosmias, are ideal for a limited planting area because of their vertical habit. Careful choices will enable you to accommodate an attractive range of plants of different species in a space that might otherwise be occupied by one wide-spreading plant.

True climbers – honeysuckle (*Lonicera*), jasmine (*Jasminum*) and clematis, for example – are an obvious choice for growing on boundary walls, fences and overhead structures, such as arches and pergolas. There are also many shrubs that can be trained to grow on trellises and wires fastened to walls and fences. Most of these do require additional, regular pruning and tying in, so if you're not looking for extra work it's best to avoid them.

Mix and match

Boundaries and dividers

Containers and beds

Decking

Decoration and ornaments

Edging

Furniture

Gravel and rocks

Index

Acknowledgements

Alamy/blickwinkel/Jagel 116 top; /Neil Holmes/Holmes Garden Photos 73; /Geoff Kidd/Garden World Images 116 centre top. **Corbis UK Ltd**/Mark Bolton 84 bottom right; /Tim Street-Porter/Beateworks 45. **Flowerphotos** 116 bottom. **GAP Photos**/Jonathan Buckley/Design: Christopher Lloyd 135; /Ishihara Kazuyuki Design Laboratory 55 bottom right; /J S Sira 99; /Friedrich Strauss 27; /Rob Whitworth/Design: AOA Corporation. **Garden World Images**/Sarah Lee 42 bottom right. **Jerry Harpur** 109, 147, 158 top, 177, 207, 234 bottom right, 237; /Design: Fiona Brockhoff 48 bottom right; /Design: Tim Du Val and Dean Payne 150 bottom right; /Design: Luciano Giubbilei 1, 30 bottom right; /Design: Bunny Guinness 243; /Design: Mel Light for Raymond Hudson 222 bottom right; /Design: Jimmie Morrison 66 bottom right; /Design: Ulf Nordfjell 9; / Design: Robin Williams for Melanie Edge 7. **Marcus Harpur** 111, 123, 171; /Design: Brinsbury Campus, Chichester College 192 bottom right; /Design: Justin Greer, for Mrs and Mrs Laing 8. **Andrew Lawson** 20 bottom, 26 bottom, 38 centre top, 38 centre bottom, 62 top, 74 centre top, 80 centre top, 92 centre top, 98 centre bottom, 110 centre top, 128 bottom, 164 centre bottom, 170 top, 176 centre top, 194 top, 206 top, 212 centre bottom, 218 centre bottom, 248 centre bottom, 248 bottom, 26 centre bottom, 62 centre bottom, 120 bottom right, 128 centre bottom, 200 centre top, 200 bottom, 246 bottom right/Design: Mary Keen; /Torie Chugg/26 centre top. **Clive Nichols** 108, 132 bottom right, 186 bottom right, 230 centre bottom, 235; /Copton Ash, Kent 75; /Design: Olivia Clarke 168 bottom right; /Design: Sarah Layton 93; /Design: Hilary McPherson 96 bottom right; /Design: Stephen Woodhams 25 bottom right. **Octopus Publishing Group Limited** 194 bottom, 242 top; /Mark Bolton 97, 138 bottom right, /Design: Christopher Costin Scenic Design Landscape 210 bottom right, /Design: Lloyd-Morgan 180 bottom right, /Design: Xa Tollemache with Jon Kellett 39, /Design: Geoffrey Whitten 189; /Michael Boys 32 centre top, 44 centre bottom, 62 centre top, 74 centre bottom, 86 centre top, 98 centre top, 98 bottom, 104 bottom, 104 top, 128 centre top, 146 centre top, 146 centre bottom, 152 centre bottom, 158 bottom, 200 top, 212 centre top, 236 centre bottom, Neil Holmes 158 centre bottom, 188 centre top; /Jerry Harpur 14 centre bottom, 32 bottom, 38 top, 44 bottom, 50 centre top, 56 bottom, 62 bottom, 68 top, 68 centre top, 68 centre bottom, 80 bottom, 86 top, 98 top, 122 bottom, 122 top, 134 top, 140 top, 152 bottom, 152 centre top, 182 top, 182 bottom, 188 centre bottom, 200 centre bottom, 206 bottom, 206 centre top, 212 bottom, 224 bottom, 230 centre top, 230 bottom, 236 bottom, 248 centre top; /Marcus Harpur 170 bottom, 218 bottom; /Andrew Lawson 3 picture 4, 14 top, 14 centre top, 26 top, 50 centre bottom, 56 top, 68 bottom, 80 top, 92 centre bottom, 110 centre bottom, 134 centre top, 146 bottom, 152 top, 164 bottom, 170 centre bottom, 194 centre bottom, 218 centre top, 224 top, 236 top; /Howard Rice 20 centre top, 50 top, 56 centre top, 74 top, 102 bottom right, 134 bottom, 153, 188 bottom, /C.U.B.G. 44 top, 44 centre top, 224 centre top, /Mr. & Mrs. H. Rice 3 picture 3, 170 centre top; /David Sarton 162 bottom right, /Design: Chris Beardshaw 195, /Design: Jinny Blom 87, /Design: Lesley Bremness (East West Garden Design) 126 bottom right, /Design: Burntwood School, Tooting 204 bottom right, /Design: Cherry Burton 240 bottom right, /Design: Julian Dowle Partnership 141, /Design: Guy Farthing 18 bottom right, /Design: Adam Frost 12 bottom right, /Design: Sarah Lloyd 249, /Design: Angel Mainwaring 19, /Design: Paul Martin 3 picture 2, 37 bottom right, /Design:Ulf Nordfjell 54 bottom right, /Design: Carol Smith 90, /Design: Linda Upson & Carole Syms 63; /Freia Turland 72 bottom right, 158 centre top, 159, 165; /Mark Winwood 78 bottom right; /George Wright 3 picture 1, 20 top, 86 centre bottom, 92 top, 92 centre top, 110 top, 122 centre top, 140 centre top, 140 centre bottom, 140 bottom, 146 top, 164 top, 176 top, 188 top, 212 top, 224 centre bottom, 242 bottom; /James Young 14 bottom, 32 top, 32 centre top, 38 bottom, 50 bottom, 56 centre bottom, 86 bottom, 104 centre bottom, 122 centre bottom, 128 top, 176 centre bottom, 230 top, 236 centre top, 242 centre top, 242 centre bottom. **Photolibrary**/Mark Bolton 156 bottom right; /Will Giles 33; /John Glover 80 centre bottom, 228 bottom right; /Paul Hart 225; /Francois De Heel 216 bottom right; /Michele Lamontagne 21; /Martin Page 57; /Jerry Pavia   116 centre bottom; /Didier Willery 176 bottom; /Steven Wooster 174 bottom right, /Design: Cherida Seago 36 bottom right. **Photos Horticultural** 182 centre bottom; /Design: Allison Armour in assoc. with Peter Rogers Associates. Sponsor Hone & Gardens Magazine 37 top left; /MJK/Southend-on-Sea Borough Council 183. **S & O Mathews** 74 bottom, 104 centre top, 110 bottom, 134 centre bottom, 164 centre top, 182 centre top, 194 centre top, 206 centre bottom, 218 top, 248 top. **The Garden Collection**/Liz Eddison 15, /Design: Deborah Oakley 144 bottom right; /Andrew Lawson 117; /Marie O'Hara/Design: Earth Designs Ltd. 55 top, /Design: Paul Williams 60 bottom right; /Derek St. Romaine 81; /Derek St. Romaine/Design: Rupert Golby 201, /Design: Phil Nash/Garden: Robert van den Hurk 198 bottom right; /Nicola Stocken Tomkins 20 centre bottom.

Publisher: **Jane Birch**

Managing Editor: **Clare Churly**

Editor: **Lydia Darbyshire**

Deputy Creative Director: **Karen Sawyer**

Design: **Ome Design**

Illustrations: **Gill Tomblin**

Diagrams: **Ome Design**

Picture Library Manager: **Jennifer Veall**

Production Manager: **Ian Paton**